Writing Madness,
Writing Normalcy

Writing Madness, Writing Normalcy

Self and Stigma in Memoirs of Mental Illness

LISA SPIEKER

McFarland & Company, Inc., Publishers
Jefferson, North Carolina

This book has undergone peer review.

Excerpts from *Wasted* by Marya Hornbacher.
Copyright © 1998 by Marya Hornbacher-Beard.
Used by permission of HarperCollins Publishers.

Excerpts from *MADNESS: A Biopolar Life* by Marya Hornbacher. Copyright © 2008 by Marya Hornbacher. Reprinted by permission of Houghton Mifflin Harcourt Publishing Company. All rights reserved. Also, reprinted by permission of HarperCollins Publishers Ltd., © 2008 by Marya Hornbacher.

LIBRARY OF CONGRESS CATALOGUING-IN-PUBLICATION DATA

Names: Spieker, Lisa, 1987– author.
Title: Writing madness, writing normalcy : self and stigma
in memoirs of mental illness / Lisa Spieker.
Description: Jefferson, North Carolina : McFarland & Company, Inc.,
Publishers, 2021 | Includes bibliographical references and index.
Identifiers: LCCN 2021013219 | ISBN 9781476682273 (paperback : acid free paper) ∞
ISBN 9781476644844 (ebook)
Subjects: LCSH: Anger—United States. | Mental
illness—United States. | Self—United States.
Classification: LCC BF575.A5 S66 2021 | DDC 152.4/7—dc23
LC record available at https://lccn.loc.gov/2021013219

BRITISH LIBRARY CATALOGUING DATA ARE AVAILABLE

ISBN (print) 978-1-4766-8227-3
ISBN (ebook) 978-1-4766-4484-4

Front cover image © 2021 Shutterstock

Printed in the United States of America

*McFarland & Company, Inc., Publishers
Box 611, Jefferson, North Carolina 28640
www.mcfarlandpub.com*

Table of Contents

Acknowledgments

No project of this size is ever finished without some serious help, and this one is no exception.

My family—Ulrike, Theo, and Robert Spieker as well as Kurt and Renate Linden—provided emotional and financial support. Thomas Oschwald kept me grounded through the rough patches.

My advisors Astrid Franke and Ingrid Hotz-Davies gave me both the space to develop my own thoughts and crucial advice when I needed it. I am particularly grateful for Astrid Franke's comments regarding comparisons to victims of the Holocaust which helped me to put this form of stigma management in perspective. I also benefited immensely from Ingrid Hotz-Davies' insight regarding Russian Formalism and the management of shame. It enabled me to reframe my entire thinking on the literariness of memoirs in my corpus.

In the Department of American Studies at the University Tübingen, I want to thank Isabell Klaiber for her comments regarding narratology and tons of encouragement, Luvena Kopp for pointing me toward Bernd Ostendorff's text on minstrelsy, Ferdinand Nyberg for his feedback on my terminology, Aileen Priester, Lars Rieger, and Tom Dirkschnieder for their help with research tasks and the thorough proofreading of the bibliography, and Albrecht Raible, who patiently listened to my ideas in their earliest stages and provided valuable feedback when I was stuck, as well as all the students in the seminar on shame I taught with Ingrid Hotz-Davies and everyone who helped me by participating in the department's monthly colloquium. I'm also thankful for Nathalia Lemos Müller's valuable feedback on Chapter Two.

But most of all, I want to thank Annika Brunck, a speaker of hard truths about my writing, a persistent cheerleader who helped me to keep going when I didn't think I could, a source of too many great insights to list here, and one of the main reasons why I made it through the dissertation process with a semblance of sanity.

Preface

To hear people tell it, we're all mad from time to time. People are madly in love, mad at or about somebody. Humorous signs in offices proclaim, "You don't have to be mad to work here—but it helps." The leaking faucet drives you insane, and he is cleaning like crazy before his partner comes home. We go out of our mind with grief or lose it when we cannot take a situation anymore. The term mad and its synonyms are highly evocative and are "widely applied to many people besides the clinically certifiable and include all manner of abnormalities and extremes of thought and emotion" (Porter, *Faber* xi). It is only when an invisible, ever-shifting line has been crossed, and behavior becomes threateningly transgressive, or else when a member of the psychiatric dispositive has proclaimed an individual mad, insane or—more recently—mentally ill or mentally disordered, that a behavior, mood or opinion condenses into a highly stigmatized trait, whose meaning is extremely variable: Even the most cursory glance at contemporary cultural products and discourses reveals instances where those with the stigma of madness are represented as a threat, others where they are alternately the object of ridicule, paternalistic concern, medical inquiry or adulation.

This study investigates how madness is discursively constructed by those who bear its stigma and which effects their constructions of meaning have. To this end, I analyze memoirs by people who have been diagnosed with a mental illness and published accounts of their lived experience in late twentieth- and early twenty-first-century America.[1] I pay special attention to the kinds of narrative structures, tropes, and discourses they draw upon to make sense of their lived experience, fashion themselves textually, and negotiate stigma beliefs. Moreover, I analyze how authors legitimize their knowledge claims, attach meaning to terms like *madness*, how these meanings interact with each other, and how they are utilized in advocacy, identity claims, and "cultural work" (Tompkins 200).[2] In this manner, this study considers the cultural and political impact of a popular and highly prolific genre that functions as a platform for a traditionally marginalized group.[3]

I follow Michel Foucault's seminal claims in *Madness and Civilization* and *Psychiatric Power* as well as basic tenets in Mad Studies and hold that madness is a discursive construct: Its meaning is shaped by various agents in fields such as psychiatry, psychology, philosophy, high and popular culture, news media, advocacy groups, the humanities, and legislature. This definition does not deny the suffering caused by the conditions currently identified as mental disorders, by side effects of their treatment or by the discrimination experienced by those who are diagnosed with them. However, treating madness and mental disorders as discursive constructs allows for analyses of how the condition is conceptualized and experienced within contemporary social, intellectual, economic, and cultural structures as well as how life writing can change those meanings and experiences.

To analyze the cultural work done by mental illness pathographies, I assembled a corpus of seventeen book-length accounts of first-person experience of madness. The corpus includes a variety of mental disorders, which represent different facets of the general *gestalt* of madness: disturbance of thought, mood, personality, and sense of identity as well as transgressive behavior. These features are the diagnostic cores of schizophrenia, major depressive disorder, bipolar disorder (previously called manic depression), borderline personality disorder, dissociative identity disorder (formerly known as multiple personality disorder), and eating disorders, more specifically anorexia nervosa and bulimia nervosa. They are among the most prevalent[4] mental disorders in contemporary US society and stigma-based representations of them feature extensively in popular culture and journalistic coverage.[5] Additionally, life writing on these conditions is especially prolific. Authors in my corpus are therefore part of relatively large marginalized populations, which have mostly been (kept) silent and now use the memoir as a site of self-representation. Thus, my corpus provides insight into the cultural tensions around the phenomenon of madness and the self-expression of those with lived experience.

I chose to include only one text about borderline personality disorder to reflect the relative silence of those with the condition.[6] I maintain that a corpus of seventeen memoirs is large enough to make claims about the genre as a whole, yet small enough to conduct close readings of individual passages from each text.

Beyond the diversity of conditions, my corpus is relatively homogenous. While some authors in my corpus, like William Styron, Mark Vonnegut or Cherry Boone-O'Neill, have some claim to fame because of their previous literary pursuits, a singing career or because of their fathers Kurt Vonnegut and Pat Boone, most authors are not public figures. What connects all of them is that they present themselves as heterosexual, cis-gendered, upper-middle-class or upper-class people of European descent.[7] This relative uniformity allows me to pursue an analysis that is not complicated by issues of intersectionality.[8]

Author	Title	Date of Publication	Diagnosed Disorder
Apostolides, Marianne	*Inner Hunger: A Young Woman's Struggle Through Anorexia and Bulimia*	1998	Eating disorders
Beers, Clifford Whittingham	*A Mind That Found Itself: An Autobiography*	1956	Bipolar disorder
Boone-O'Neill, Cherry	*Starving for Attention*	1982	Eating disorders, bipolar disorder
Chase, Truddi	*When Rabbit Howls*	1987	Dissociative identity disorder
Cvetkovich, Ann	*Depression: A Public Feeling*	2012	Depressive disorder
Hornbacher, Marya	*Madness: A Bipolar Life*	2009	Bipolar disorder
Hornbacher, Marya	*Wasted: A Memoir of Anorexia and Bulimia*	1998	Eating disorders
Jamison, Kay Redfield	*An Unquiet Mind: A Memoir of Moods and Madness*	1995	Bipolar disorder
Kaysen, Susanna	*Girl, Interrupted*	1993	Borderline personality disorder
Morgan, Kristina	*Mind Without a Home: A Memoir of Schizophrenia*	2013	Schizophrenia
Oxnam, Robert B.	*A Fractured Mind: My Life with Multiple Personality Disorder*	2005	Dissociative identity disorder
Phillips, Jane	*The Magic Daughter: A Memoir of Living with Multiple Personality Disorder*	1995	Dissociative identity disorder
Schiller, Lori, and Amanda Bennett	*The Quiet Place: A Journey out of the Torment of Madness*	2011	Schizophrenia
Smola, David R.	*A Waltz through La La Land: A Depression Survivor's Memoir*	2010	Depressive disorder
Styron, William	*Darkness Visible: A Memoir of Madness*	1991	Depressive disorder

Author	Title	Date of Publication	Diagnosed Disorder
Vonnegut, Mark	*The Eden Express*	1975	Schizophrenia
Wurtzel, Elizabeth	*Prozac Nation: Young and Depressed in America*	1994	Depressive disorder

Table 1: Overview of this study's corpus.

The main finding and structuring principle of this study is that memoirs of mental illness are characterized by two central tensions. To reflect the centrality of these tensions, this project is organized into two parts. Part one discusses the tension that exists in the authors' self-fashioning as *both* normal and mad, and part two analyzes the tension in truth production, i.e., the reliance on methods of so-called objective and subjective truth. This arrangement allows me to demonstrate that seemingly disparate textual elements such as narrative structures, intertextual references, imagery, and tone work together in an intricate fashion in self-fashioning and truth production. While no single memoir incorporates every strategy discussed in this project, all rely on several from each side of each tension. Throughout, I analyze particularly salient examples of narrative structures, tropes, and appropriations from my entire corpus to show the prevalence of these textual features in memoirs of madness. However, due to the size of my corpus, I will mostly consider memoirs in relation to my larger thesis rather than offer in-depth readings of all of them. Nevertheless, I include a more sustained reading of Marya Hornbacher's *Madness: A Bipolar Life* throughout this study to demonstrate the cultural work and stigma-political effects of these tensions in an individual text.

According to sociologist Erving Goffman, all stigmatized individuals consider themselves to be both normal and blemished or, in this case, mad. Despite being treated as blemished through the label "mentally ill," confinement to a mental hospital or the administration of psychotropic drugs, the stigmatized individual still harbors "a sense of being a 'normal person,' a human being like anyone else" (Goffman, *Stigma* 7). However, the obtrusive nature of their condition and "the standards he [the stigmatized person] has incorporated from the wider society equip him to be intimately alive to what others see as his failing, inevitably causing him, if only for moments, to agree" that he is indeed not normal. This double sense of self is also expressed in textual self-fashioning, and memoirs never completely resolve the tension between an individual's claims to normalcy and to madness. By maintaining this tension, memoirs not only represent the lived experience of stigmatized persons but problematize attempts to conceive of madness and normalcy as binary oppositions which performs stigma-political functions.

The second tension in these memoirs concerns the truth of madness, or more specifically how it is produced and by whom. Here, a tension exists between so-called objective, i.e., academic, journalistic, and scientific, methods of truth production and subjective, artistic ones. By relying on both objective and subjective, literary means of truth production without privileging one over the other, memoirs problematize simplistic distinctions between the two methods. This destabilizes existing truths on madness and thereby creates more favorable circumstances in which stigmatized subjects may claim a voice.

Chapter One, "Self-Fashioning as Normal (Again)," focuses on how memoirs produce the meaning of normalcy and how narrating selves attempt to mitigate the stigma their diagnosis incurred. To this end, narrating selves stress that they retained a core of normalcy, distance themselves from other mad persons or draw upon the discourse of anti-psychiatry to claim that they may be transgressive but not mad in the sense of debilitated or incomprehensible. Moreover, authors inscribe themselves into culturally valued narratives of overcoming like the US national fantasy of rational self-making or the conversion narrative to "expunge a deviant identity and replace it with a positive one" (L. Anderson 107). These explicitly didactic narratives not only provide practical advice to the mad among readers but also narrate or enable an individual's return to social acceptance. In other words, Chapter One is about textual features that help establish the return to normalcy or the normalcy beyond madness and addresses how this contributes to the tension in self-fashioning as both normal and mad.

Chapter Two, "Self-Fashioning as Mad," discusses how memoirs acknowledge the textual selves' Otherness and reveal the multiplicity of meanings madness can take on when it is not restricted to the framework of mental illness.[9] Authors endorse mutually exclusive, yet deep-seated beliefs about madness when they portray their experiencing selves as both incapacitated *and* inspired, both monstrous Others *and* lovable eccentrics. They present madness as a formative, even enjoyable experience *and* as a destabilizing sense of alienation from themselves. Memoirs thus encourage more nuanced ways of thinking about madness as a signifier and—in their very contradictions—provide an alternative to the totalizing, bureaucratizing discourse of psychiatry. Moreover, spectacular confessions of madness not only contribute to the commercial success of the genre but also increase the visibility of marginalized subjects and their perspective.[10] The conflicting ways of self-fashioning therefore engage in important cultural and stigma-political work by representing the lived experience of the mad—and their normalcy—in complex, culturally situated ways.

Chapter Three, "Producing Objective Truth," discusses how memoirs in my corpus draw upon the scientific truth of the psychiatric discourse[11] and its understanding of madness *qua* mental disorder as well as other forms of truth production associated with authenticity and reliability. I suggest that the supposedly objective truth produced by the psychiatric dispositive organizes the disorienting experience of madness into the more narrowly defined conceptual framework of disorder and thus supports the meaning-making process.[12] Moreover, these appropriations of the markedly scientific language of psychiatry constitute a textual performance of normalcy in the sense of rationality that not only reinforces the central tension in self-fashioning but also contradicts stigma beliefs that the mad are too impaired to contribute insight or produce legitimate knowledge about their condition (cf. Martinez 90–103, Prendergast 191; Pryal). Established academic and journalistic methods of researching and referencing, the inclusion of medico-administrative documents and witness testimony further authenticate first-person accounts of mental illness and present authors as credible sources with an inside perspective on madness. The memoirs' appropriation of psychiatric knowledge and production of objective truth therefore supports the claiming of voice.

Chapter Four—"Producing Subjective Truth"—investigates how memoirs use markedly poetic means to produce a personal, literary truth of madness that exists in a tension to the psychiatric understanding of mental disorders. Arguably, a literary rendition of madness can (re-)produce madness textually and convey the ambiguities, affective intensity, and multiple truths of lived experience that are missing from the abstract generalities of diagnostic handbooks (cf. also L. Zimmerman 465). Through affective language, defamiliarizing imagery, and "personalized, experientially oriented means of narration" (Vickroy 3) texts recreate a weaker, mediated experience of the narrated self's madness for the reader.[13] Memoirs in my corpus combine this affective way of conveying the subjective truth of madness with the extensive use of the confessional mode to produce the impression of authenticity and intimacy which helps present accounts as truthful narratives of the meaning of madness, normalcy, and the author's life "such as it was" (Lejeune 23). Ultimately, these textual features establish the mad as legitimate producers of truth claims and contribute to discussions on how madness can be known.

These unresolved textual tensions represent the lived experience of madness, which is one of contradictions. According to the memoirs in my corpus, the intra-psychic experience of madness is characterized by the loss of distinctions between self and Other or sanity and madness. Authors feel that their madness is both intimately entwined with those aspects that make us who we are *and* that it is an utterly alien, intrusive force. Madness is a coping strategy that protects the mind from trauma *and* a traumatic experience in itself. It is a precondition for creative genius *and* the ultimate incapacitation. Because of symmetries between the appropriation of contradictory discourses on madness, the textual representation of the contradictory experience of (the self in) madness, and the refusal to resolve these tensions narratively, memoirs discussed in this study exhibit a high degree of complexity and encourage a reading as literature. Authors further support this reading through the use of markedly literary means. These texts are therefore representative in the sense of mimetic, that is, as works of art they imitate life (Couser, *Memoir* 57).

As becomes increasingly clear throughout my analysis, memoirs of mental illness do not reject stigma beliefs in the straightforward manner of political manifestos. Instead, they reveal that madness, in contemporary US culture, is the dissolution of clear boundaries and binaries. As an experience and as a discursive construct, madness is the simultaneous presence of contradictory attributes. It is a complex, historically grown network of tensions between opposing states of mind and moods, definitions, ascribed characteristics, and (stigma) beliefs that have accumulated in the cultural consciousness. Memoirs reveal this through references to culturally valued representations in high culture, wide-spread and deep-seated popular beliefs, and various methods of truth production. While these memoirs may emphasize a specific meaning of madness, all texts in my corpus also include fissures and contradictions so that no individual understanding of madness is ultimately privileged. This complicates the cognitive categories that are the basis of the stigmatization process (Goffman, *Stigma* 3).

Even though none of the authors discussed in this project claims allegiance to advocacy groups, their memoirs also perform important political functions and are similar to what Bradley Lewis calls "biocultural activism" (116). While the Women's Health Movement, the AIDS Coalition to Unleash Power or the Mad Pride movement are political in a different way than literary memoirs of madness, all are "located at the interface of bioscience and politics" (Lewis 116) and struggle over questions of epistemology as well as traditional political issues such as the group's representation and position in society. In other words, they all "struggle over both truth and values" (Lewis 116). Memoirs are political insofar as they contribute to the politics of representation and the discursive production of the truth of madness.

The memoir is a uniquely suitable genre for the complex identity-political work discussed here because it is so deeply ambiguous itself.[14] A tension between objective and artistic, subjective truth permeates the genre of memoirs. According to Philippe Lejeune, an implicit agreement exists between authors and readers of life writing which he calls "the autobiographical pact": The author's proper name on the title page functions as "the pledge of responsibility of a *real person*" (Lejeune 11) that guarantees "the identity ... of the *name*"—and thus the irreducible subjectivity—of author, narrator, and protagonist (Lejeune 14, 10).[15] This pact entails the need for truthfulness about any identity categories such as age, gender, or ethnicity as they pertain to the subjectivity in question. The autobiographical pact furthermore assures readers of the text's fidelity to the *meaning* of the life described (Lejeune 22). However, unlike a promise of accuracy, which requires the correctness of all verifiable information, a promise of fidelity makes allowances for the highly selective processes of remembering and writing that organize the contingency and ambivalence of lived experience into sharp contrasts and recognizable narrative structures. The narrative order that results may not have been obvious at the time it was experienced, yet it still portrays a life "such as it was" (Lejeune 23). Memoirs thus retain a degree of faithfulness to extratextual reality while also embellishing, condensing, and altering it to live up to its "aspirations as art" (Couser, *Memoir* 80). In other words, memoirs can "be read as 'true stories,' but the emphasis must be as much on the word 'stories' as the word 'true'" (Hawkins, *Reconstructing* 14).

According to Thomas Couser, this balancing act between fidelity to truth and creativity is essential to the cultural work memoirs do. "[T]he genre has an identity claim at its core" (*Memoir* 81), and memoirs serve as "a threshold genre in which some previously silent populations have been given voice for the first time" (*Memoir* 12). Memoirs have done vital cultural work like providing a platform for the self-representation of members of marginalized populations, especially those afflicted with HIV/AIDS, oppressed ethnicities, women, individuals with physical or mental impairments, and survivors of the Holocaust (cf. Cvetkovich 74–75; Couser, "Some" 7–8). They contain testimony of the lived experience of these groups and the cultural and political force of this testimony—such as the depathologization of the HIV survivor—depends on the belief in their authenticity (cf. Couser, *Memoir* 79–107). Authors thus need to establish their right to make truth claims about the first-hand experience of madness and do so by relying upon medical-administrative documents, confession, and statements by witnesses to their lived experience.[16]

At the same time, memoirs do not simply translate a fully formed identity into writing but actively produce it. Moreover, life writing creates a split between a present, narrating self who tells their story with the benefit of hindsight and a past experiencing self who lives through events as a character.[17] Memoirs in my corpus shape their stories as culturally-valued narratives of transformation and thus emphasize the difference between the two selves. This division of selves, however, does not resolve the tensions of identity by creating a past, mad self and a present, sane one. For one thing, many authors have chronic conditions that can be managed but not cured. Secondly, the narrating self repeatedly assumes the perspective of the past, mad self to represent the narrated self's madness. In these instances, the narration is characterized by fragmentation, associative logic, neologisms or unusual sentence structure. In other words, recognizable representations of madness intrude into the narrative voice. The distinction to the past, mad self is momentarily erased as the purportedly transformed, narrating self dons the mask of madness for a greater sense of immediacy and affective intensity, making madness something that can be performed. Narratives of transformation are furthermore undermined by essentialist claims about madness being a part of one's personality. Because of these contradictions, memoirs establish neither a stable identity as mad nor one as normal but shift back and forth or claim both simultaneously. It is because they establish themselves as persons with a credible claim to an inside perspective that authors in my corpus can draw upon the significant cultural force of life writing and contribute to the instability of madness as a discursive construct.

I refer to the texts in my corpus as memoirs of madness or mental illness pathographies. The latter is a specification of Anne Hunsaker Hawkins' term "pathography," which she introduced in her groundbreaking monograph *Reconstructing Illness: Studies in Pathography* (1993; 2nd ed. 1994).[18] Hawkins read more than 350 book-length accounts of physical affliction for their use of myth in meaning-making. Her approach allows her to access deep-seated, culture-wide beliefs about illness and its treatment that influence how they are narrated and experienced. Hawkins furthermore makes fruitful connections to the field of trauma studies to illuminate how narrativization can return voice and a sense of agency to patients: In narrative, authors can reduce disorienting and traumatic events to a contained, familiar story. As such, pathography can serve as "a kind of vicarious support group" (Hawkins xi) that not only shares practical information but also coping strategies with readers who are—or might become—similarly afflicted. In short, Hawkins provided much-needed groundwork on the social and cultural functions of pathography, and my analysis of narratives of overcoming is partially inspired by her chapter on the myth of rebirth.

Beyond that, my focus and methods are very different. Hawkins' study draws a straight line from contemporary pathographies written by Americans to the writings of Dante, Augustine of Hippo, or Roman and Greek mythology. As a result, her analysis disregards how narratives of transformation have been used in the more immediate US literary history and the stigma-political work these texts can do: For example, the conversion narrative has been appropriated by several marginalized groups who sought (re-)admittance to the social order, such as nineteenth-century drunkards who told the story of their newfound sobriety or immigrants who narrated their Americanization. However, Hawkins largely ignores the impact illness has on an individual's social standing and instead focuses on its potential for meaning-making and what a predominance of certain myths says about a culture. By contrast, I analyze how authors of mental illness pathographies inscribe themselves into US literary history, current psychiatric discourses, as well as long-standing and contemporary practices of self-fashioning. This focus enables me to engage with texts in a more specific cultural and historical context which is necessary for the analysis of cultural, identity-political, and stigma-political work.

Another central difference between Hawkins' study and mine is her desire to impose order and provide orientation within the rapidly growing genre. In her introductory overview of the genre of pathographies, she organizes them according to "authorial intent" (4), i.e., testimonial, denunciation of depersonalizing medical treatment, and promotion of alternative forms of treatment. She provides examples for each "group of pathographies" (9) as well as a timespan when they occur most frequently. By contrast, I hold that literature is characterized by its radical openness of meaning and that attempts at organization tend to fail in the face of the complexities of actual texts.

However, Hawkins is far from alone with this approach. Arthur Frank's *The Wounded Storyteller: Body, Illness and Ethics* (1995) created a schema of illness narratives, namely "restitution stories" of quick, uncomplicated, and full recovery, "chaos stories" where suffering eclipses the self's capacity for narrative, and "quest stories" about the protagonist's journey and transformation through illness. Jennifer Radden suggests that contemporary first-person illness narratives operate according to two models, depending on the stance narrating selves assume towards their mental disorder: In the "symptom-alienating model," metaphors of distance and control conceive of the condition as inconsequential to someone's personality, whereas the "symptoms-integrating model" embraces madness as a central aspect of the self (cf. also Beilke). Which model authors choose depends largely on the narrating self's condition. These approaches unduly simplify the mechanisms of meaning-making through narrative and textual self-fashioning, and reveal the impulse to categorize, systematize, and bureaucratize expressions related to the disorienting experience of sickness and mental illness in particular. By contrast, my understanding of tensions that permeate mental illness pathographies avoids these pitfalls and essentialist distinctions based on the narrating self's diagnosis and instead allows for an analysis of the conflicting forms of self- and meaning-making in literature.

In many ways, this project shares the scope and approach of Thomas Couser's work on narratives of somatic illness and disability, most notably *Recovering Bodies: Illness, Disability, and Life Writing* (1997) and *Signifying Bodies: Disability in Contemporary Life Writing* (2009). *Recovering Bodies* focuses on how illness narratives relate to other forms of life writing and how authors negotiate conventions such as point of view and narrative formulas to "represent previously unrepresented conditions" (14). Both works furthermore explore the interactions of life writing and identity politics, and the potential of self-representation through narrative to counter stigmatizing portrayals. In other words, Couser also deals with issues at the heart of this project. However, I contend that somatic illness and disability occupy a different cultural space than madness and that those who write memoirs of the latter need to confront a different history of representation.[19] Furthermore, Couser holds that "[o]ne common purpose [of memoirs about illness and disability] is to invalidate dominant cultural narratives of invalidism" (*Recovering* 12) and that memoirs are "a response—indeed a retort—to the traditional misrepresentation of disability in Western culture generally" (*Signifying* 7).[20] I, by contrast, suggest that the effects of memoirs of mental illness are more ambiguous and complex than the straightforward contestation of stigma beliefs about the mad.

While research on life writing by individuals with somatic illnesses or disabilities has flourished, monographs on contemporary memoirs by individuals with mental illnesses are relatively few and tend to have a limited scope. Either works focus on a very small corpus such as three primary sources (cf. Martinez) or life writing by individuals who share the same diagnosis such as schizophrenia (cf. Wood). In other cases, studies focus on historical narratives of madness (cf. Porter, *Social*), or on gendered accounts of hospitalizations (cf. Walter). While these projects and edited collections (cf. Clark, *Depression*; Donaldson) do valuable work, their perspectives are limited. My project takes a broader view and can therefore make claims about the larger category of madness as it is represented in a very prolific genre.

The collection *Pathology and Postmodernism: Mental Illness as Discourse and Experience* (2000), edited by Dwight Fee, lays out many of the theoretical assumptions on which this study is based. It analyzes how social constructionism and the postmodern strategy of undermining totalizing knowledges can be brought to bear on the discussion of mental illness (Fee 4–6). However, a key difference between Fee's edited collection and my study is that *Pathology and Postmodernism* considers the implications of postmodern theory for the conceptualization of mental illnesses and relates many aspects of the experience of madness to the postmodern, fragmented sense of self. These analyses are in danger of having the specificity of the mad experience evaporate into the postmodern moment or of reducing the mad person to the postmodern subject *par excellence*.[21] While I acknowledge the impact of postmodernism on my corpus, I offer close readings of how fragmented, instable selves and texts can do concrete stigma-political and cultural work.

This project charts the tensions in truth production and self-making, as well as the stigma-political strategies and the potential for meaning-making they enable and thus fills a gap in existing scholarship. It employs an interdisciplinary perspective that, however, relies heavily on the methods of literary and cultural studies and concepts from the fields of sociology and Foucauldian discourse analysis.

Introduction

As I elaborated in the preface, this project considers how madness and the stigma that is attached to it are discursively and narratively constructed by those who were declared mentally ill or mentally disordered by members of the psychiatric dispositive. I show how memoirs as literary texts create tensions by emulating narrative structures that suggest conflicting things about the nature, etiology, and overcoming of madness as well as diverse modes of writing that encourage contradictory reactions towards the mad.

However, before a meaningful analysis of mental illness pathographies can take place, I need to elaborate on my use of the terms "madness," "mental illness," "mental disorder," and "normalcy." Afterward, I provide an overview of the meanings madness has acquired over time and situate the genre of pathography in its cultural and literary context.

Writing About Madness: Terminology

As this project focuses on how authors of mental illness pathographies use language and narrative to fashion themselves and their condition textually, a few words on the cultural context of their—and my—choice of words are in order. I use the terms "madness," "mental illness," and "mental disorder" to refer to the conditions that stigmatize authors in my corpus. To contextualize the authors' and my own choice of words, the following provides an overview of the terminological preferences of important discursive agents, namely advocacy groups, scholar-activists, and members of the psychiatric dispositive. This section also illuminates what sets texts in my corpus apart from traditional, non-literary stigma-political efforts by advocacy groups and scholar-activists.

Like any marginalized group, persons with mental illnesses and their various advocacy groups are very concerned with language. After all, "the power to name and define the experience of the self is at stake" (Morrison xii). Who does the naming is crucial, since language shapes individual and social perceptions and has the power to denigrate, exclude, conceal or delegitimize (Goffman, *Stigma* 24; Burstow 79–83). For this reason, advocacy groups endorse very specific terms that speak to their political stance and their understanding of the condition which the psychiatric dispositive calls mental illness or, more recently, mental disorder.[1] As a consequence of the ever-growing number of self-help and advocacy groups, there is a plethora of identifying terms currently promoted for those with conditions of the mind, including but certainly not limited to "person with (or labeled with) a mental illness," "person with lived experience," "person with a psychiatric disability," "person with a brain disorder," "neurodiverse," "mad"/"Mad," "mad-identified," "survivor," "service user," "ex-patient," and "voice hearer."[2] Each of these terms has specific political connotations and emphasizes different aspects of the experience such as "use or survival of mental health services; first-person experience in general or … [emphasis on] protected legal status; distancing from or centring [sic] of mad experience as a core sense of personhood (that is person-first or mad-first language)" (Jones and Kelly 46). Therefore, every term is criticized by other groups for the political stance it represents and defended by its adherents. For example, to the mind of some advocacy groups, the term "person living with a mental illness" accepts the psychiatric framework that pathologizes the experience of madness and privileges a psychiatric account over that of the patient (cf. Russo and Shulkes 32–33). However, those who employ it insist that the term enables coalition politics and the stigma-political strategy of equating mental illnesses with all other illnesses, a rhetorical move that arguably reduces ascriptions of personal responsibility for madness.[3]

Even though authors in my corpus do stigma-political work, their use of terms deviates greatly from that of advocacy groups. Authors in my corpus avoid terms with specific political or legal connotations such as survivor, mad-identified, neurodiverse, or person with a psychiatric disability. Instead, they reproduce the tension between objective and subjective truth through their choice of labels and euphemisms. On the one hand, each author uses identifying terms based on psychiatric diagnostic labels such as schizophrenic, depressive or bulimic or describes themselves as mentally ill. On the other hand, the same authors use non-medical, colloquial terms and call themselves "mad," "crazy," "insane" or "nuts." This appropriation of both psychiatric and colloquial labels is central to the ambiguity of memoirs on the questions of what madness is—a medical disorder or something else—and which terms are appropriate for discussing it. Both kinds of labels furthermore enable distinct kinds of self-fashioning and stigma-political maneuvers.

Among other things, drawing upon psychiatric labels and thus the conceptualization of madness as mental illness enables a self-fashioning as well-informed in the currently dominant discourse on madness and allows authors to engage mental healthcare professionals in their dialect. The appropriation of psychiatric terms can therefore be read as a form of empowerment and is illustrative of the authors' interest in coalition politics and the reform (rather than the dismantling) of the psychiatric dispositive. At the same time, authors engage critically with these terms and problematize the language of psychiatry for its essentializing impetus (cf. Vonnegut xi) and its inability to convey the intensity of experiencing the disorienting but also sublime loss of one's mind (cf. Jamison, *Unquiet* 179, 181; Styron 66; Kaysen 75; cf. also Beilke 30). Authors convey that intense experience with the term mad and colloquial expressions, thereby illustrating the distinct communicative potential of different labels.

Many major advocacy groups such as the National Alliance on Mental Illness (NAMI) condemn the use of stigma terms and instead promote the usage of supposedly softer social labels and person-first language—that is, "individuals living with mental illness" rather than "the mentally ill"—to "respect the integrity and individuality of people affected by these illnesses" ("Public" 2).[4] By contrast, all authors in my corpus defiantly, ironically, and self-deprecatorily reclaim terms which "haunt the popular imagination, while technically belonging to a regime of ruling that predates psychiatry"—a practice shared by the Mad Pride Movement (Burstow 82).[5] Among these terms are "loony," "crazy," and "nuts" but also more light-hearted expressions like "taking the fast train to Squirrel City" and "being a few apples short of a picnic" (Jameson, *Unquiet* 180). Erving Goffman proposed that the appropriation of a humorously "self-abusing language and style" is an attempt by well-adjusted discredited individuals "to show that they have not forgotten about the ways of the group or their own place" through performances of a "humorous caricature of their identity" (*Stigma* 134). My analysis in Chapter Two shows how this "humorous caricature" also allows for complex processes of signification that reveal stereotypical depictions of the mad to be constructions and insists on the individuality of persons with lived experience of madness.

In the humanities, the most widely used terms are "mad" and "Mad," and a surge of interest in recent years has even led to the creation of the field of Mad Studies.[6] Scholars in this field are frequently mad-identified and allied with advocacy groups that challenge the biomedical paradigm of mental illness by considering its symptoms within the wider social, institutional, and economic context of the person who exhibits them. Academics in Mad Studies furthermore aim to uncover symbolic, epistemic, and structural violence in the psychiatric dispositive, try to find new ways of conceptualizing the mind and its processes, and do so by "linking the struggle against biopsychiatry with other movements organized around gender, race, disability, social class, culture, and generation" (LeFrançois et al. 3).[7] Because of the latter, Mad Studies are theoretically indebted to the fields of Queer, Black, Disability, and Fat Studies. Researchers in those fields are extremely critical of dominant constructions of identity categories and "recogniz[e] the flawed nature of simplistic dichotomous and oppositional constructions of difference" (LeFrançois et al. 17). As did the embrace of "queer" and "fat," appropriating the word "mad" represents an "expressly political act" with the goal of "invert[ing] the language of oppression, reclaiming disparaged identities and restoring dignity and pride to difference" (LeFrançois et al. 10).

While the terms "madness" and "mad" in both capitalized and non-capitalized versions are still contested among scholars in Mad Studies, the various usages generally revolve around the same issues that shape the fields of Queer, Disability, and Fat Studies, namely resistance, lived experience, and attempts to institute it as a central, non-pathological category of identity. In their definition of the capitalized "Mad," Poole and Ward stress that it is a term of oppression reclaimed by individuals who have been pathologized as mentally ill and then expand it to also refer to "a movement, an identity, a stance, an act of resistance, a theoretical approach, and a burgeoning field of study" (96). They furthermore invoke the social model of disability which "locates difficulties that Mad folk face not simply in our 'conditions' but in a 'disabling society' permeated by oppressive power relations ... that divide, ostracize, individualize, medicalize, and prescribe" (96).[8] In this way, Poole and Ward inscribe themselves into discourses by marginalized groups that have previously been effective in garnering support for social change and express their rejection of the psychiatric understanding of madness as mental illness.

Whereas Poole and Ward organize their usage of "Mad" around various forms of resistance, Liegghio adds experiential components and more explicitly elevates it to the realm of recognized identity categories: According to her, "madness refers to a range of experiences—thoughts, moods, behaviors—that are different from and challenge ... dominant, psychiatric constructions of 'normal' versus 'disordered' ... [and is] a social category among other categories like race, class, gender, sexuality, age, or ability that define our identities and experiences" (122). Similarly, Diamond uses "mad" as an identity category but one so broad that it becomes "an umbrella term ... used in place of naming all of the different identities that describe people who have been labeled and treated as crazy (i.e., consumer, survivor, ex-patient)" (66). Liegghio and Diamond attempt to establish "mad" as a more general label that can "represent a diversity of identities" (Diamond 66) and thus unite disparate strands within the identity-political efforts of persons diagnosed with mental illnesses. As this brief overview of prominent voices in the academic discourse showed, scholars tend to use the label "mad" to signify nothing more specific than a group of people with a history of marginalization, disenfranchisement, and maltreatment by a powerful dispositive who have a wide variety of experiences that diverge from a narrowly defined norm. This usage allows them to conceive of madness as "a more inclusive and culturally grounded human phenomenon that encompasses various historically and contextually specific terms such as insanity, feebleminded, mental disorder, and mental illness" (White and Pike 250).

As in academia, the term "madness" is most widely used in both the main text and paratextual elements of memoirs in my corpus—albeit to different ends and effects. In academia, the use of the term is explicitly and exclusively identity-political. While authors in my corpus certainly use it to identity-political effects, such as destabilizing binary oppositions, reclaiming sanist slurs, and transcending individual psychiatric conditions, they also profit from the term's tabooization. Even though it also has positive connotations, the term was previously seen as pejorative since it evokes stigma beliefs of spectacular derangement, depravity, and dangerousness (cf. Perring 4; Corrigan et al. "Challenging"). Because of these associations, the use of the terms "mad" and "madness" can entice readers to buy and engage with the memoir, which reveals the political and commercial usefulness of the terms.

Furthermore, the term "madness" lends itself to complex acts of self-fashioning, as it is tied to a long history of thought and has "salience for the social order and the cultures we form part of and … [its] resonance in the world of literature and art and religious belief" (Scull, *Madness* 14). Unlike "mental illness" and "mental disorder," which were coined much more recently and are conceptually more restricted, madness carries connotations of nonconformity, romanticized suffering, and artistic genius which authors use for positive self-fashioning. Moreover, the term helps authors to implicitly and explicitly address issues of discrimination and shame because the term itself "implies stigma … [which] has been and continues to be a lamentable aspect of what it means to be mad" (Scull, *Madness* 14). As the following chapters show, "madness" in the sense that authors in my corpus use it, is a *palimpsest* of meanings that contains a broad array of positive and negative associations, deep-seated cultural tropes such as the (wise) fool or the dangerous madman/madwoman, and ties in with multiple discourses such as pre-nineteenth-century medicine, philosophy, art, literature, and religion as well as the supposed causes these discourses suggested for extremes of mood and thought. Only a term with such a broad meaning can accomplish what happens in pathographies, namely that established meanings are destabilized through marginal or submerged connotations which are brought to the surface (cf. also Cross, *Mediating* 31).

As for myself, I use "madness" as an umbrella term for behaviors and states of the mind that diverge from the norm, because it conveys a "dizzying superabundance" of meaning (L. Zimmerman 478) and can support a wide variety of apparently opposing rhetorical strategies. However, when I discuss specific conceptualizations of madness, such as the contemporary pathologization of extremes of thought and emotion by the psychiatric dispositive, I also use the terms "mental illness" and "mental disorder" as well as the specific psychiatric labels that experiencing selves received. When referring to understandings of madness in a specific historical context, I emulate the language of the period, using, e.g., "insanity" or "lunacy." While I understand that nowadays these historical terms and conceptualizations are widely considered to be slurs or misconceptions, I insist that, in order to study stigma, it is central to analyze not only current discourses on a subject matter but to also examine older discursive formations that still underlie contemporary ones. Terms such as "mental illness" and "lunacy" thus not only mark when I refer to a specific, historical understanding of madness but also allow me to problematize and analyze older discursive formations through the language they use.

By the same token, I at times employ a generalizing language to succinctly call up culturally salient tropes, types, and stigma-based categories that have structured debates about individuals deemed mad, such as "the dangerous madman" or "the mentally ill." Likewise, I use terms such as "truth," "authenticity," or "natural" to refer to commonsense notions around the complex processes that are at work in producing these effects. In other words, whenever I use any of these terms, I don't take them at face value but understand them to be discursive constructs, i.e., concepts that are produced by authoritative individual and institutional voices and perpetuated in journalistic and popular debates. It furthermore means that the understanding of these concepts varies across time and cultures and that there is no essential quality to any of them.

I concede that blanket terms like "madness" and "mental disorder" unduly suggest homogeneity when, in fact, my corpus contains very different experiences regarding the duration, severity, and impairment that resulted from the condition: While some authors like Truddi Chase, Jane Phillips, Kay Redfield Jameson, and Marianne Apostolides never had to stay at a psychiatric hospital, others like Marya Hornbacher, Lori Schiller and Kristina Morgan faced repeated and extended hospitalizations for their conditions. There are also differences in the content and severity of stigma between different types of madness: Whereas authors with psychotic conditions such as schizophrenia and certain types of bipolar disorder are more strongly affected by stigma beliefs about the dangerousness of the mad, authors with eating disorders or depressive disorder report that they found it hard to have their condition taken seriously (cf. Chapter Three). However, I suggest that there is a deeply ingrained, general conceptual category of madness that refers to extreme states of mind and carries multiple negative and supposedly positive stigma beliefs with it. The uniformity of stigma-management in my corpus suggests that authors react to this general category rather than their individual experience of symptoms and social reactions. It is thus because of the widespread use of the term madness by important discursive agents and because of the term's multifaceted meaning that I choose to employ "madness" and "mad" as well. I furthermore suggest that my understanding of madness as discursively constructed and the term's *palimpsest* of meaning provide a suitable basis for an analysis of the complex stigma- and identity-political negotiations of meaning which authors in my corpus conduct.

As this study also focuses on self-fashioning as normal, a few words on that term are in order as well. Following Lennard Davis, I understand normalcy as a concept that originated in mid-nineteenth-century statistics to describe entities that either conform to a standard or have a feature that is present in most of the population (2). Because normalcy arises through comparison to different samples, normalcy, like madness, can never be stable but is utterly relational. The boundaries between normalcy and madness are therefore constantly renegotiated and porous rather than solid. However, to provide a starting point for my analysis, I transitorily define normalcy as the absence of madness as well as all features textual selves—i.e., the totality of textual self-representation—share with the implied reader, such as a basic humanity, the capacity for suffering and rational thought, and a belief in US national myths. Normal furthermore has strong normative connotations and will therefore be used as the semantic opposite of the stigmatized traits of madness: Normalcy is the opposite of badness, irrationality, helplessness, mad genius, and general Otherness. However, these definitions are constantly renegotiated throughout this study.

The Stigma of Madness

Negotiations of meaning take place against the backdrop of historically elaborated discourses on madness and culturally embedded meanings. Simon Cross suggests that while older notions of the dangerous, depraved, incomprehensible madman have "supposedly receded in importance in art as well as medicine," these assumptions nevertheless continue to underlie the current understanding of madness and influence how we perceive the mad (*Mediating* iii). Moreover, these assumptions are easily revived, as Cross shows in his analysis of contemporary tabloid press treatment of the subject (*Mediating*). Authors in my corpus are also very concerned with them, and nearly all state that they wrote their memoirs to dismantle common misconceptions. To better understand the self-fashioning in my corpus and to outline which notions underlie the perception of the mad in contemporary US society, I will outline and contextualize the most pervasive stigma beliefs in this section.

Like Ian Hacking, I understand these general beliefs about madness and the mad within a framework that combines Erving Goffman's theory of stigma and Foucauldian discourse analysis. As I already elaborated on Foucault's theories in the preface, I now introduce Goffman's sociological concept of stigma and illustrate its mechanisms through the diverse meanings of madness that have accumulated in popular and scientific thought. This section does not attempt a comprehensive account of the history of madness.[9] Instead, my focus is how the attribute "mad" influenced how its possessors were seen and, generally, discriminated against.[10]

Discrimination, in both the sense of "the ability to recognize the difference between things that are of good quality and those that are not" and "the practice of unfairly treating a person or group of people differently from other[s]" ("Discrimination"), is at the root of the process of stigmatization. When the term *stigma* originated in Ancient Greece, it referred to bodily signs inflicted to "expose something unusual or bad about the moral status" of the bearer to make avoiding them easier (Goffman, *Stigma* 1). While the term was later also applied to bodily signs of divine grace in a Christian context, contemporary usage has returned to its original sense. However, rather than referring to the inflicted sign thereof, stigma nowadays refers to the disgrace itself (Goffman, *Stigma* 1–2).

According to Goffman, humans have developed means of categorizing people to reduce the cognitive effort required by encounters with strangers. We have normative expectations what kinds of people we are likely to meet in specific settings and convictions which attributes are "ordinary and normal" for them (Goffman, *Stigma* 2). We generally only become aware of these normative expectations when individuals differ from them. If the attributes in which the person deviates are found to be less desirable, these attributes constitute a stigma. Regardless of other, positive traits, an individual is then "reduced in our minds from a whole and usual person to a tainted, discounted one" and is in extreme cases considered to be "not quite human" (Goffman, *Stigma* 3, 5). As such, the bearer of the stigma is likely to become the recipient of discriminatory actions, which are justified by "a stigma theory, [i.e.,] an ideology to explain his [the stigmatized person's] inferiority and account for the danger he represents" (Goffman, *Stigma* 5).

In the case of madness, these stigma theories—which are expressed in myth, art, and medical discourses—focus on the mad person's responsibility for the condition, their supposed biological inferiority, animalism or monstrosity. Assumptions about the mad person's responsibility for their madness are as old as the Hebrew story of Saul, first king of the Israelites. After defying God, Saul was plunged into intense mental turmoil and was in turns full of fear, murderous rage, and despair. Similar stories about the divine and often punitive origin of madness can also be found in the Hellenic world and in the New Testament (Scull, *Madness* 16–24). In these myths, madness has a twofold function: On the one hand, the torment of madness is a form of punishment, and on the other hand, it is a sign that marks sinners. In the former case, madness is the result of previous sinful behavior, in the latter case, madness constitutes a stigma in the Ancient Greek sense of the word. These myths thus conduct complex stigma-based negotiations about the genesis and nature of madness.

The notion that the mad person is responsible for their condition has remained a pervasive trope in literature as well as an enduring theory in medical and laypeople's discourse: For example, Lady Macbeth is punished for her lust for power with madness. Similarly, eighteenth-century medical discourse held that melancholics and hysterics had irritated their nervous systems by indulging in too many worldly passions, abstract knowledge, and the artificial arousal of sentiments by theater-going and novel-reading (Foucault, *Madness* 213, 157; Cross, *Mediating* 94–128). The assumption of responsibility is retained in popular thought until the present, as studies found that lay people still blame individuals with mental illnesses for causing and maintaining their condition (Monteith and Pettit 485). Madness therefore constitutes a type of stigma Goffman called "blemishes of individual character" (*Stigma* 4): Negative traits such as immorality, worldliness, and weak will are *inferred* based on a person's madness.

A related stigma theory that furthermore produced the mad person's supposed biological inferiority originated in the second half of the nineteenth century with the publication of Bénédict-Augustin Morel's *Treatise on the Intellectual, Moral, and Physical Degeneracy of the Human Race* (1857). Based on the Lamarckian theory of the inheritance of acquired characteristics, Morel understood madness as the prize of sin, which was, however, "sometimes paid not by the original sinner for fornication, excessive drinking or other violation of conventional morality … but by his or her children, grandchildren or great-grandchildren" (Scull, *Madness* 243). Once acquired, the trait of degeneracy would become increasingly pronounced in each generation, leading first to madness and idiocy, then sterility, and finally the extinction of the blemished group. The theory of degeneration brought a biological component to the discourse about the nature and etiology of madness. As a result, the mad were no longer only regarded as moral deviants but also as a "biologically inferior lot" (Scull, *Madness* 243). This in turn provided justification for the incarceration of the insane in asylums: Unless they were confined to the moral and geographical margins of society, these "tainted creatures," who by definition lacked self-control, were prone to "attend upon the calls of their instincts and passions as does the unreasoning beast" and "to act as parents to the next generation" (Strahan 337, 334, qtd. in Scull, *Madness* 244–245). As Strahan's quote shows, nineteenth-century medical discourse negated the humanity of the mad through animal imagery and perceived of them not only as polluted but as actively, biologically polluting agents and a danger to society—a notion that a little later justified rites of purification like the eugenics movement.

However, the association of madness and animalism was not particular to nineteenth-century mad doctors.[11] Textual tropes of the animalistic appearance and behavior of the mad can be found throughout Western literature and as early as the Old Testament: When struck with madness, Nebuchadnezzar ate "grass as oxen" and "his hairs were grown like eagles' feathers, and his nails like birds' claws" (*English Standard Bible*, Daniel 4:33). In a similar vein, Shakespeare described the mad as "mere beasts" (*Hamlet* 4.5.85) and Charlotte Brontë's titular character Jane Eyre witnesses the animal spectacle of Mrs. Rochester who is on all fours, growls, and goes for her husband's throat. Stigma beliefs about the mad person's lack of humanity are therefore well established in Western literature.

The character of Bertha Rochester furthermore embodies the related stigma theory of monstrosity in madness, and the theatrical flourish with which her husband reveals her to Jane Eyre resembles how the mad were publicly displayed until the beginning of the nineteenth century. Her feral, unpredictable attacks, her bodily strength, and her supernatural cunning are a striking reversal of contemporary feminine ideals and signify her monstrosity: Positioned in the space between human and beast, the monster transgresses supposedly natural laws and is a threat to the social order (Federman et al. 45, 52). Like Mr. Rochester to his wife, nineteenth-century reason no longer felt any relation to madness and its potential for monstrosity (cf. Foucault, *Madness* 70). Reason's increasing disavowal of any relation to madness and the new shift in medical discourse towards the theory of degeneration led to an understanding of the mad "as creatures of a different ontological order" (Scull, *Madness* 188) that should be feared, disciplined or displayed.

Traces of the stigma belief in the fundamental difference of the mad remained, although its foundations changed: In 1950, a survey on the conceptualization of mental illness found that many respondents saw it as "a loss of what people consider to be the distinctly human qualities of rationality and free will, and [that] there is a kind of horror in dehumanization" (Star 6). Moreover, a 2004 review of research suggested that more recent understandings of madness as an imbalance of neurotransmitters "imply that people with mental illness are fundamentally different or less human … almost a different species" (Corrigan and Watson 478). These findings show that the belief in the mad person's inferiority and Otherness are deeply rooted and still persist in the twenty-first century.

The belief in the dangerous Otherness of the mad gave rise to their confinement in asylums and houses of correction all over Europe (Foucault, *Madness* 38–45; Scull, *Madness* 49). This confinement, in turn, allowed for the observation of (and experimentation on) large numbers of lunatics, and the medico-scientific discourse on madness made rapid advances. Yet, it was only in the nineteenth century when mad doctors, as they were called then, started to become an organized and self-conscious profession, that their conceptualization of madness became widely accepted and the condition was increasingly limited to the field of disease. The four major forms of madness distinguished until the end of classicism—melancholia, mania, hypochondria, and hysteria—were reconceptualized as mental illnesses and integrated into increasingly elaborate nosologies. This trend continues to the present day, as can be traced in the ever-growing number of mental disorders listed in each new edition of the *Diagnostic and Statistical Manual of Mental Disorders* (*DSM*) of the American Psychiatric Association (Scull, *Madness* 264–265, 388). The reconceptualization of madness as (mental) illness not only determined the language with which we predominantly speak about its origins (etiology) and its expression (symptoms), it also became the most widely accepted frame through which contemporary Western society views differences in temperament and perception as well as transgressive behavior.

This symbolic imposition of order on the disorder that is madness must also be seen as "a specific mode of subjection [that] was able to give birth to man as an object of knowledge for a discourse with a scientific status" (Foucault, *Discipline* 24). Madness, since the Classical Age held to be a loss of reason, could by its very definition not participate in the rational, objective discourse on itself.[12] This exclusion from the privileged form of discourse and the "legal and moral death-in-life" (Scull, *Madness* 133) that comes with the confinement to a mental hospital discredited the mad in two ways: In the Goffmanian sense of "discredit," it made the undesirable differentness of those diagnosed as mentally ill visible or known about (*Stigma* 4). In a literal sense, the discrediting attribute of madness thoroughly "cause[s] disbelief in the accuracy or authority" ("Discredit") of a person's statements—a conceptual mechanism that leaves the mentally ill particularly vulnerable to abuse and discrimination (cf. Cross, *Mediating* 20–24).

While madness is thus excluded from the realm of scientific truth, it is strongly connected to "another possible way of 'seeing': Bacchic, erotic, creative, prophetic, transformational" (Scull, *Madness* 36). From biblical accounts in which raving individuals "divine the future, and, if true prophets … spoke the words of the Lord" (Scull, *Madness* 18) to the visions of medieval saints, frenzied behavior and hallucinations have also been understood as divine blessings in Judeo-Christian thought. In the Hellenic world, madness is similarly connected to divination but also to art, philosophy, poetry, and love. In Plato's *Phaedrus*, Socrates states that "[m]adness, provided it comes as the gift of heaven, is the channel by which we receive the greatest blessings … madness is a nobler thing than sober sense … madness comes from God, whereas sober sense is merely human" (46–47). Poets, untouched by the divine fire of madness, would always be "utterly eclipsed by the performance of the inspired madman" (Plato, *Phaedrus* 48). From Antiquity, madness thus not only had a connection to a loss of reason but also to artistic genius.

This connection between madness and artistic genius eventually lost some of its cultural salience only to be rediscovered during the Renaissance when melancholia became a somewhat fashionable affliction with the intellectual elite: Since the melancholic humor, i.e., black bile, was believed to stimulate the intellect and imagination, poets and scholars were particularly prone to it. Galenic and Hippocratic theories of bodily humors were soon to be replaced with the notion of nerves as the body's animating principle, but the conflation of desirable attributes and conditions that had previously been understood as humoral imbalances remained: Nervous disorders signaled the refined nature of those they afflicted. Furthermore, Romantic poets, especially William Blake and Lord Byron, repopularized the Ancient Greek concept of the mad artist during the first half of the nineteenth century (Scull, *Madness* 86–120; Feder) and contributed to the continued relevance of this stigma theory.

The belief in a connection between madness and artistic genius also found its way into scientific discourse. In the early nineteenth century, the American physician Benjamin Rush and several contemporary European doctors published their observations about the relationship between specific kinds of mania and talents for the artistic use of language, music, painting, and some of the mechanical arts (Jamison, *Touched* 52–53). Rush stated that "[f]rom a part of the brain preternaturally elevated, but not diseased, the mind sometimes discovers not only unusual strength and acuteness, but certain talents it never exhibited before" (153; qtd. in Jamison, *Touched* 53). Rush's choice of words ("preternaturally") suggests a recourse to an ancient notion of divine madness and thus illustrates the overlap and exchange between different discourses on madness.

This history of the changing assumptions about madness not only illustrates the oscillation between the demonization and romanticization of madness but also reveals a key mechanism of stigmatization: Once a disgrace is discovered, "[w]e tend to impute a wide range of imperfections on the basis of the original one" (Goffman, *Stigma* 5), e.g., sinfulness, monstrosity or animalism. At the same time, "some desirable but undesired attributes, often of a supernatural cast" (Goffman, *Stigma* 5) are also ascribed to the bearer of the stigma, as could be seen in the case of prophets and mad artist. Stigma beliefs are therefore not unequivocally negative but have an inherent tension between supposedly positive and negative traits.

As this outline of the history of madness furthermore showed, the meanings of madness are ever shifting: Throughout history, madness was alternately a moral, a medical, a social, and an individual issue. However, the shifts in how madness was seen are not complete in the sense that newer theories supersede old ones. Instead, older assumptions about madness accumulated and formed a *palimpsest* of meanings that is discernible in contemporary US media, cultural products, and "common sense" (Gramsci 419–425) assumptions about the condition.[13] Older meanings may take a more covert form in contemporary culture and science than they did at their height of discursive power, yet they still form the basis of deeply rooted and pervasive stigma theories.

The Confessional Mode

When authors in my corpus negotiate the stigma of mental illness and fashion themselves as mad, their texts interact with a rich history of cultural practices that center on revealing oneself to be blemished in the Goffmanian sense. To contextualize these practices, I briefly outline a Foucauldian understanding of the mechanisms of confession, discuss several seminal texts and literary movements, and illustrate the additional effects which confessions can produce for authors and readers.

According to Michel Foucault, Western society ascribes multiple functions to confession: It produces the truth of the speaking subject, imposes social control, redeems transgressive individuals, provides emotional relief, tantalizes, and creates a sense of intimacy between confessor and confessant. To account for this diversity of functions, I adopt Foucault's definition of confession, i.e., a "ritual of discourse in which the speaking subject is also the subject of the statement" (Foucault, *Sexuality* 61) as well as "all those procedures by which the subject is incited to produce a discourse of truth" (Foucault, "Confession" 215–216). Because of its complex effects, Western society has relied heavily on confession in religion, medicine, literature, and popular culture, and these cultural practices influence how confessional memoirs of madness are received. As several more extensive genealogies of confession in the fields of religion, medicine, literature, and popular culture can be found elsewhere, this section restricts itself to confessional practices that directly impact readings of memoirs of madness.[14]

One use of confession is to authenticate transformations of the speaking or writing subject. This deployment of confession in literature began with Augustine's of Hippo *Confessions* (397–401 AD) in which he considers his life from the perspective of his conversion from Manichaeism to Christianity. Augustine's use of the first-person pronoun and the past tense not only "set up a mode of writing for Western literary practices thereafter" (Tambling 8) but is also central to the construction of the subject via confession. It constructs the writer of I as "an inward being," while the use of the past tense creates the expectation of a change from the experiencing I to the narrating I (Tambling 19). Although they are never completely fulfilled, the expectation of a transformation enables confessions in my corpus to support the self-fashioning as normal again. This type of self-fashioning allows authors to demand a stop of discrimination since they no longer have the stigmatized trait.

Linked to the authentication of transformations is the use of confession as a ritual of purification that offers redemption to penitents. In *Confessions*, Augustine structured his conversion through a "chronological narrative of errors and self-indulgence" (Smith and Watson 105) and insisted that this public admission of faults purified the soul (Wills 98). The belief in confession as a means of purification remains salient to the present as the success of confessional talk shows and the media trope of the confessional press conference prove: Scandal-ridden celebrities and transgressive unrenowned individuals publicly admit their wrongs and if audiences find them sincere, they are granted "rectitude and reentry into the social order" (Lofton 90). Similarly, confessions of former madness can redeem authors and ritually purify them.

A second key figure in the literary history of confessionalism is Jean-Jacques Rousseau who published his *Confessions* in the second half of the eighteenth century. The text not only established several tropes of autobiographical writing such as the insistence on the truthfulness of the account, the focus on the inner life rather than actions, and what Rousseau claimed was unpoetic language to convey that passages were emotionally authentic rather than carefully scripted (Yagoda 62). Moreover, it exemplified that confessions can be intensely pleasurable as they cater to prurient interest. In Rousseau's *Confessions*, "the development of a personality was explained in print by relating ... shameful events" (Rak, *Boom* 5). Each confession renews the curiosity of the reader, thus imbuing confessionalism with "the logic of ... infinite regression" (Olson 132; cf. also Foucault, *Sexuality* 44–45): The more intimate details one learns about someone, "the more truth about that individual shall be known" (Olson 132). By this logic, the use of unpoetic language and the inclusion of particularly intimate details are a trope or a mode of writing that "can be deliberately, even cynically, assumed" (Brain 13). Confessions of spectacularly transgressive behavior—such as those made in the memoirs in my corpus—can create the impression of having intimate knowledge of what is produced as the true experience of madness.

Furthermore, personal revelations can create a sense of intimacy between the reading and the writing subject. Smith and Watson suggest that the current popularity of memoirs may be due to "increasingly depersonalized and dispersed communities of late capitalism, [in which] readers seek the intimacy of a one-on-one reading experience ... [and a] connection with a narrator whose story ... resonates with their own struggles to find 'wholeness' and 'meaning'" (148). For similarly mad readers, mental illness pathographies can therefore create the impression of being intimately understood.

However, excessively intimate confessions can also create the desire for distance, as can be seen in reactions to confessional poetry. Confessional poetry is a US literary movement that emerged in the late 1950s and whose best-known representatives are Robert Lowell, Sylvia Plath, and Anne Sexton. Similar to Jean-Jacques Rousseau, confessional poets used a "rawness of ... address" (Yezzi 15), free verse, and "fervor [of expression] and associative logic" (Yezzi 15) to write in the first-person singular about taboo subjects such as madness, addiction, sexual transgressions, and bodily functions (cf. Gregory 34). Due to frequent references to persons and circumstances linked to the historical author, contemporary critics, most prominently M.L. Rosenthal, expressed unease about the intimacy forced upon them as readers. Despite his admiration for the "beautifully articulated poetic sequence[s]" in Lowell's work (110), Rosenthal was appalled by a speaker taken to unequivocally represent the poet as well as the "rank" confessions and "rather shameful [personal confidences] that one is honor-bound not to reveal" (110, 109). As I elaborate in Chapter Four, excruciatingly visceral confessions in pathographies can be read as "hostile bravado" (Goffman, *Stigma* 17), i.e., a reaction to stigma in which authors aggressively perform their abjection to scandalize readers and to manage the level of intimacy. In this case, confession strengthens the mad side of the tension inherent in the texts in my corpus and helps authors to manage shame.

Another property ascribed to confession is spiritual or psychological healing. Psychoanalytic and psychological theory as well as its adaptation into popular psychology have established the notion that the mere verbalization of transgressions produces changes in the speaking subject and liberates them from various mental ills that would otherwise surface as some form of pathology (Jones 94–95; Grobe 6–15). Trauma therapy therefore encourages patients to narrate overwhelming events to assist the meaning-making process[15] and to "give coherence to the distinctive events and long-term course of suffering" (Kleinman 49; cf. also Lifton 367). They suggest that reducing a disorienting experience to events in narrative structures creates a sense of agency and control (Tal 6; Kleinman 49). Additionally, communicating disorienting events helps to reestablish a sense of connection between the speaking self and others (Lifton 367). Because of these functions, narratives of madness, physical illness or trauma "not merely reflect … [but] shape and even create experience" (Kleinman 49). In this manner, confessional narratives of madness can have a healing effect on their authors while simultaneously providing new interpretations of lived experience.

As this section showed, the confessional mode influences how mental illness pathographies are received and has complex, even contradictory effects on both the confessant and the confessor. On the one hand, the ritual of confession can create a sense of intimacy and help penitent individuals to regain social acceptance. On the other hand, shockingly private confessions can increase the readers' desire for distance to the confessant and lend credence to the author's claims to madness. Furthermore, literary confessions are both seen as meaningful work that helps both confessants and confessors make sense of overwhelming events, and as a self-absorbed spectacle that only caters to prurient interest. The confessional mode therefore does not resolve but aggravates tensions already present in memoirs of madness. I will now turn to these tensions, first to the one that exists between the self-fashioning as normal and as mad, and then to the one between objective and subjective truth.

PART I

Self-Fashioning as Normal (Again) and as Mad

There is a basic tension that underlies mental illness pathographies, and that is never resolved. This tension exists between a textual self-fashioning as normal and one as mad. While some memoirs put more focus on either the selves' normalcy or their madness, these texts still contain too many ambiguities and inconsistencies to produce unequivocally normal or mad textual selves. The next two chapters analyze how these tensions are created and maintained through appropriations of culturally valued narrative structures, tropes, discourses, and modes of writing. I furthermore discuss how these tensions contribute to the discursive production of madness and the literary negotiation of stigma. What interests me in particular is how textual constructs such as the experiencing and the narrating self react to the label mad, how they interact with those who share their stigma, and how they embrace or problematize stigma beliefs about the mad.

For the sake of a structured argument, I divide this part into two chapters, turning first to textual features that produce the textual selves' normalcy and then to those that lend themselves to the production of their madness. This division allows me to reveal the full extent to which each textual identity is developed and throws the conflict in self-fashioning into relief. As in all parts of this study, I analyze particularly salient examples of tropes or narrative structures from different texts to show how pervasive these textual features are. However, I always also include examples from Marya Hornbacher's *Madness: A Bipolar Life* to demonstrate that tensions between vastly different meanings of madness and types of self-fashioning are present not only in my corpus as a whole but in individual texts as well.

However, even among the textual features that produce the same state of mind, tensions arise between the meanings that are produced for either the normalcy or the madness of the textual selves. The reasons for these tensions are the wide variety of subject positions, tropes, and narrative structures that are culturally available in the American tradition of life writing and the authors' appropriation of several of them to make sense of their life. For example, they draw upon the national myth of self-making through self-reliance, hard work, and perseverance as well as the narrative of conversion and passive redemption through the grace of a higher power. While both are narratives of overcoming and aid the production of a mad experiencing self and a normal narrating self, they suggest very different things about agency: In the myth of self-making, mad experiencing selves work hard to raise themselves above the circumstances of their neurochemistry and trauma. In conversion narratives, experiencing selves must see the error of their ways and give themselves up to a higher power, either God or the healing power of the psychiatric dispositive. By extension, these narrative structures suggest contradictory things about madness and its treatment, namely that it is in the responsibility and power of the patient to overcome it or that madness is beyond their control and they require outside help. Moreover, Gothic tropes collapse previous distinctions between mad experiencing self and normal narrating self and furthermore raise questions about the unity and distinction between self and madness. Since memoirs draw upon a mix of these narrative structures and other tropes, both madness and normalcy receive highly conflicting meanings.

The tension between normalcy and madness as well as these internal ambiguities destabilize clear binary oppositions such as mad and normal, victim and perpetrator, self and Other. Memoirs in my corpus thus produce subjectivities unmoored from central organizing labels. As a result, the label "mad" loses its essentializing impetus, and the process of stigmatization, which operates on the assumption of stable, inherent blemishes, breaks down. In other words, memoirs in my corpus undermine the stigma attached to mental illness not by decrying its hurtful effects or disproving stigma theories—although they do that as well—but by disabling the central mechanism of the process itself: The creation of order by distinguishing clearly between those who are blemished and those who are not.

While many authors state that their stigma-political goals caused them to write their memoirs, this does not mean that this destabilization of the process of stigmatization is the result of a conscious strategy shared by all authors in my corpus. Instead, the texts' literariness enables the move away from a unified self and towards openness of meaning. This literariness is marked by tensions, contradictions, the inclusion of multiple intertextual references, and self-referentiality which also show that texts in my corpus are highly postmodern.[16] Since postmodern techniques are currently regarded as a high-brow form of writing, they allow authors to claim "cultural capital"[17] (Bourdieu, "Forms" 247) and legitimize the position from which they speak (cf. Gilmore, "Mark" 6).[18] This high-brow status further points to the stigma-political work completed in these texts because "literature is a focal point for the expression of cultural tensions" (Olson 4).

Memoirs in my corpus also do other important cultural work. The appropriation of narratives of overcoming inserts those labeled mad into US fantasies of self-hood, shows that they embrace American values, and thus allows supposedly normal readers to bridge the gap of Otherness to the mentally ill. Detailed descriptions of hardship that are common to narratives of conversion and self-making furthermore establish the experiencing selves' basic human capacity for suffering and contradict stigma beliefs about the monstrous mad person which are embraced again through the appropriation of Gothic tropes. The resulting complex forms of self-fashioning furthermore interact with discourses on madness in contradictory ways: For example, the self-fashioning challenges the totalizing structure created by the diagnostic categories of the psychiatric dispositive. Conversely, many texts endorse the psychiatric discourse on madness when they (also) narrate their lived experience as stories of conversion to the truth of the psychiatric dispositive. In this simultaneous affirmation and rejection of the allegedly objective truths of psychiatry, mental illness pathographies produce an uncertainty that is both fundamentally postmodern and that evokes ancient notions of madness as a truth that transcends "sober sense" (Platon, *Phaedrus* 46). Mental illness pathographies thus engage with stigma beliefs and dominant discourses on madness on the level of narrative in a highly postmodern manner.

Despite their complex cultural work and their postmodern contradictions and fragmentation, memoirs of mental illness remain accessible enough to become commercially successful. This has to do with their embrace of three modes of writing, namely the confessional, the sentimental, and the spectacular mode. While the confessional mode is also undermined by the marked constructedness and artificiality of formulaic narrative templates such as the conversion narrative, the use of confession as a means of truth production is so deeply embedded in Western culture that it still creates the impression of authenticity and increases the effect of the latter two modes. The sentimental mode encourages sympathy for the plight of the mad, whereas the spectacular mode offers up pitiful or monstrous experiencing selves to the voyeuristic desires of the reader. The combination of these three modes creates texts that fit well into the contemporary culture of extreme confessionalism and thus ensures that the stigma-political work in these memoirs reaches a wide audience (cf. Gilmore, "American").

Despite their status as literature and the openness of meaning it entails, memoirs are also platforms individual authors use to address stereotypes about their social group and to fashion themselves textually (Couser, "Some" 7–8). Chapter One therefore begins by considering the problems in self-fashioning encountered by discredited individuals before turning to the textual selves' nuanced claims to normalcy and narratives that produce the narrating self as normal *again*. Chapter Two discusses the authors' embrace of the label "mad" as well as the meanings they produce for that label. Authors in my corpus carve out greater freedom in self-fashioning by problematizing any single interpretation of madness be it pathology, impairment, a blessing in disguise, a way of being in the world or a label to oppress transgressive individuals. Moreover, Chapter Two addresses similarities between memoirs of madness and stigma-political work by other marginalized communities by considering the deployment of the humorous mode as well as the ways in which texts in my corpus charge the discourse emotionally through claims to extreme suffering and victimization. The self-fashioning as an innocent victim is immediately complicated by the appropriation of the Gothic mode which confounds the boundaries between self and madness and alternately depicts the condition as a demonic or seductive Other or an expression of a repressed true self. The first part of this project therefore analyzes the contradictory forms of self-fashioning in mental illness pathographies that are never resolved and that contribute to the multiple, opposing meanings that memoirs in my corpus produce about madness as well as normalcy.

Dealing with Discredit

Individuals who have been diagnosed with mental disorders cannot simply insist that, despite or beyond their madness, they are quite ordinary people: The discredit which is incurred by psychiatric diagnoses or confinement to a mental hospital is so extensive that it threatens to delegitimize claims made by authors in my corpus, especially those to normalcy. Because the psychiatric dispositive holds so much discursive weight in Western societies, authors need to employ multiple, nuanced strategies to present themselves as *essentially* or *relatively* normal (again), regardless of the diagnostic labels they have received.

Authors in my corpus are well aware how confinement by the psychiatric dispositive can restrict the patient's ability to fashion or see themselves as normal (cf. Foucault *Psychiatric*). During her first hospitalization, Lori Schiller, who was diagnosed with schizophrenia, points to the structural delegitimization of patients' claims to sanity when she rages, "naturally they [Schiller's friends and family] thought I was sick! If you are in a mental hospital you must be sick" (Schiller and Bennett 89; cf. also Smola 51). Moreover, Marya Hornbacher and Susanna Kaysen express their sense that hospitalization is not restricted to a medico-psychiatric assessment of their mental health but implies moral deviance as well. Kaysen states, "In the world's terms … all of us [she and her fellow patients] were tainted" (124) by their hospitalization, and Marya Hornbacher explains that her admission to a mental hospital is a removal from the world because she has been found "flawed and wanting" (*Wasted* 145). Authors thus realize that their self-fashioning and stigma management needs to take the discursive weight and delegitimizing impetus of psychiatric diagnoses or hospitalizations into account.

The discredit incurred by psychiatric diagnoses cannot be countered by straightforward rejections of the attribute of madness because these rejections generate an uncomfortable contradiction between the textual selves' statements and the assessment of psychiatrists. Readers likely resolve this contradiction between a dominant dispositive and a discredited person in favor of the former. An example of this reaction can be found in Roy Porter's discussion of Samuel Bruckshaw's pamphlets. Bruckshaw was confined to a Lancashire asylum in 1770 where he claims he was abused rather than treated as part of a conspiracy aimed at cheating him out of his property. Musing about the reliability of Bruckshaw's writings for historical research into asylum conditions, medical historian Roy Porter writes,

> Bruckshaw presents himself as a lamb led to the slaughter by diabolical conspiracies hatched by his fellow citizens. Yet his tone is, to say the least, fractious, suspicious, and litigious. And though he upholds his sanity, he records that while confined he had heard disembodied voices. In this and many similar cases, it would take a bold psycho-historian to judge whether such writings reveal persecution, paranoia, or both [*Madness* 168].

Even though Porter admits that it would be "bold" to attempt a psychiatric evaluation based on a historical document, his dramatic summary of Bruckshaw's version of events ("*lamb* led to the *slaughter* by *diabolical* conspiracies") suggests that he is highly critical of the account. Likewise, Porter's assessment of Bruckshaw's tone and the inclusion of a well-established sign of madness—hearing voices—speaks to his doubts about the accuracy of the pamphleteer's allegations against the asylum. This passage exemplifies that the discrediting power of the psychiatric dispositive can pose serious problems to any person diagnosed as mad who wants to criticize the treatment of mental illnesses or contest their diagnosis.

This phenomenon is also visible in Katarzyna Szmigiero's discussion of women's first-person accounts of madness. Szmigiero distinguishes between "Unconvincing Accounts of Sanity" (56) and "brave depictions" of "the often-devastating effects of a mental illness" (58). In her analysis of the former, Szmigiero—an assistant professor in an English department—diagnoses authors of historical and contemporary life writing with multiple conditions. Her corpus includes two texts dealing with the sensational abuses in nineteenth-century asylums whose authors claim that they were hospitalized when they developed unorthodox religious beliefs. Though Szmigiero acknowledges that the psychiatric dispositive more readily pathologizes transgressive behavior in women than in men and that this pathologization is not based on objective, stable diagnostic criteria (50), she categorically overrules the female writers' claims to sanity. Szmigiero states, "An objective modern reader would easily notice that mania and paranoid delusions are present" (53), thus supposing the objectively verifiable existence of a mental disorder in these two women. Like Roy Porter, she resolves incongruences between self-evaluations in life writing and a psychiatrist's assessment in favor of the latter. The reactions of Porter and Szmigiero illustrate that, once discredited as mentally ill, individuals cannot successfully lay claim to an identity as completely normal anymore but need to employ more complex modes of self-fashioning.

CHAPTER ONE

Self-Fashioning
as Normal (Again)

Authors in my corpus avoid proclamations of total sanity in favor of more nuanced approaches. The first of these approaches consists of rejecting the label "mad" in its stigmatizing meanings as a dehumanizing, utterly debilitating, all-encompassing condition by fashioning themselves as *relatively* or *essentially* normal. To depict themselves as *relatively* normal and reject stigma-based ascriptions of complete debilitation, narrating selves distinguish between the experiencing self's condition and patients whose madness is more obtrusive and incapacitating. In this manner, the meaning of madness as "a defiling thing to possess" (Goffman, *Stigma* 7) remains unchallenged, but the discredit is redirected through relativization, a process Leon Anderson calls "role distancing" (108). Texts in my corpus also negotiate the meaning of madness as dehumanization or an all-encompassing Otherness with a strategy Goffman calls "normification" (*Stigma* 31): When textual selves insist that experiencing selves retain the capacity for suffering and rational thought, which arguably makes them "a human being like anyone else" (Goffman, *Stigma* 7), or else when they differentiate between a normal, core self and an intrusive, Othered madness, they fashion themselves as *essentially* normal.[1] Texts therefore produce textual selves as normal in the sense that they do not certain possess negative characteristics associated with madness.

The second approach is a related mechanism that takes place when authors enable normalizing readings of madness as a normal reaction to an insane society that is pathologized by the psychiatric dispositive. Drawing upon arguments of the anti-psychiatry movement, some authors seek to delegitimize the dispositive that discredited them and reject the discursive construction of madness as a disorder with the same verifiable existence as cancer or infections. In other words, they question the legitimacy of anyone being labeled "mad," thus deflecting the discussion of their personal madness to more general epistemological concerns.

Relativization, normification, and the rejection of the entire frame-work of madness as mental illness can also be read as manifestations of one[2] response to stigma, namely shame.[3] Following Léon Wurmser, I hold that these expressions of shame are masked and surface in the form of denial or reversal, the latter being the application of stigma beliefs to those more visibly blemished than oneself (Wurmser 9). This reading does not intend to unmask persons with mental disorders in denial about their condi-tion—after all, the texts *do* include affirmations of madness, and even those narrating selves that stress their normalcy refer to themselves as "luna-tics" (Kaysen 51), "mental incompetent" (Beers 21) or "a nut" (Smola 73). Instead, it reveals the complexity of self-fashioning in my corpus, shows the extent to which authors have internalized common stigma beliefs, and thus illustrates the cultural background against which these texts were written.

Relativization and Claims to Essential Normalcy

One way of dealing with the stigma of madness is to embrace stigma beliefs and to apply them to individuals whose condition is more obtrusive. This fashions narrating selves as normal insofar as they renounce kinship with the mad (cf. Goffman, *Stigma* 107). This section considers how mem-oirs discursively produce the madness of others as well as the relative or essential normalcy of experiencing selves.

This type of self-fashioning is very prominent in David Smola's account of his severe depressive episode, multiple suicide attempts, and hospitalization, *A Waltz Through La La Land: A Depression Survivor's Mem-oir* (2010). Note how the title acknowledges the author's lived experience with a mental disorder but also downplays it: "Waltz through" establishes the transitory nature of his condition and the ease with which the expe-riencing self overcame it, whereas "La La Land" suggests eccentricity and being a little out of touch with reality rather than a serious affective disor-der. The fashioning of his depressive episode as a relatively short, minor crisis continues throughout the memoir and is contrasted with the seri-ous, enduring madness of Smola's fellow patients. The memoir thus opens up a distinction between mental crises and genuine madness, which is pre-sented as a stable blemish that, however, does not affect the experiencing self.

The difference between Smola's experiencing self and his fellow patients is repeatedly emphasized by everyone: the narrator, the expe-riencing self, his parents, fellow patients, and mental healthcare pro-fessionals.[4] They frequently marvel "how a good looking [sic], college educated, popular young man could end up here [in a mental hospital]," among people many of whom the narrator describes as either recognizably "wacko," "mentally retarded" or "a combination of mentally retarded and mentally ill" (Smola 73, 43, 91). Staff and patients furthermore single Smola's experiencing self out as the only one who has a realistic chance of recovery: A nurse remarks that Smola "can be saved. He's not like the rest of the folks up here" (87) and other patients agree (73). Likewise, Smola's experiencing self exclaims: "I am not like these people. I am not crazy, damn it" (60). Whereas the experiencing self's mental crisis is transient and at odds with his usual all–American, high achieving, fun-loving, frat boy ways (13), the other patients' conditions are incurable, utterly incapacitating, and in line with stigma theories that conflate madness and intellectual disabilities.

In this manner, Smola acknowledges the discrediting power of the psychiatric dispositive that labeled him "depressive" but also distances himself from those he perceives to be justifiably stigmatized by their disorders. To convey this distinction, Smola's memoir dwells on the symptoms and incapacitations of other patients. To give just a few examples, the narrator derisively comments on other patients in the experiencing self's therapy group: He explains that the "awful hygiene" of one man, who was "clearly also mentally retarded" (90–91), was the topic of debate for an entire therapy session because it "offended everyone" (51). Introducing another patient, the narrator explains that "the rather messy gentleman … [was] convinced his father was none other than Lucifer … [and that the patient] needed heavy doses of Haledol [sic] to keep him just a babbling fool instead of an angry, violent babbling fool" (47). These comments show that Smola does not protest the stigmatization of the mad as such, only the application of this stigma to them personally. Analyzing the coming-out narratives of scholar-activists that self-identify as mad and disabled, Elizabeth Brewer points out that that "crip-casting" or categorizing certain stigmatized conditions as less desirable than others "effectively buys status" for persons with one condition at the expense of others and undermines the possibility of community and coalition politics (24). Smola's memoir therefore not only illustrates the urgency with which individuals want to escape stigmatization but also shows that mental illness pathographies contain the same conflicts and challenges that characterize contemporary advocacy work and that pathographies can provide insights for sociological inquiries.[5]

Even though the narrator in Smola's memoir embraces multiple stigma theories about the mad as well as a derisive tone and language when describing the other patients, *A Waltz Through La La Land* is more complex than the mere attempt to buy status at the expense of those whose madness is more obtrusive. When the narrator calls group therapy a "three-ring circus" (66) and "the loony line dance" (47), he ascribes a certain entertainment value to the noise and agitation of the patients, thus evoking stigma beliefs about the entertaining oddity the mad (cf. Wahl, *Media* 14–35). As the experiencing self is unwilling to contribute to group therapy, the text aligns him with the audience and readers rather than the patients and performers. Smola thus performs his normalcy by distancing himself from the carnivalesque spectacle of madness. However, this imagery can also be read against the grain, i.e., as an allusion to the history of exhibiting the mad in freak shows and as an implicit critique of the constant surveillance of patients. Smola's experiencing self notices the nurses' station, "a large wooden creation … where the nurses and counselors could keep an eye on the creatures who were there …He felt as if he were a tortured animal at the zoo, one who had been injured and then left on display" (26). In his first days, "[h]e spent most of his time observing the *other* creatures around him" (45; emphasis added). Note how Smola acknowledges the dehumanizing panopticism of the psych ward through animal imagery as well as his status as a creature *among others*. In this vein, his reluctance to share his thoughts in group therapy could be seen as a refusal to perform his improving or deteriorating condition in a "three-ring circus" or "line dance" for the staff. This passage therefore further exemplifies the threat of dehumanization and stigmatization which Smola's memoir attempts to escape as well as the ambiguity of all literary texts.

R. David Smola is not the only author who produces his experiencing self as normal—at least in comparison to his fellow patients. Kaysen's narrating self explains that the experiencing self and her roommate Georgina were well enough to go outside with little supervision but were assigned to the highly supervised group due to staff shortages. "[T]his made it seem that Georgina and I were as crazy as Cynthia and the Martian's girlfriend. We weren't, and there was quite a bit of resentment on our part" (50–51). Similarly, Lori Schiller proclaims at the beginning of her first hospitalization: "The other patients were crazy. I had as little to do with them as possible. Outside the hospital were other normal people like me" (91; cf. also Hornbacher, *Wasted* 197).[6] While these proclamations of relative normalcy may be read as attempts to ward off stigma and shame about being confined to a mental hospital, they also produce madness as utterly relational: The conditions of the authors' experiencing selves may have well been less obtrusive or incapacitating than those of the other patients on the psych ward. It just goes to show that most people can lay claim to either madness or normalcy—it all depends on the group of people they compare themselves to.

Jane Phillips' and Robert B. Oxnam's memoirs of dissociative identity disorder—formerly known as multiple personality disorder—make this relativization more explicit. Phillips finally agrees with *their[7] psychologist that "mental illness is not behavior different from what is found in the rest of the population; mental illness is only its more extreme manifestation" (217). Likewise, Oxnam suggests, "a lot of people, possibly all people have multiple personae.... Many describe them as 'roles' or 'masks,' and that his 'experience may be an extreme exaggeration of what is normal human behavior'" (5). In these quotes, narrating selves reject binary oppositions between madness and normalcy, reduce distinctions to a matter of degree, and fashion *themselves as relatively normal. Moreover, the notion of a spectrum that connects normalcy and madness undermines the sharp distinctions needed for the process of stigmatization.[8]

Additionally, authors in my corpus present themselves as *essentially* normal distinguishing between a personified, intrusive madness and a normal core self, thereby producing madness as a less global a taint than stigma beliefs suggest. Memoirs thus "challenge the humanist assumption of a unified self and an integrated consciousness" (Hutcheon xii; cf. also Fee 6) and resist totalizing discourses such as those of psychiatry in a highly postmodern manner (E. Young 56). Clifford Beers, who was diagnosed with what is now called bipolar disorder, firmly establishes this distinction between his mad and his normal self on the first pages of his memoir. He introduces the text as "an autobiography, and more: in part it is a biography; for, in telling the story of my life, I must relate the history of another self—a self which was dominant from my twenty-fourth to my twenty-sixth year. During that time, I was unlike what I had been, or what I have been since" (3). This passage implies that his "unnatural self" (3) is so alien to his regular, sane self that it warrants a modification of the "autobiographical pact" (cf. Lejeune) and an adjustment of the genre. This not only protects Beers from charges of a global madness and to a certain extent rids him of responsibility for his actions during his period of Unreason, but the reference to an "unnatural *self*" still allows him to claim the authority of experience on which he bases his truth claims about madness.

The self-fashioning as *essentially* normal is further supported by Beers' assertions that he retained a core of rationality even at his most delusional. Going against the stigma belief "that no insane person can reason logically" (28), he states that upon "unreasonable premises" he made "most reasonable deductions ... [b]ut, such as they were, they were deductions, and essentially the mental process was no other than that which takes place in a well-ordered mind" (28–29).[9] In this quote, the narrating self reduces the processes of "a well-ordered mind" to deductive reasoning whereas the experiencing self's "unreasonable premises," i.e., his delusions of persecution, receive a secondary, almost accidental status, which allows him to lay claim to normalcy.

These claims to a normal core are also central to Beers' advocacy for asylum reform.[10] Since Classicism, reason was seen as one of the necessary conditions for humanity. The loss of reason—madness—was "man in immediate relation to his animality … [and] animality could be mastered only by *discipline* and *brutalizing*" (Foucault, *Madness* 74–75). Because of this history of thought, Beers' claim to a core of reason also functions as a claim to humanity and a plea against brutalization. The self-fashioning as normal therefore not only conveys Beers' double sense of self but also supports his calls for the abolition of harsh treatment in mental hospitals.

Several authors in my corpus, then, appropriate stigma beliefs and discursively produce other mad persons as incurable or mentally incapacitated, thus presenting experiencing selves as normal by comparison. In addition to disavowing those who share the stigma of hospitalization, narrating selves insist that whatever madness they exhibited, it is not something that defines them as a person, and that they are normal at their core. This self-fashioning as relatively or essentially normal is likely received more favorably than the proclamations of full sanity that were discussed above. Authors who relativize or normify don't ask readers to take the word of a discredited person—themselves—over that of a dominant dispositive. Instead, they affirm deep-seated stigma beliefs but demonstrate that madness has various degrees of severity. In this manner, they complicate established beliefs about madness and selfhood.

Normalization and Depathologization

Another way for authors in my corpus to fashion themselves as normal is to reject the pathologization of the experiencing self's condition by the psychiatric dispositive. Drawing upon arguments of the anti-psychiatry movement[11] to challenge the psychiatric understanding of madness as a mental disorder and to present the psychiatric dispositive as an instrument of social control (Szasz, *Myth* 67, 102; Foucault *Psychiatric*). They hold that their condition is not pathological at all but a normal reaction to an oppressive society (Laing, *Divided* 23–24, 107) or else that they are systematically discredited for being particularly liberated individuals. In this manner, authors not only reject the discredit that a psychiatric diagnosis entails but also use romanticized, anti-psychiatric notions of madness for positive self-fashioning.

Although all authors in my corpus criticize aspects of their treatment or individual practitioners and represent their madness in a manner that is at odds with the psychiatric discourse, few *explicitly* reject the pathologization of their condition as mental disorders. In fact, only the memoirs by Susanna Kaysen and Ann Cvetkovich supply strong examples of this fundamental critique. The relative rarity of depathologization not only speaks to the discursive weight of the psychiatric dispositive but also illustrates how extensively authors rely on psychiatric truth for meaning-making, stigma management, and the promise of a cure (cf. Chapter Three). Another reason for the rarity of a self-fashioning as normal through depathologization is that authors seek to engage psychiatrists and psychologists in a dialogue about the conceptualization and treatment of their conditions. Rejecting the most basic tenet of psychiatry—that madness is a disorder of the mind—likely makes this dialogue impossible. However, depathologization enables different kinds of stigma-political work.

Susanna Kaysen, who was diagnosed with borderline personality disorder, engaged in multiple self-harming behaviors, and attempted suicide, was confined to the renowned McLean Hospital for two years in the late 1960s. Kaysen's memoir begins with an account of how the experiencing self's psychiatrist "tricked" (39) her into signing herself into the hospital, even though she was not mentally ill. She returns to this topic several times over the course of the text, and the depathologization of the experiencing self's condition is one of the main themes of *Girl, Interrupted* (1993).

To produce the textual selves' normalcy, Kaysen's narrating self points out that psychiatric truth claims about the etiology and nature of madness have changed so dramatically over time that the truth value of current interpretations needs to be questioned. To this end, she presents a list of the conflicting meanings which madness has acquired throughout history in a chapter titled "Etiology." The list contrasts Classicist, Modern, psychoanalytic, psychiatric, and anti-psychiatric interpretations of madness and the treatment it requires, and *asks the reader to decide* if

this person is (pick one):
1. on a perilous journey from which we can learn much when he or she returns,[12] …
5. bad and must be punished;
6. ill, and must be isolated and treated by (pick one):
  (a) purging and leeches,
  (b) removing the uterus[13] if the person has one,
  (c) electric shock to the brain, …
  (d) Thorazine or Stelazine,[14] …
7. ill, and must spend the next seven years talking about it;
8. a victim of society's low tolerance for deviant behavior;
9. sane in an insane world;
10. on a perilous journey from which he or she may never return [15].

By listing vastly different and, to modern eyes, preposterous claims about madness and its treatment ("purges and leeches," "removing the uterus"), Kaysen expresses her doubts about psychiatric truth claims: Why would contemporary theories on madness be more on point than older ones? Kaysen emphasizes this skepticism by denying the current neuropsychological model of madness as mental illness the last position in her list, which would imply that this view is the most advanced or even final truth of madness. In this manner, she rejects the authority of the psychiatric dispositive to discredit her by pointing to its history of now disproven theories.

Kaysen continues her critique when she reveals that psychiatric theories are not formulated on the basis of supposedly disinterested science but that they are deeply rooted in specific historical contexts as well as notions of morality and that, ultimately, the psychiatric dispositive is an instrument of social control. She states that the authors of the *Diagnostic and Statistical Manual of Mental Disorders* (*DSM*) "do get rid of things—homosexuality, for instance…. Maybe in another twenty-five years I won't be in it [the *DSM*] either" (152). By creating equivalencies between the pathologization of her own condition and homosexuality, Kaysen implies that the diagnosis she received is an act of discrimination rather than a medical assessment. Moreover, she suggests that borderline personality disorder could and should one day be seen as a facet of human diversity. Kaysen thus not only fashions madness as an identity category akin to sexual orientation but also rejects the moral authority of the psychiatric dispositive by pointing to its history of oppression.

Kaysen further undermines the scientific authority of the psychiatric dispositive when she gestures towards the performativity of madness and the lack of objective evidence that a person is mentally disordered. Unlike other specialties in medicine, psychiatry cannot use physical examinations to determine a patient's condition. Instead, psychiatrists rely on patients' reports of symptoms and observations of their behavior which means that madness and sanity can be performed. Kaysen's narrating self thus questions the validity of diagnoses when she discusses her own perceptions: When she looked at oriental rugs, tile floors, printed curtains or even faces, she saw "other things within them … patterns [that] seemed to contain potential representations, which in a dizzying array would flicker briefly to life" (41). She repeatedly emphasizes that these perceptions may *sound* like hallucinations but that they were not, adding, "I was at all times perfectly conscious of my misperceptions of reality" (41). She finally claims, "This clarity made me able to behave normally, which posed some interesting questions. Was everybody seeing this stuff and acting as though they weren't? Was insanity just a matter of dropping the act?" (41) The narrating self thus suggests a definition of normalcy as the ability to *act* normally. She thereby rejects notions of an essential difference between normals—as Goffman call persons without the stigma in question (*Stigma* 5)—and the mad which form the basis for processes of discrimination. Moreover, she undermines psychiatry's self-fashioning as the producer of an objective, quasi-medical truth.

Kaysen's musings on perceptions and performativity are indebted to anti-psychiatric discourse, specifically R.D. Laing's writings. Laing states that "what we call 'normal' is a product of repression, denial, splitting" (*Divided* 23–24) of a person's fantasies, sense of self, and the capacity to think beyond the limits of conformity. Someone who expresses alienation in ways that are statistically the most common, who "*acts* more or less like everybody else, is taken to be sane" (24; emphasis added). In this line of thought, the psychiatric dispositive is reduced to an instrument of social oppression which disciplines less repressed individuals by discrediting them. By appropriating anti-psychiatric thought, Kaysen implicitly produces madness to mean nonconformity and psychological liberation.

Kaysen's narrating self also appropriates arguments from another prolific writer in the anti-psychiatry movement, Thomas Szasz, to present her hospitalization as the result of systemic sexism rather than madness on her part. Szasz emphatically stated that a complex of (mis-) behaviors is no illness in the traditional medical sense (Szasz, *Psychiatry* 2–5) but that it is presented as such to lend weight to attempts "to stigmatize, and thus control, those persons whose behavior offends society" (Szasz, *Myth* 102) like turn-of-the-century women whose grievances were delegitimized through the diagnosis of hysteria (*Myth* 188–190).[15] Kaysen alludes to this history of sexism when her psychiatrist tells the experiencing self, "You need a rest" (7), thus evoking the so-called rest cure.[16] The rest cure became a popular treatment in the second half of the nineteenth century, and, "perhaps not coincidentally, had more than a touch of the punitive and the disciplinary about it" (Scull, *Madness* 276). Upper-middle-class and mostly female patients, who exhibited various nervous symptoms were believed to be overwhelmed by the pace of modern life and therefore confined to the bed without any stimulation such as work, visitors, reading, or craft projects. The authors Virginia Woolf and Charlotte Perkins Gilman prominently underwent the rest cure and wrote scathing indictments of it, Perkins in "The Yellow Wallpaper" (1892) and Woolf in *Mrs. Dalloway* (1925) (Scull, *Madness* 275–276). While Kaysen's experiencing self does not have to stay in bed, she does complain about the unceasing monotony, surveillance, infantilization as well as the sense of being "behind bars" (Kaysen 117). The allusion to the rest cure therefore places Kaysen in the tradition of outspoken women who were victimized by the psychiatric dispositive, thus suggesting that the main goal in her hospitalization was disciplining, not curing her.

Similar to Kaysen's memoir, Ann Cvetkovich's *Depression—A Public Feeling* depathologizes the experiencing self's condition by rejecting the medico-psychiatric model and instead analyzing how "anxiety and what gets called depression are ordinary feelings embedded in ordinary circumstances" (79; cf. also Wurtzel 34, 337; Hornbacher, *Wasted* 283). As the "affective dimensions of ordinary life" (11) include the felt effects of neo-liberalism, globalization, and toxic corporate culture, Cvetkovich conceives of depression "as a cultural and social phenomenon rather than a medical disease" (1), and thus dismisses psychiatric "discussions about the biomedical causes of depression … [as] trivial" (15). Moreover, the definition of "pathology" as "structural and functional *deviations from the normal* that constitute disease" ("Pathology"; emphasis added) suggests that any *ordinary* condition loses its status as pathology.

According to Cvetkovich, the ordinariness of depression derives from the fact that "we live in a culture whose violence takes the form of systematically making *us* feel bad" (15; emphasis added), and where biopower works "insidiously by making people feel small, worthless, hopeless" (13). Here, the narrating self normalizes madness by playing on the implied reader's feelings of alienation and victimization in late capitalism and equating them with her lived experience of depression. Ann Cvetkovich's memoir therefore extends the meanings of madness—here: depression—to signify a general cultural affliction or the result of biopower and encourages readers to relate. Additionally, she rejects the deep-seated assumption that madness has its root cause in the individual thus rebuffing the stigma belief that mad individuals only have themselves to blame for their condition.

Marya Hornbacher also appropriates anti-psychiatric thought when she presents psychiatric diagnoses as subjective evaluations. After an accidental overdose, Hornbacher's experiencing self is in the hospital where she paces and cries, which, she realizes, "won't look good" (*Madness* 266). She adds, "I'm trying to come off as perfectly sane, but this pacing and crying makes me look crazy," and all of the sudden she realizes, "I honestly don't *see* myself as crazy. Which, I realize, means I definitely am" (266). In this passage, Hornbacher alludes not only to the stigmatized person's double sense of self as both normal and blemished (Goffman, *Stigma* 7) but also suggests that judgments of a person's state of mind are necessarily subjective, as phrases related to outward appearance and sensory perception suggest ("won't look good," "come off as," "look crazy," and "*see* myself as crazy"). Additionally, she problematizes the trope that the mad are ignorant of their state, which can be used to justify forced treatment and involuntary hospitalization. However, rather than merely decrying the oppressive, circular logic of this trope, Hornbacher gives the passage an additional twist when she attributes this insight to her experiencing self who is in the midst of a manic episode and acts stereotypically crazy, e.g., by hopping out of her psychiatrist's office like a chicklet (cf. *Madness* 264). Because the trope of the mad person who is ignorant of their madness seems perfectly logical to a mad person, the memoir activates another long-standing trope, namely that psychiatrists are just as mad as their patients. In this manner, Hornbacher destabilizes well-established and oppressive tropes about the mad and undermines psychiatry's self-fashioning as objective in a thoroughly anti-psychiatric fashion.

As the last two sections have shown, authors in my corpus fashion themselves as normal by using strategies that deviance scholar Leon Anderson calls "*distancing*" (108). More specifically, authors "emphasiz[e] the difference between oneself and others who fall into a particular deviant [here: stigma] category" or else they "separate themselves from the stigmatized acts and conditions with which they fear they are associated" (Anderson 108) by calling attention to their core normalcy, depicting madness as a common reaction to the maddening world we live in or reinterpreting their diagnosis as a moral rather than a medical judgment. In any case, they present themselves as normal in the sense that they are not mad in its stigmatizing meanings, i.e., dehumanized, debilitated, and pathological. Because authors put so much effort into demonstrating their normalcy and because discredited individuals are likely more sensitive to stigma beliefs about their social group, mental illness pathographies can function as seismographs for deep-seated beliefs when direct verbal expression becomes socially discouraged.[17] Similarly, rejections of kinship to fellow patients can provide insight into the internal hierarchies of marginalized groups. Mental illness pathographies can therefore be informative for qualitative research into the processes of stigmatization. However, as this study primarily considers memoirs of madness as literary texts, I turn to appropriations and pastiches of culturally valued narratives of transformation now.

Narratives of Transformation

Another way of textually producing one's normalcy is to establish a distinction between a mad, past experiencing self and a sane, present narrating self in culturally valued narratives of transformation. The appropriation of these narratives constitutes a stigma management strategy called "destigmatization" which "involves an effort to expunge a deviant identity and replace it with a positive one" (L. Anderson 107; cf. also Mercer 71–73). This can either be achieved by presenting oneself as "morally purified" through a secular or religious conversion experience or else by demonstrating that one has "ris[en] above" one's madness through hard work and other modes of self-making (L. Anderson 107). Here, authors not only renounce the experiencing self's prior madness but they also establish their normalcy by demonstrating that they embrace the US national values that are propagated in narratives of transformation.

Authors draw upon two well-established genres in life writing—the conversion narrative and the self-made man[18] narrative—to represent their transformation from mad persons to recovered, saved or carefully managed individuals. Through the appropriation of these genres, authors not only produce madness as sin or as a condition that can be overcome but they also do cultural work by inscribing themselves into US literary traditions as (former) mad persons. Furthermore, shaping memoirs according to these conventions contributes to the commercial success of mental illness pathographies: The didactic and inspirational impetus of both conversion and self-made man narratives link mental illness pathographies to self-improvement literature, a genre that enjoys consistent popularity. Moreover, confessions of sinfulness and degradation can greatly increase reading pleasure as texts allow for "the simultaneous knowing of salacious details and a certitude of his [the confessant's] triumphant return" (Lofton 90).[19] Readers are privy to suicide attempts, overdoses, and a life in depression and squalor, yet they have the certainty that the author will eventually recover enough to finish the taxing and lengthy project of publishing a memoir. The appropriation of these narratives therefore allows authors to do cultural work and to access the didactic mode as well as the intensely pleasurable sensational and confessional mode.

Further effects of the choice of narrative structure differ among the three groups of potential readers: Those who are similarly mad and whom Goffman calls "the Own," those who are not—Goffman's "normals" (*Stigma* 5)—and psychiatrists. For the Own, narratives of transformation can provide hope: After all, authors confess to highly transgressive behavior and extreme states of mind, and if they overcome them, so can anyone. Additionally, memoirs provide an interpretive framework for the disorienting experience of madness as well as detailed advice regarding the path to normalcy. In a way, mental illness pathographies are self-help books for the Own.

In the address of normals, narratives of transformation constitute a plea for the return to the social fold. Within the framework of conversion narratives, narrating selves conceive of their madness as a debased condition or even sinfulness and thus endorse deep-seated stigma beliefs. However, they also textually repent for the error of their ways, and their narrative "helps to define and constitute the writer's conversion" (Gordis 371). Narratives of self-making, by contrast, frequently stress the virtue of protagonists and present madness as hardship rather than moral failure. Those who overcome madness by themselves may claim the US national virtues of self-reliance and resourcefulness and fashion themselves as success stories rather than previously blemished subjects. This process is aided by the embrace of US values and markers of identity: authors show that they, too, are American or a sinner among sinners and invite readers to bridge the gap of Otherness incurred by the label "mad."

Lastly, appropriations of these genres can engage psychiatrists in a dialogue. In most memoirs of my corpus, the conversion narrative is removed from an explicitly religious context and instead recounts the experiencing self's salvation through the acceptance of psychiatric truths. The depiction of the psychiatric dispositive as a source of salvation not only speaks to the relief and meaning authors derived from it but can also be read as an overture to dialogue via flattery. The narrative of self-making, by contrast, can voice criticism of psychiatric treatment, e.g., when the experiencing self's self-reliance is a virtue born out of necessity, such as the lack of adequate treatment from mental healthcare professionals. As this quick overview showed, the choice of the genre allows authors to execute multiple communicative functions that are geared towards different audiences.

For the sake of a structured analysis, I consider the appropriation of the conversion narrative and the myth of the self-made man in individual sections. However, even the most striking emulations of either genre—Cherry Boone-O'Neill's conversion from anorexic to recipient of divine grace and Clifford Beers' descent into madness and gradual rise to sanity through resourcefulness and hard work—include elements of the other. Boone-O'Neill's quest to remake herself into a more glamorous and controlled person exhibits many hallmarks of the self-made man's journey to success. The experiencing self continuously resisted offers of her favorite foods (65–66) and demonstrated her self-discipline, hard work and determination through a daily exercise regimen that "would have made an Olympic trainer feel right at home" (52). Similarly, Clifford Beers, an author so committed to the myth of self-making that medical historian Roy Porter called him "[t]he Benjamin Franklin of psychiatry" (*Social* 190), describes the return of reason as a "miracle," "salvation," and rebirth (Beers 41–42), thereby fashioning himself as the passive recipient of divine grace in an otherwise markedly secular narrative of self-reliance. This mix of narrative tropes and interpretive frameworks therefore contributes to the conflicted self-fashioning in my corpus as well as the radical openness of meaning that is a hallmark of literature.

The mixing of tropes and narrative structures further marks my corpus of mental illness pathographies as distinctly postmodern since the "[p]ostmodern genre is ... characterized by its appropriation of other genres, both high and popular, by its longing for a both/and situation rather than one of either/or" (Gilmore, "Mark" 8). The tension created in these memoirs between a narrative that places the self-reliant individual at the center and one which stresses the importance of complete submission to a higher power further mirrors the conflicts and uncertainties that surround the postmodern self: As Dwight Fee put it, "self-definition becomes progressively more elusive as subjectivity becomes 'populated' with multiple and often discordant voices" (6). These tension-laden mixtures of tropes and narratives, uncertainties, and conflicted productions of selfhood in mental illness pathographies, then, contribute to the elevation of life writing to literature in the normative sense and represent selves and narratives that transcend boundaries and genre conventions in a thoroughly postmodern fashion.

Moreover, the mixing of tropes, interpretive frameworks, and narrative structures can be explained by the authors' desire to respond to several conflicting stigma beliefs simultaneously: The conversion narrative absolves the mad self of responsibility for (maintaining) their condition as only a higher power can truly save them, yet also fashions them as incapable of making their own decisions. The narrative of self-making, by contrast, returns agency to those who wish to overcome their madness, yet this potentially exposes the mad person to blame. The need to respond to both stigma beliefs means that memoirs have to produce narratives with contradictory types of self-fashioning. I begin my analysis of how these effects of literariness play out in my corpus with an investigation of the appropriation of conversion narratives.

Religious Conversion Narratives

Conversion narratives hold an important place in US literary and cultural practices and were most frequently written by subjects who sought (re-)acceptance into the social fold. Since a wealth of analyses already exists, I restrict myself to a quick overview of the forms and mechanisms of this culturally valued genre before I discuss their appropriation in mental illness pathographies.[20]

By the beginning of the 1640s, several Puritan denominations used conversion narratives as a ritual of initiation and asked aspiring members of their church to publicly confess their sins as well as their experience of salvation. Prospective church members were interpellated to *prove* that they had indeed been saved, and the confessional aspects of conversion narratives served as a method of truth production. Additionally, conversion narratives marked the ritualized rejection of old, sinful ways and a transition to a new phase in life (Bauer 23–24).

Because conversion narratives serve to convince both author and audience that the author's transformation is complete and permanent, many kinds of marginalized subjects have appropriated their structure, tropes, and language. By the early 1840s, several temperance societies required repenting drinkers to present confessional first-person accounts of their drunken depravities and their "conversion to teetotalism" (Hendler 29) in so-called "experience narratives" (Hendler 30; cf. also Cannon) or "*temperance narratives*" (Crowley, *Drunkards* 4). Similarly, immigrants emulated form and language of conversion narratives to narrate their Americanization (cf. Wasson) while former slaves used them to describe their transformations "from slave to man" (Gordis 383). In the context of the temperance and abolitionist movement, conversion narratives were central vehicles for the movements' didactic and political discourse, but their sentimental and sensational aspects also made printed narratives a popular commodity and ensured the widespread dissemination of their messages (Crowley, "Slaves" 116, 119). Conversion narratives therefore have a history of being highly effective stigma-political tools.

Like other stigmatized subjects, authors in my corpus appropriate conversion narratives to produce the truth of the abject depths of their madness as well as their salvation. By ritually humbling themselves through confession, authors reduce the symbolic threat which their mad Otherness poses to the social order and instead acknowledge the reader's "right to judge them and to take part in the cleansing ritual of forgiveness" for their transgressions (Bauer 7). In this manner, the practices surrounding conversion narratives allow authors of mental illness pathographies to prove their transformation and to ask for a restoration of their status as normal.

In the following, I will draw upon three texts to illustrate how mental illness pathographies produce two distinct variants of the conversion narrative.[21] First, I will turn to Cherry Boone-O'Neill's memoir of eating disorders which is told in the language and conceptual framework of the Puritan conversion narrative. Then, I will move on to Marya Hornbacher's and Kay Redfield Jamison's secular versions of the conversion narrative which narrate how they left behind false conceptions of mental illness as well as their resistance to pharmacological treatment and were subsequently saved by the psychiatric dispositive. The main distinction between the two variants is how they produce the meaning of madness. Whereas Boone-O'Neill's memoir fashions madness as a spiritual crisis and a form of sinfulness that can only be overcome through divine grace, Hornbacher and Jamison narrate their journey towards the ideal of submission to psychiatric treatment and thus produce madness as a biomedical condition. These differences show that similar narrative structures can produce very different meanings.

Cherry Boone-O'Neill's *Starving for Attention* (1982) relates her struggles with anorexia and bulimia as well as her experience of growing up as a member of the family band *The Pat Boone Family*. Together with her father, the successful pop singer Pat Boone, and the rest of the family, Cherry toured the country, produced gospel albums and did her best to convey the celebrity image of a wholesome young girl, who was raised to live by strict religious standards. Her memoir reveals the lasting impact of her religious upbringing when it produces madness as sinfulness and spiritual crisis and by sticking closely to the highly formulaic narrative structure of religious conversion narratives: Her memoir begins with her descent into sinfulness and self-deception, moves to grief over her sinful nature, and then oscillates between a sense of God's support and relapses (cf. Watkins 37; Caldwell 2–11; Shea 97–101). Finally, the experiencing self receives help from a therapist whose scripture-informed counsel enables her to be reborn through the love of God. By narratively reframing her condition as sin, the memoir negotiates stigma beliefs that conflate madness and badness, presents her condition as a state that can be overcome, and enables supposedly normal readers to bridge the gap of difference by presenting Boone-O'Neill as a sinner among sinners.

However, rather than tracing the entire elaborate structure of conversion narratives, I show the memoir's indebtedness to the genre by illustrating the use of key tropes in Boone-O'Neill's text and one of the more well-known Puritan conversion narratives by a lay-person, *The Experiences of God's Gracious Dealing with Mrs. Elizabeth White* (1669).[22] Similarities include a misplaced need for self-reliance, sins relating to holy communion, the oscillation between hope and relapses, and, finally, the experiencing self's spiritual rebirth that coincides with the birth of an actual child. Though the inclusion of distinctly feminine experience is by no means typical of the genre, the transmutation of life events into "the reenactment of biblical truth" is very common (Caldwell 12). In Boone-O'Neill's case, this transmutation further supports her interpretation of madness as sin: To binge is "gluttony" (35), to compare oneself to other women is to "covet the bodies of fashion models" (38), to have an intense and vaguely sexual relationship with food is "whoring after food" (100). This comparison of key tropes and modes of interpreting experience, then, illustrates how extensively authors in my corpus draw upon established genres in life writing and which productions of meaning their appropriations enable.

Like all authors of conversion narratives, Cherry Boone-O'Neill tells her story from the point of salvation, i.e., after her "restoration to health" (Boone-O'Neill ix).[23] This perspective allows the narrating self to assume a critical distance to the "evolving point of view of a person who becomes imprisoned by, and then ultimately freed from, invalid fears and misperceptions" (ix). Through the immediate evaluation of her fears as "invalid," the narrating self establishes that she has overcome the sin and madness that is her eating disorder and is only incorporating her former misperceptions to "best shed light on this terrifying disorder" (ix), i.e., for the edification of her readers. The narrating self's distance to her former, eating disordered self is so great that she does not claim any relation at all but refers to her with the generalizing and anonymizing phrase "a person." By thus marking the completeness of her transformation, the narrating self implies that she is free of the taint of madness and should no longer bear its stigma (cf. also Beers 100).

The generalizing and anonymizing impetus of "a person" also speaks to the didactic intent that permeates both conversion narratives and *Starving for Attention* (cf. Caldwell 2; Shea 89). When Boone-O'Neill omits the first-person pronoun, she does implicitly what Puritan authors do explicitly, namely erasing the specificity of their story and presenting their salvation as one of many examples of the works of grace (cf. Hawkins, *Reconstructing* 33). This self-fashioning allows both Boone-O'Neill and Puritan authors of conversion narratives to make sense of their lived experience within the framework of religion, to encourage others to do the same, and to provide hope to those still struggling with doubts. Boone-O'Neill explicitly states the latter in her memoir's dedications: "This book is written for … [t]he people who endure the personal, hidden hell of anorexia nervosa; … and for hope, that they may emerge victorious from this nightmare" (n. p.). Boone-O'Neill's appropriation of the genre therefore illustrate how stigma management strategies—like the narrative transformation from a stigmatized self to a morally purified self—not only affect the lives of individual authors but also have "an inspirational quality" (L. Anderson 107).

The cornerstone of this hope is that no state of depravity is so great that God cannot save a penitent. To emphasize this, Boone-O'Neill begins the prologue by assuming the perspective of her seventeen-year-old and severely eating-disordered experiencing self and gleefully explains that "[f]asting on Thanksgiving Day had really *saved* me" (xi, emphasis added).[24] On one level, the narrating self (donning the mask of the experiencing self) states that fasting *saved* her from unwanted meals and questions about her eating behavior. She explains, whenever someone inquired about her empty plate, "I just answered with spiritual overtones, 'I'm fasting today,' and that was that!" (xi). The experiencing self thus used religious devotion to mask her madness which makes her guilty of deceit. On another level, the term "saved" speaks to the experiencing self's desire to influence her state of grace actively through ascetic practices. In Puritan conversion narratives, including the one by Elizabeth White (8), the attempt to actively achieve redemption is frequently presented as a heretic misconception (Shea 105, 146). Before she learned to cast herself upon Christ, Elizabeth White believed that she "must do something to merit Salvation," prayed five times a day, and found temporary comfort in a routine that helped her to forget her "vile Heart" (8). Though her actions were more removed from spiritual practices than White's prayer regimen, Boone-O'Neill's experiencing self also numbed her sense of inadequacy with exercise and a restricted diet, thus reframing her madness as the result of sinful misconceptions. Moreover, she allows normal readers to understand the experiencing self's motivation as well as emotional and spiritual investment in her madness by drawing upon the more familiar framework of sin and redemption.

Boone-O'Neill's further connects her madness to sinfulness when she confesses spectacular religious transgressions that mirror those of Elizabeth White. When White's experiencing self went to receive communion for the first time, she began to doubt whether she had enough "Knowledge, Faith, Love, Repentance, &c" (4) to partake in the ritual and remembered a bible passage that reads, "He that doubteth is damned if he eat [sic]; for whatever is not of Faith, is Sin" (Romans 14:23, qtd. in White 4). Unwilling "to eat and drink [her] own Damnation" (4), she prayed for grace and quickly deluded herself that she had truly repented. She passed the exam by the minister and the narrating self laments, "so unworthy I went to the Lord's Table" (4). Similarly, Boone-O'Neill's narrating self also recalls sins relating to communion when she explains that the experiencing self was so worried about the calories contained in Christmas Day communion that she resolved only to pretend to drink the grape juice and to "just smash it [the wafer] between my fingers and sprinkle the crumbs on the floor. No calories!" (xii). The prologue ends with the experiencing self proclaiming herself unworthy of God's help and falling asleep "on the vomit-stained carpet" (xvi), which leaves her to wallow literally and symbolically in her own abjection. As in Elizabeth White's text, partaking in communion also incurs damnation, if only within Boone-O'Neill's personal eating disordered model of redemption through thinness. This incident therefore not only presents madness as sinfulness but also illustrates the power eating disorders can have over a person by showing how it alienated Boone-O'Neill from her faith, thereby educating her audience about the serious, destructive effects of the condition at a time when it was not widely known, i.e., in 1982.

To further stress the seriousness of her condition, Cherry Boone-O'Neill's narrating self describes the alternations between hope and despair, that are typical of the structure of conversion narratives, through the metaphor of slavery. She refers to her eating disorder as "overpowering bondage" (123) and "enslavement" (154), and the experiencing self repeatedly thinks "my emancipation had commenced" (87), is disappointed when gaining insights about herself does not lead to "the unlocking of [her] chains" (74), or when pure willpower cannot prevent her renewed "groaning collapse into captivity" (75). Unlike her previous representation of madness as sinful behavior, Boone-O'Neill's allusion to the biblical trope of comparing pre-conversion life to slavery (e.g., *New English Translation,*

John 8:34; Romans 6:1–8:15) relativizes her transgressions and presents her condition as one variant of human frailty, thus presenting herself as a sinner among sinners.

Moreover, Boone-O'Neill's imagery evokes the US discourse on slavery and thereby establishes the suffering connected to madness. In the mid-nineteenth century, temperance narratives by recovering alcoholics also exploited these associations when they called themselves "slaves to the bottle" and even proposed that their condition was worse than that of African Americans because their bondage was of both the body and the mind (Crowley, "Slaves"). By (implicitly or explicitly) comparing their condition to that of African American slaves, Boone-O'Neill and authors of temperance narratives actively victimize themselves, ask for their readers' sympathy and—to a certain extent—reject responsibility for their transgressions (cf. also L. Anderson 107). This shows that texts in my corpus not only take up stigma management strategies used previously by other discredited groups but also that memoirs of madness produce highly conflicting meanings of madness and stances about the mad person's responsibility for it.

Despite these conflicting meanings, Boone-O'Neill's account, like White's, ends on a hopeful note and stresses her salvation. In an interesting similarity, the final transformation of both White's and Boone-O'Neill's experiencing self is marked by the birth of a child, turning the event into the "double birth" of both a new and different self and an actual child (Caldwell 12). Elizabeth White states, "I was much dejected, having a Sense of my approaching Danger [death by childbirth], and wanting an Assurance of my everlasting Happiness" (10). As Patricia Caldwell explains, "Mrs. White is 'dejected,' that is, literally thrown down … and in the labor of childbirth, aided by the 'begetting' Word of God, she feels for the first time the joys of deliverance" (11). In her narrative, Elizabeth White draws upon the scriptural imagery of salvation as childbirth (cf. *New English Translation,* Psalm 53:15, James 1:18) to transmute a personal event into the reenactment of biblical truth (cf. Caldwell 12). Continuing the metaphor, White's narrating self explains that she soon needed to distract herself from sinful thoughts, managed to do so by breastfeeding her child, and also experienced a sense of being nourished by God's love. Like her child, Elizabeth White was eventually weaned from all earthly supports to rest in God alone. The completion of this process is the end of her narrative which, despite Puritan insistence on the need for perpetual self-examination, is very neat and optimistic (Caldwell 12–13).

Likewise, Cherry Boone-O'Neill's experiencing self reaches the limits of dejection before her rebirth takes place. After her husband finds her crouching on the floor and confronts her about debasing herself by eating out of the dog bowl, Boone-O'Neill declares, "we had sunk to the depths of our own private hell" (107). The scene therefore expresses the same literal and metaphoric downward movement as Elizabeth White's dejection in childbed and soon after this event, Boone-O'Neill also finds comfort and salvation: First through a therapist who ushers her towards rebirth by quoting scripture—the central source for transformation in Puritan conversion narratives—and then through the conception of a child which is "a special message" (161) from God: "With Brittany's birth I felt that God was giving me His official stamp of approval on my recovery. In a sense He was saying to me, 'Okay, Cherry, you have proven that you can be responsible for your own life. Now I can trust you with another one'" (161). Her memoir thus provides an ending that is just as neat and uplifting as that of Elizabeth White's narrative and fashions Boone-O'Neill's transformation as complete, permanent, and authenticated by the highest power.

While the appropriation of the structure and tropes of conversion narratives provides Boone-O'Neill with a framework that makes sense of her condition and powerfully argues for her reintegration into society, it is not without its problems. In line with Thomas Couser's comment on a memoir by a woman with cerebral palsy, I hold that the "rhetoric of spiritual compensation" supports the classic "symbolic paradigm of disability [here: madness], according to which an impairment is a mark of sin or God's displeasure with an individual" ("Rhetoric" 36). In other words, Boone-O'Neill appropriates the stigma-based conflation of madness and sinfulness, which legitimizes the stigmatization of the mentally ill. "The effect of her mystical validation is to remove stigma not from cerebral palsy [here: eating disorders] as a condition but rather from her as an individual … [This] precludes any attempts to seek a remedy in worldly efforts toward reform, short-circuiting any movement toward the competing political paradigm of disability" (Couser, "Rhetoric" 38). Therefore, literary attempts at stigma management may evade some problems of more straightforward advocacy work, but they have pitfalls of their own, as this study will continue to show.

Secular Conversion Narratives

In addition to Cherry Boone-O'Neill's account of salvation through divine grace, my corpus also includes memoirs that appropriate the template of conversion narratives to describe a more secular conversion. In these texts, the conversion revolves around the experiencing self's initial reluctance and final submission to a secular force, namely the psychiatric dispositive. In this variant of the narrative, the sins of experiencing selves consist of their unwillingness to take medication as prescribed and of their failure to conceive of their condition as mental illness rather than an integral part of their personality or a source of creativity. This section analyzes how Kay Redfield Jamison and Marya Hornbacher represent their salvation through the psychiatric dispositive, i.e., how they were lifted from a life of chaos and unhappiness towards a state of relative, carefully managed stability. As in the previous subchapter, I refrain from tracing the entire structure of conversion but instead focus on passages that illuminate key similarities to and differences from the traditional narrative template: This includes the representation of supposedly misguided perceptions of mental illness, the eventual conversion to the psychiatric dispositive, as well as the use of ironic detachment and metafictional techniques. This allows me to consider the complex meanings of madness that Hornbacher and Jamison create as well as the nuances of their stance towards the psychiatric dispositive.

Secular conversion narratives enable many of the stigma-political strategies of traditional religious conversion narratives, namely an inscription of marginalized subjects into the literary tradition of redemption stories (cf. McAdams) and a positive self-fashioning. Additionally, secular versions produce some of the same social and communicational effects of traditional conversion narratives. For one thing, Hornbacher's and Jamison's memoirs of bipolar disorder constitute a secular confession of faith directed at psychiatrists: Just as Puritans produced and authenticated their redemption and gained full admittance to the community of believers, authors in my corpus testify to the healing powers of the psychiatric dispositive to confirm their return to (carefully managed) normalcy, possibly gain admittance to the psychiatric "fellowship of discourse" (Foucault, *Discourse* 225; see Chapter Three), and claim a voice. In other words, these secular confessions of faith can be read as an (optimistic) attempt to enter the discourse on mental disorders by way of flattery. Secondly, memoirs like Hornbacher's and Jamison's share the didactic intent of traditional conversion narratives and encourage readers who are not yet saved to turn to the psychiatric dispositive for healing and meaning-making. In this manner, secular conversion narratives contribute to stigma-political efforts through representation, stigma-management, attempts to claim a voice, and advice to the author's Own.

Much like traditional conversion narratives, Hornbacher's and Jamison's memoirs are written from the position of salvation, and narrating selves repeatedly comment on the experiencing selves' actions in an openly didactic fashion. Kay Redfield Jamison begins her memoir with a description of a time when her experiencing self was "manic beyond recognition" (*Unquiet* 4) and states, "I was beginning a long, costly personal war against a medication that I would, in a few years' time, be strongly encouraging others to take … [and] that ultimately saved my life and restored my sanity"

(*Unquiet* 4; cf. also Hornbacher, *Madness* 200). The phrase "beyond recognition" establishes the distance between the normal narrating and the mad experiencing self and emphasizes the radical nature of Jamison's transformation, thereby producing madness as curable but also deflecting responsibility and shame about her actions to a past self.

Moreover, the passage quoted above supports the narrating self's pharmacological missionary efforts: "[L]ike all the best preachers with their personal sinner-turned-saint tales" (Porter, *Social* 190), Jamison authenticates her gospel by claiming that she spoke from experience, more specifically the experience of "a long, costly personal war" against lithium. True to the trope of the sinner-turned-saint, Jamison's experiencing self strayed from living according to the psychiatric truth, was reluctant to seek help but was ultimately "saved" and "restored" by her medication-savior, which fashions her return to normalcy as a quasi-religious experience. What makes the experiencing self's initial rejection of pharmacological treatment all the more dramatic is that Jamison is a psychiatrist by training, and one specialized in mood disorders to boot. Through this trope, Jamison creates a powerful didactic narrative of conversion that encourages medication compliance in unconverted readers. These missionary efforts also fashion Jamison as a potential asset to the psychiatric dispositive and imply the need to include the perspective of individuals with lived experience of mental illness like Jamison—if only to convince other recalcitrant patients to comply with their treatment.

Marya Hornbacher also produces a highly didactic account of her pre-salvation life but uses the trope of self-delusion. In Puritan conversion narratives, experiencing selves frequently convince themselves of their state of grace through outward performances of devoutness and self-serving comparisons to the less pious (cf. White 3). Similarly, Hornbacher's narrating self exposes how her experiencing self continually deceived herself with attempts to assess her sanity through outward signs of a successful life, such as having

> nonstop dinner parties—the glorious food, the fabulous friends, the gallons of wine.
> I sometimes feel as if I've raced off a cliff and am spinning my legs in midair, like Wile E. Coyote. But I'm fine. It's fine. It's all going to be fine. Crazy people don't have dinner parties, do they? No.
> … I make the fancy meals and wash the wedding dishes and write the thank-you notes for all the million wedding gifts on stationary stamped with my married name.
> Crazy people don't have stationary, do they? [*Madness* 55].

While the present tense does obscure distinctions between the present normal and the past mad self, the composition of the passage also privileges the reformed point of view, thereby exposing Hornbacher's former self-delusions. For example, the repeated insistence that she is fine arouses suspicions rather than dispersing them. Additionally, a single word answer firmly negates the first question and the shift to a new paragraph suggests conviction, whereas the second question is left unanswered and conveys a growing uncertainty about the relation of bourgeois consumer goods and normalcy. Furthermore, by likening her pursuit of a perfect life to the futile exploits of Wile E. Coyote—a member of Warner Brothers' *Looney* (!) *Toons*—Hornbacher's narrating self not only exposes previous misconceptions—such as the belief that true madness only exists in the margins of society—but also alerts readers to the undifferentiated and narrow understandings of madness they might harbor themselves. In this manner, she both educates the reader on the diverse manifestations of madness and fulfills the genre conventions of conversion narratives, namely the exposure of past mistakes.

    Hornbacher's memoir also *emphasizes and then deviates* from tropes of conversion narratives and thus produces the experiencing self as a particularly reluctant convert to the psychiatric dispositive. After the experiencing self's psychiatrist implores her to stop drinking to avoid aggravating her mental disorder, the narrating self announces,

> Now, this is the part of the book where I emerge from the hospital into the July sunshine, fresh-faced, rosy-cheeked, eyes a-twinkle, and gung ho [sic] to embark on my journey, the obvious journey, the recommended journey, the acceptable journey from sickness to health, from dark to light, from inside the locked door to outside it, freedom!
>
> Here I am, striding with newfound purpose into my house, collecting the bottles ... shocked, just shocked to realize how much I'd been drinking, but full of strength, the strength of the totally sensible sane, strength enough to dramatically flush all the booze down the toilet…. Well, no. That's not exactly what happened. Just kidding. Really, it embarrasses and frankly baffles me to write this, but the next part of the book is where I'm at my house, knocking back my meds with a beer…
>
> You may be asking at this point, Why? Or more to the point, What the fuck is wrong with you? Are you completely dense? Are you—ha ha!—insane?
>
> Ladies and gentlemen, yes I am [*Madness* 81–82].

Conversion narratives, and especially temperance narratives, generally describe a specific moment when experiencing selves see the error of their ways and subsequently transform their life (Cannon 2–5). Hornbacher's memoir draws attention to this trope through both her metafictional reference that the narrative template requires a conversion at this point and through the clichés of personal transformation: e.g., she emerges into the July sunshine that symbolizes her moral journey "from dark to light." The experiencing self's failure to embark on "the obvious journey" at "this part of the book" is a metafictional variation of the trope of the greatest sinner. Like the vilest sinners, Hornbacher's experiencing self requires many signs and much support from a redeeming entity before she can be saved.

However, the assumption "[t]he more benighted a sinner ... the more glorious the redemption" (Clark, "Repenting" 59) also holds true: Her eventual conversion to normalcy speaks to the healing power of psychiatry, just as dramatic spiritual transformations speak to the glory of God. As such, Hornbacher's narrative not only gives hope to those who share her madness but also flatters mental healthcare practitioners through this testimony to the power of their work.

Additionally, the marked deviation from the structure of conversion narratives creates the impression of truthfulness or authenticity. The straightforward narrative trajectory of conversion or temperance narratives appears exceedingly artificial when compared to the general messiness that governs most lives. This artificiality is thrown into relief not only through the clichés addressed above but also through exaggerated claims. For example, the phrase "the strength of the totally sensible sane" appears excessive because it includes a global assurance and a synonymy which is further emphasized by the alliteration. This excessiveness ultimately questions whether any transformation can be that neat and complete. When the narrating self subsequently confesses her deviation from "the recommended journey" and acknowledges the shame she feels, it creates the impression of a more intimate perspective that grants a glimpse behind the socially accepted tropes of the redemption narrative, i.e., a more truthful account. Yet, as Michael Lewis points out, "[c]onfession also has another role. If one feels shame about a global self, to confess to this shame somehow is a virtue that allows some relief in terms of one's global evaluation. Such ideation may take the form of 'Well, I'm not good, but at least I can own up to my faults'" (132). In these ways, the narrating self uses the deviation from well-established narrative tropes to authenticate the memoir, to manage her shame, and to redeem herself.

While the flaunting of deviations from the tropes of conversion narratives is an example of "hostile bravado" (Goffman, *Stigma* 17), i.e., an aggressive, exaggerated performance of attributes that are imputed on the basis of the original stigma, in this case unreasonableness, the passage also ends in an admission of madness that constitutes Hornbacher's true conversion. After confessing that she deviated from the trajectory of transformation, the narrating self addresses the implied reader's incredulity and accepts ascriptions of madness: "Are you—ha ha!—insane? Ladies and gentlemen, yes I am" (*Madness* 82). Note how the full passage quoted above initially maintained a division between the narrating and experiencing self: Metafictional devices marked the present tense as a stylistic device that creates a sense of immediacy while the narrating self remained on the extradiegetic level. In the narrating self's answer to the anticipated questions, this division of selves dissolves. The narrating self, which is marked as such by her reader address, affirms that she is just as insane as the experiencing self. This confession of madness constitutes the major difference to the experiencing self who denied the seriousness of her condition. The narrating self concedes a need for consistent treatment *because* she knows that she is insane. Paradoxically, it is this insight into her madness which enables the textual selves' conversion which in turn allowed Hornbacher to be normal in the sense of functional enough to write a memoir. This paradox furthermore illustrates that tensions between a self-fashioning as normal and as mad remain even in passages that initially suggest the affirmation of one or the other.

Kay Redfield Jamison conveys her struggles with medication compliance in a similarly multilayered fashion and also uses the language and conceptual framework of Christian conversion. After describing her attempts to adapt to the side effects of medication and to let go of costly beliefs about self-reliance, Jamison's memoir presents "Rules for the Gracious Acceptance of Lithium into Your Life" (*Unquiet* 97), a tongue-in-cheek emulation of religious pamphlets that encourage readers to accept Jesus Christ as their savior. The title to the segment of rules is an ironic comment on the memoir's missionary zeal and on the preposterousness of placing quasi-religious faith in a medication-god. Nevertheless, the term "[g]racious" in the sense of thankful for an act of mercy, enables a reading of her rules as a confession of faith in the efficacy of pharmacological treatment. The tension between a tongue-in-cheek admission of the preposterousness and genuine gratefulness shows that the ways in which authors position themselves towards the psychiatric dispositive are just as complex as the authors' self-fashioning.

Despite this complexity, Jamison's rules primarily encourage the submissive attitude of a true believer, even if they do so in a humorously fatalistic way. Regarding lithium's severe side effects such as blurred vision and cognitive impairment, they advise "not to let the fact that you can't read without effort annoy you. Be philosophical. Even if you could read, you couldn't remember most of it anyway" (97). Rule number seven makes this thrust most explicit as it states, "[b]e patient when waiting for this leveling off [of moods]. Very patient. Reread the book of Job" (97). Whereas the section title equates lithium with Jesus Christ and thus stresses the saving power of the medication, Jamison's reference to the book of Job compares the drug to the more wrathful, unpredictable God of the Old Testament and the compliant patient to God's most faithful servant, Job (cf. *New English Translation*, Job 1:1). Since the book of Job gives ample room to his lamentations, Jamison's comparison implicitly acknowledges the suffering that may afflict those who take lithium religiously. Just like Job loses his wealth, family, and health, Jamison loses the ability to dress herself quickly and efficiently (97) as well as the "enthusiasm and bounce that [she] once had" (98;

cf. also *New English Translation*, Job 1–2:7). However, through the Job reference, Jamison also stresses the importance of enduring those hardships and submitting to the superior judgment of the psychiatric dispositive and implies that it will all pay off: Even though Job curses the day he was born and begs God for mercy, he also agrees that God's superior strength and wisdom place him beyond the council of mere humans (*New English Translation*, Job 13:3, Job 40:4–5). For his acquiescence and continued faith, God rewards Job with renewed health, a long life, new children, and even greater wealth (*New English Translation*, Job 42:10–17). The overall impetus of the conversion narrative therefore remains undisturbed by the ironic undertones of the segment title. Like Hornbacher's memoir, Jamison's text insists that psychiatric treatment was central to her return to normalcy in the sense of not being floridly mad. She furthermore informs her Own that the process of restoring normalcy is trying but ultimately worth it.

By contrast, the passage that describes the final submission of Hornbacher's experiencing self to psychiatric treatment complicates the straightforward encouragement of deference to a higher power by illustrating how it robs patients of their sense of agency and self-determination. According to Hornbacher, a typical post-salvation day looks like this:

> I go into my kitchen. Take my handful of meds. Take the supplements *they tell me* will help. Take anything *they tell me* to take. I eat the food *they tell me* to eat; a little protein, *they say*, takes the edge off the anxiety.... *They want me* to be functional. *My doctors' goal*, ultimately, is for me to return to a normal life.... *They tell me* the gym will help stabilize my moods.... *They tell me* it will make me happier. *They tell me* it will decrease the ever-present, crippling anxiety [*Madness* 243–244; emphasis added].

Notably, Hornbacher's descriptions lack the joy and sense of love that experiencing selves of Puritan conversion narratives felt after they succumbed to God (cf. White 11). Hornbacher's thoughts and actions are dominated by the directions of an anonymous group of mental healthcare professionals ("they") rather than her own volition, which expresses her sense of lost agency. The repeated use of the third-person plural pronoun without specifications about the referents speaks to several things. First of all, its anonymizing impetus makes it clear that Hornbacher, who extensively criticizes incidents of malpractice (see Chapter Three), submits to the abstract wisdom of the psychiatric discourse rather than its individual representatives and that it is through this emphasis on the larger-than-human discourse that the appropriation of the conversion narrative works. However, the paratactic sentences evoke an automaton or a person sedated by psychotropic drugs which not only suggests resignation but also creates a sharp contrast to the expressive language that characterizes her descriptions of madness. In this manner, the passage expresses the suffering due to side effects of Hornbacher's medication, like numbness and cognitive impairment, but also explains why her madness was so tempting and why she repeatedly went off her meds. It also shows that Hornbacher is as conflicted about the experiencing self's secular conversion to the psychiatric dispositive as she is of any element in her narrative that aids a stable conceptualization of madness.

Marya Hornbacher and Kay Redfield Jamison thus appropriate the conversion narrative to give advice to their Own and to present themselves as potential assets to the psychiatric dispositive. But mostly it assures themselves and others of their restored normalcy—that is it produces the first half of their double sense of self. Moreover, (secular) conversion narratives produce madness both as a medico-psychiatric disorder and resistance against that understanding as a quasi-religious transgression, thereby contributing another denotation to the tension of meanings that exists in my corpus.

Whereas conversion narratives suggest that the adequate response to madness is submission to a worldly or divine higher power, authors also appropriate another culturally valued narrative which suggests that the condition can be overcome by the mad person alone. It is this narrative, the myth of the self-made man, that I turn to now.

Narratives of Self-Making

The narrative of the hero who rises from humble circumstances to various forms of success is by no means a North American invention, but it has significantly shaped US national as well as personal modes of self-fashioning and remains a core national myth (Cawelti 1, 4). Variants of this myth were propagated prominently by Benjamin Franklin, who chronicled his rise from printer's apprentice to successful entrepreneur and respected statesman, the former slave and noted abolitionist Frederick Douglass, and Horatio Alger who wrote popular rags-to-riches narratives during the Gilded Age. In this section, I analyze how authors of mental illness pathographies produce madness as a type of hardship, that may befall experiencing selves as unexpectedly as Alger's protagonists find themselves in poverty. Moreover, their return to normalcy is presented as the result of hard work, resourcefulness, and self-reliance—that is, attributes thought to be prototypically American (cf. Carden 38). By pointing to shared national values, authors in my corpus allow supposedly normal US readers to bridge the gap of Otherness created by the diagnosis of a mental illness. Moreover, authors inscribe themselves into US literary history, claim cultural capital, and access prestigious forms of self-fashioning.

Although the acquisition of wealth through aggressiveness and frugality is also central to the literary history of narratives of self-making (see Wyllie), I focus on the variant espoused by Franklin, Douglass, and Alger who represent success as individual fulfillment and social welfare through rationality, self-reliance, self-discipline, and hard work (Cawelti 4–6, 15; McGee 19). I furthermore point to the narratives' "thinly veiled didactic aim" and discuss how they "cater to sensationalism, sentimentalism, and voyeurism" (Paul 374) through spectacular representations of abused mad persons whom a virtuous protagonist helps. I therefore address not only the content but also the mode in which narratives were frequently written which allows me to discuss a broader range of effects which these appropriations have.

The life writing and speeches of Frederick Douglass also illustrate why the myth of self-making is attractive to marginalized subjects such as people of color and the mad. Douglass' texts *narrate and establish* the transformation from a slave to a self-made man who embodies some of the most cherished national values. Douglass' propagation of these values not only constitutes an implicit rejection of common stigma beliefs about the helplessness, idleness, and simple-mindedness of people of color—which are also applied to mad persons—but allows him to fashion himself as American and thus demand social inclusion. Moreover, his use of the sentimental mode contributed to the popularity of his life narratives and demonstrates that the narrative template of self-making in combination with certain modes of writing aids the widespread dissemination of texts that guide moral judgment on stigmatized individuals.[25]

All of these features can also be found in Clifford Beers' *A Mind That Found Itself* (1909), which narrates his lived experience of what is now called bipolar disorder. Beers' text was intensely popular at the time of its publication and became the "bible" of the Mental Hygiene Movement, which Beers founded (Porter, *Social* 194). It advocated a decrease of the stigma of madness, the improvement of conditions in asylums, and the application of psychiatric methods in "all the educational and industrial spheres, courts, and homes" to ensure a "collective social psychological evolution" towards emotional stability and mental health (Porter, *Social* 198, 197). Furthermore, the memoir featured such striking emulations of the self-made man narrative that medical historian Roy Porter states, "Clifford Beers wrote psychiatry into the American dream. The Benjamin Franklin of psychiatry, his talks and writings offered *Poor Richard's Almanac*-style advice on how to renounce mental malady and embrace mental muscle power" (*Social* 190). Beers' text is therefore readily recognized as a narrative of self-making that understands success as mental health and that sees psychiatry as a tool to achieve it. Moreover, it was both popular and able to effect social change, thereby illustrating the ability of mental illness pathographies to be both commodities and stigma-political tools.

A central strategy to reduce stigmatization and the ascription of essential Otherness is to demonstrate one's similarity to normals. Beers' memoir does so by establishing a shared national identity with US readers. In addition to the implicit self-fashioning as American through the appropriation of a core national myth, the narrating self makes his Americanness explicit and foreshadows his propensity for overcoming hardship. At the very beginning of the memoir, the narrating self states that his ancestors "settled in this country not long after the *Mayflower* first sailed into Plymouth Harbor" (1). He continues, "the blood of these ancestors, by time and the happy union of a Northern man and a Southern woman—my parents—has perforce been blended into blood truly American" (1; cf. also Smola 166). In this short passage, Beers fashions himself as the quasi-mythological American in three ways. First, he links his family temporally to the iconic journey of the pilgrims—a journey that has become synonymous in popular imagination with both the solidarity of the Mayflower compact and the subsequent overcoming of the hardships of New England winters (cf. Paul 137–150). Secondly, the marriage of his parents recalls the reunion after the trauma of the Civil War and supplies Beers with roots in both the North and the South. Lastly, the insistence that the blood of his pilgrim ancestors, his Northern father and Southern mother "has been blended into blood truly American" (1) not only evokes the myth of the melting pot but also suggests that his very life force is permeated by archetypal American identities and experiences of overcoming (cf. Paul 257–298). By tying his family history to these iconic US experiences, Beers enables a mode of belonging that counterbalances his Otherness as a (former) mad person and encourages readings that focus on the narrative of overcoming, thereby temporarily stressing the normal side of his double sense of self.

Beers' emphasis on his "truly American" blood as well as his connection to significant historical national experiences furthermore evokes the discourse on sympathy. Sympathy has been considered the basis of a stable, cohesive, democratic society and arguably fueled US reform movements such as temperance and abolitionism by encouraging a sense of connection between normals and stigmatized subjects (Boudreau x, 7). Because the social bonds within the young American republic were envisaged as familial bonds, "the fiction of shared blood [had to] be maintained by imaginary leaps across spaces of difference, leaps enabled … by a common language and national and historical origin" (Boudreau x). Beers thus taps into a discourse which had previously aided the (re-)integration of marginalized subjects and implicitly reminds supposedly normal readers of their connection and obligation to their fellow citizen.

Even though the narrating self highlights the bonds between himself and US readers, he doesn't evoke their sympathy to call for assistance explicitly but instead fashions himself as self-reliant. Self-reliance is a characteristic generally associated with the myth of the self-made man since the publication of Benjamin Franklin's bestselling *Autobiography* (1793), where he "affirms that everyone is responsible for their own fate and success in life" (Paul 372). The memoir's title already announces Beers' emulation of this sentiment: *A Mind That Found Itself*. As a play on the phrase "losing one's mind," the title not only suggests the successful recovery of sanity but also frames the memoir as a narrative of self-help and agency rather than a religiously connotated tale of being lost and found.[26] Through the paradox—a mind that is lost but finds *itself*—the title also evokes the idiom of "pulling oneself up by one's bootstraps," i.e., getting out of an impossibly difficult situation without help. In this way, the title gestures towards Beers' rejection of the stigma belief that all mad persons are helpless which empowers himself and his Own. However, this self-fashioning also implies that those who do not return to normalcy by their own devices may lack determination or strength and thereby runs the danger of increasing ascriptions of blame to those stigmatized individuals.

Another characteristic ascribed to self-made men is the willingness to work hard. In his *Autobiography,* Benjamin Franklin attributed his success to industriousness and disciplined work (Paul 371–372), a view emulated by Frederick Douglass in his popular speech "Self-made Men." In that speech Douglass states, "we may explain success mainly by one word and that word is WORK! WORK!! WORK!!! WORK!!!! Not transient and fitful effort, but patient, enduring, honest, unremitting and indefatigable work into which the whole heart is put, and which … is the true miracle worker" (n.p.). Authors in my corpus adapt this view to their situation when they reframe psychotherapy as painstaking but necessary work towards mental stability. Jane Phillips calls therapy "a lot of work" (48), and Marya Hornbacher claims that getting better involves "more work than you ever thought possible" (*Wasted* 285). Though she does not use the term "work," Ann Cvetkovich evokes Douglass' emphasis on persistent efforts when she states that her process of overcoming depression did not involve "an instantaneous conversion, resurrection, or cure. It's the result of the slow and painstaking accumulation of new ways of living" (55). This shows that authors in my corpus access a positive self-fashioning as hard workers and implicitly assure their Own that they have agency to overcome their condition.

Marya Hornbacher also emphasizes her agency in managing her bipolar disorder when she illustrates how her experiencing self embraced the work ethic and methods of "rational self-mastery" that were popularized by Benjamin Franklin in his *Autobiography* (McGee 7). In a process that has since become known as "the Franklin method" (cf. McGee 6), he chose thirteen "necessary or desirable" qualities and recorded his transgressions against them (Franklin 63). For example, one virtue was industry, i.e., losing no time by always doing "something useful" (Franklin 63), another was order, which required that *"every part of business should have its allotted time"* (Franklin 87). The Franklin method also reserves some time each morning to contemplate the resolution for the day as well as some time at night to evaluate the success (Franklin 85–87). Franklin—and by extension Hornbacher—thus ascribes his success to self-control, rationality, regular self-examination, the daily formulation of goals, and planning, that is, virtues and practices that rely on individual agency, will power, and determination.

Like Franklin, Hornbacher's experiencing self records her transgressions against the ideal of being *"Without impairment—No symptoms"* (*Madness* 274). In other words, she works towards being normal—in the sense of not showing symptoms of madness—and shares her strategies in an implicitly didactic fashion. She also begins her day by planning what she will do, but unlike Franklin she does not strive for maximum efficiency but wants to avoid states of anxiety that are triggered by "too much unscheduled time" (*Madness* 273). Just as Franklin tracked his progress towards virtues, Hornbacher's keeps extensive records of the actions she took to stabilize her mood and she furthermore takes note of her level of irritation, anxiety, depression as well as her progress in work projects. Lastly, like Franklin's practice of setting a resolution for the day, Hornbacher's narrating self claims, "I Try to Change My Thoughts. I Shift My Perception. I Choose Peace of Mind" (*Madness* 274). Hornbacher thus embraces markedly controlled, rational practices of self-mastery which not only shows how indebted memoirs in my corpus are to other types of self-help literature but fashions her experiencing self as normal—in the sense of rational and self-disciplined—despite the occasional recurrence of symptoms of madness.

Beers' narrating self also negotiates the co-existence of rational thought and madness when he explains how the experiencing self used logic and resourcefulness to overcome his delusions. When he was still floridly psychotic and confined to a mental hospital, Beers' experiencing self decided to submit his main delusion—that all his family members were doubles and police officers who tried to frame him for crimes—to a test of logic. Enlisting the help of a fellow patient, Beers' experiencing self confirmed that the most recent city directory still listed his relatives as residents of his family home. Thereby convinced that a letter to that address will reach his true relatives, he composed a note that instructed his brother to bring said note as a method of identification on his next visit. When his brother arrived with the letter, the experiencing self was able to let go of his delusion (36–40). Beers even included the letter as proof "that sometimes a mentally disordered person, even one suffering from many delusions, can think and write clearly" (39). In this manner, Beers introduces a paradox into his self-fashioning. On the one hand, he shows that the experiencing self was always normal, in the sense of capable of rational thought, and on the other hand, he embeds this self-fashioning in a narrative of overcoming which shows that he used rationality to return to normalcy. This complicates binary distinctions between normalcy and madness as well as the conflation of madness and unreasonableness, and therefore undermines widespread and stigma-based assumptions about mental disorders.

The myth of the self-made man also includes conceptualizations where the drive for self-making is tied to the desire "to improve blatant social and moral injustices" (Mieder 22) and which incorporates aspects of sentimentalism that "entrea[t] the spectator to show his or her moral fiber by feeling deeply with the sentiments they [the texts] offe[r]" (Boudreau 23). For example, Frederick Douglass claims that self-making must always be "joined to some truly unselfish and noble purpose. Patriotism, religion, philanthropy—some grand motive power other than the simple hope of personal reward must be present" ("Trials" 302). For Clifford Beers, this noble purpose was "to protest in [sic] behalf of the thousands of outraged patients in private and state hospitals whose mute submission to … [the] indignities [of brutalizing and humiliating treatment] has never been recorded" (21) and to eventually effect reform in institutional practices (44) as well as the way the public views the insane (98). To effect this change, Beers' experiencing self physically defended helpless inmates against rough treatment (51), and wrote about these events in the sentimental mode, i.e., in the same way that was employed in fictional and non-fictional texts by the temperance and abolitionist movement to encourage social change.[27] In this manner, he not only establishes his determination and indomitability of spirit—qualities frequently ascribed to self-made men (Cawelti 95–96)— but also creates empathy for the insane and began "the greatest psychiatric reform movement of this [the twentieth] century" (Peterson 164).

Beers' use of the sentimental mode is especially visible in his emotional descriptions of the spectacularly cruel treatment of his fellow patients but also in his self-fashioning as a determined, virtuous hero in the style of Horatio Alger's novels. During his stay, Beers' experiencing self was repeatedly assaulted by attendants, denied necessities like food, water, and baths, and cut off from communication with his family. However, rather than keep his head down and focus on his release, Beers' experiencing self defended the rights of others. In this respect—though not in many others, especially humility—Beers' experiencing self greatly resembles the protagonists of Horatio Alger's novels as well as those of other sentimental writers

(Cawelti 111–112). As in Alger's *Ragged Dick* novels, Beers' encounters with helpless patients allowed him "to demonstrate his kindness, courage and generosity" towards those who "depended on him for protection against the harsh … world" (Cawelti 112). One benefactor of the experiencing self's help was a "well educated, traveled, refined" older man "whose abnormality for the most part consisted of an inordinate thirst for liquor" (51). Beers reports that the man "had been trapped into the institution by the subterfuge of relatives" (51) and in "as heartbreaking an ordeal as one can well imagine" (52), the man was "taken without notice from [his] home … and branded with what he considered an unbearable disgrace" (51–52). Sympathetic to the genteel man, Beers "took him under [his] protecting and commodious[28] wing" (52). When the man was forced to exercise in the yard with his fellow patients, Beers' experiencing self was outraged because "[n]o sane person need stretch his imagination in order to realize how humiliating it would be for this man to walk with a crowd which greatly resembled a 'chain gang'" (52). When Beers confronted a spiteful attendant, a scrimmage ensued which was broken up by the superintendent who called Beers a rowdy. Beers' experiencing self replied, "[i]f fighting for the rights of a much older man, unable to protect his own interest, is the act of a rowdy, I am quite willing to be thought one" (53).

The passage summarized above exemplifies Beers' appropriation of key tropes from Alger's popular novels of self-making. Alger's stories frequently include a gentle but weak character—usually the protagonist's mother—who is helpless against the scheming of second husbands or greedy relatives and depends on the manly, virtuous protagonist for protection (Cawelti 113–114). Likewise, the older man of Beers' narration is an artistically inclined, gentlemanly soul who is powerless against his scheming relatives and spiteful attendants and is feminized when he "weep[s] bitterly" about the humiliation of having to walk the yard with mental patients. By contrast, Beers' experiencing self relies on his manly grace under pressure, virtuousness, and keen sense of justice, and despite the prospect of a severe beating, he comes to the man's aid in the harsh environment of early twentieth-century asylums. In this way, he resembles the typical Alger-novel hero who, in an unforgiving urban setting, heroically prefers to be harmed himself before allowing the victimization of others (Cawelti 119). Beers' self-fashioning therefore emulates the hard work and determination as well as the sound moral compass of Alger's protagonists (cf. Cawelti 115–117), which can be read as a reaction to the stigma of madness: According to Erving Goffman, the process of stigmatization includes the ascription of moral flaws to the discredited individual such as the assumptions that they are "quite thoroughly bad, or dangerous, or weak" (*Stigma* 12). When Beers fashions himself as a virtuous champion of victimized asylum inmates, he "prov[es] that an individual of this kind [here: an asylum inmate] can be a good person" (Goffman, *Stigma* 37) and represents himself as normal in the sense of morally sound.

This type of self-fashioning is further emphasized when the narrating self not only instructs readers in the ways of sympathy and the appropriate evaluation of the drinker's treatment—it's a "heartbreaking … ordeal"— but also positions himself in the category of the sane: The narrating self claims, "[n]o sane person need stretch his imagination in order to realize how humiliating it would be for this man" to associate with mental patients. Beers thereby draws upon stigma beliefs that conflate madness and badness, or in this case, lack of empathy to produce his empathetic experiencing self as normal. By the same token, he implies that doctors and attendants are either quite mad or thoroughly sadistic for humiliating the drinker, which strengthens Beers' calls for asylum reform.

Although Beers' experiencing self also experienced repeated brutalization and humiliations, he did not become helpless and this grace under pressure contributes to a more powerful narrative of overcoming. Throughout his confinement to various asylums, Beers' experiencing self was spat upon (21), frequently subjected to physical abuse (53) and the force-feedings of meals and medication even after he had agreed to take them the regular way (64). In addition to this maltreatment, Beers claims that he never received proper assistance from "ignorant and indifferent doctors and attendants" (33) who "wrought havoc among the helpless insane" (25). He was therefore not only left to his own devices but was actively treated in a manner that is not conducive to sanity. Beers' narrative of overcoming is therefore particularly impressive due to the severity of hardships he overcame. Additionally, it functions as a critique of the asylum system because it illustrates the need for self-reliance in the very people who are incarcerated because of their presumed inability to live by themselves.

Beers also uses the sentimental mode to encourage asylum reform and empathy for some of the most vulnerable members of society, i.e., the mad, in a passage that mitigates the patient's offenses and stresses the dehumanizing environment of the hospital. During his time on the violent ward, Beers' experiencing self encounters a man over sixty who is "[b]oth physically and mentally … a wreck" (80). The man was assigned to that ward "probably because of his previous history for violence while at his own home. But his violence (if it ever existed) had already spent itself, and had come to nothing more than an utter incapacity to obey. His offence was that he was too weak to attend to his common wants" (80). Shortly after the man's arrival, a fellow patient tells Beers' experiencing self that he has seen the man "stark naked and helpless" on his bed and further informs him of "the vicious way in which the head attendant had assaulted the sick man" who could do nothing against becoming a "victim of an attendant's unmanly passion" (80). Attendants then moved the man to a new cell and "seemed as much concerned about their burden as one might be about a dead dog, weighted and ready for the river" (80). That very night the patient died, leaving the narrating self to wonder whether humane and scientific treatment could have "restored him [the old man] to health and home" (80).

This passage encourages an interest in asylum reform by relying on sentimentalism, sensationalism and voyeurism. First, the passage presents the man as a subject worthy of sympathy and responds to stigma beliefs about the dangerousness of mad people by questioning whether the man was truly violent and legitimizing the man's alleged actions. Rather than focus on the claims that he assaulted his own wife and children—the vulnerable subjects to whom sentimental literature traditionally extends sympathy—the narrating self points out that these supposed attacks took place in "his [the old man's] own home," thus implying that they are a private matter of a man asserting his patriarchal authority. Secondly, the passage establishes the man's victimization by conjuring the specter of homosexual rape, the objectification of being treated like the carcass of a dog, and the man's untimely death due to injuries sustained during the attack of the attendant with "unmanly passion[s]." In this manner, the passage not only invites cries for asylum reform and empathy but also horrified reactions at the violations and emasculation that takes place in asylums. In this case, Beers' self-fashioning as normal also produces him as a credible witness to these spectacular abuses and authenticates his report which further contributes to the memoir's voyeuristic and sensational appeal and assures its widespread consumption.

Beers shows that he is well aware of the potential political impact of sentimental tropes, such as the black and white morality in the characterization of helpless patients and sadistic orderlies and direct emotional appeals (cf. Hendler 7–19), when he states that

> "Uncle Tom's Cabin" ... had a very decided effect on the question of slavery of the negro race. Why cannot a book be written which will free the helpless slaves[29] of all creeds and colors confined to-day [sic] in the asylums and sanatoriums throughout the world. That is, free them from unnecessary abuses to which they have been subjected.... Such a book might change the attitude of the public towards those who are unfortunate enough to have the stigma of mental incompetency put on them [100].

Through his reference to Harriet Beecher Stowe's novel, which included several spectacular acts of violence by cruel slave owners against positively angelic slaves, Beers establishes that he sought to use depictions of the callous treatment of vulnerable and marginalized subjects to bring about significant social change. Moreover, through the very act of writing a text meant to free "the helpless slaves" in asylums, the narrating self equates himself with Harriet Beecher Stowe—a Northern white woman—rather than with abolitionists of color or former slaves such as Frederick Douglass. This implicit comparison suggests that the narrating self does not fashion himself as a (formerly) stigmatized person fighting for the rights of his Own but as a champion of the mad who is firmly rooted in his normalcy.

However, this claim to normalcy needs to allow for the experiencing self's previous madness—after all, Beers' lived experience authenticates the memoir. The text thus conceives of madness and normalcy as distinct, transient, yet objectively definable states rather than stable blemishes of an individual's character. To achieve this, Beers appropriates the medicalized framework of psychiatry. He proclaims, "[o]f course, an insane man is an insane man and while insane should be placed in an institution for treatment, but when that man comes out[,] he should be as free from all taint as the man who recovers from a contagious disease and again takes his place in society" (100). The comparison to contagious diseases, which one either does or does not have, suggests a binary opposition between the mad and the sane and therefore problematizes the blurring of boundaries practiced at other points of Beers' memoir. The disease simile furthermore implies that there are—or will be—objective tests to distinguish between the two groups as well as treatment for those afflicted. The tautology "an insane man is an insane man" further emphasizes the clear distinction between the mad and the sane and implies general agreement on what constitutes insanity, or rather which types of behavior, incapacitation, and danger can be expected from those who are diagnosed with it. Lastly, the quote signals the narrating self's endorsement of psychiatric treatment of the insane and thereby not only enables a close cooperation of the Mental Hygiene Movement and prominent psychiatrists (cf. Capps; Porter, *Social* 194–195) but also fashions himself as a reasonable individual rather than a disgruntled (former) mental patient. Overall, then, Beers, Hornbacher, and authors like them use seemingly straightforward narratives in complex and tension-laden ways.

As this chapter showed, authors fashion themselves as normal in multiple, frequently contradictory ways. One of these contradictions rises from the combination of self-fashioning as essentially or relatively normal all along and the appropriation of narratives of overcoming that require acknowledgments of previous madness. Another tension stems from the combination of two narrative structures which produce different meanings of madness. I have shown the full extent of the appropriation in my corpus by analyzing particularly salient examples in detail but the inclusion of passages from Marya Hornbacher's memoir of bipolar disorder, which appropriates both the narrative of self-making and the template of conversion narratives, illustrates a core phenomenon in my corpus, namely the existence of tensions between conflicting modes of self-fashioning and meanings of madness. Within the scope of the conversion narrative, Hornbacher alternately embraces a moralizing interpretive framework that depicts madness as sin and temptation but also conceives of her condition as a serious quasi-medical disorder that requires expert intervention. In any case, the experiencing self is passive, without agency, and in utter need of salvation. This self-fashioning counteracts stigma-beliefs that the mad could just pull themselves together. However, this interpretation also discredits the mad as helpless, i.e., it activates another stigma belief that historically justified forced treatment and confinement. By contrast, Hornbacher's emulation of the narrative of self-making restores her (sense of) agency and empowers herself and her Own yet reactivates stigma beliefs as it implies that anyone, whose madness did not abate, did not work hard enough to overcome it. These stigma beliefs, then, lead to social avoidance and anger on the part of normals (Corrigan and Watson 477). By drawing upon narratives that suggest opposite things about the agency the mad have in overcoming their condition, Hornbacher points to the double bind that governs beliefs about stigmatized groups, that is, one cannot reject one stigma belief without simultaneously supporting another one. Put differently, she responds to multiple different stigma beliefs simultaneously and reveals the inherent contradictions of stigmatization as well as the constructedness of distinctions between normalcy and madness.

Furthermore, Hornbacher does not separate them neatly into two halves of the text but switches back and forth between tropes from the one and the other despite their conflicting implications about agency. This has three effects: First, shifts between these templates express the changing attitudes Hornbacher's experiencing self has embraced over the years, sometimes feeling more confident and self-reliant, other times feeling readier to submit to the power, truth, and healing of the psychiatric dispositive. In other words, the mixing of tropes and structures speaks to Hornbacher's lived experience. Secondly, mixing tropes implicitly argues for a combination of methods in the management of mental disorders: Willpower and self-reliance alone cannot overcome madness, and conversely, no therapy can save a passive patient unwilling to do their part. Thirdly, structuring her memoir by drawing upon two conflicting narrative templates expresses a very postmodern distrust towards single, coherent explanatory narratives and draws attention to the constructedness of any story as well as the fragmented nature of identity.

The effect of a memoir that is governed by multiple, unresolved tensions in self-fashioning is quite aggressive in so far as it challenges common-sense assumptions about the mad as well as established patterns of narrating life. Narrative structures like the two discussed above are imposed upon lived experience to create order, ascribe meaning or to reveal larger themes. When texts combine narrative structures with contradictory claims about desirable qualities, states of mind, and potential for agency in the experiencing self, the structures undermine each other. Fissures begin to show, the experiencing self and their life spills beyond the boundaries of established, meaning-generating patterns. Considering the inadequacy of these narrative (and conceptual) patterns to create meaning, there are two options: To create new conceptual and narrative patterns that speak to the richness of lived experience or to rely less on conceptual categories such as those created by stigma. The memoir thus encourages the move away from stigmatizing notions and established patterns of thought in a roundabout way and encourages active participation by readers rather than forcing the condemnation of stigma beliefs down their throats.[30]

This chapter also showed that authors in my corpus produce normalcy to refer to more than the absence of madness. Instead, texts insist on what is normal—in the sense of a quality shared by most readers—about experiencing selves and encourage sympathetic identification based on their rationality, cultural background, values, and common religious beliefs. In other words, memoirs emphasize the experiencing self's normalcy so it can eclipse the ascription of Otherness created by a psychiatric diagnosis. Passages that normalize, relativize or depathologize the experiencing self's condition contribute to this effect as well and present madness and normalcy as utterly relational concepts that exist on a spectrum. In this manner, authors in my corpus not only claim a voice in the ontological debate on normalcy and madness, but they implicitly contradict stigma beliefs about a mad person's dehumanization, amorality, irrationality, and fundamental, all-encompassing Otherness.

The self-fashioning as normal again also encourages different readings that depend on the audience. For the Own, mental illness pathographies and their appropriation of narratives of overcoming can function as self-help literature because these narratives "have been influential locations of exchange among religious and secular languages for expressing how life ought to be lived … [as well as] vanguards of popular psychology and its revision of American values surrounding agency, morality, and the management of emotions" (Cannon 2).

Especially for those who do not share the author's stigma, confessional narratives of sensational depravity and redemption provide a titillating reading experience but also "neutralized the threat they [here: the mad] implied to this public, by acting as a mechanism to turn feared outsiders into cherished insiders. This reconciliation, in turn, re-sanctified American society as a vehicle of God's expansive grace" (Cannon 27). The story of rebirth therefore redeems two subjects simultaneously, the formerly uncontrolled mad person and the society in which they live: When the former mad person overcomes the problems exacerbated or even caused by alienating social forces and subsequently achieves reintegration into the social fold, the mad person's "redemption symbolically redeems the flaws of modern society itself" (Cannon 6). Because of this double redemption, these narratives of overcoming protect both the confessant from ostracism and have frequently been read to spare society from structural criticism and to affirm dominant notions of normalcy and well-established cultural values (cf. Peters 25).[31]

Despite their criticism, authors in my corpus also present themselves as converts to the truth of psychiatry and allies who encourage medication compliance in fellow patients. Although the template of conversion narratives requires a radical affirmation of the psychiatric dispositive, even the most fervent converts are never entirely uncritical. Even though their criticism of the dispositive (not its individual, fallible representatives!) is subdued and frequently only traceable in fissures and ironies, authors in my corpus do express misgivings about side effects and anonymizing treatment. By contrast, those who appropriate the self-made man narrative stress the need for patient agency due to shortcomings in the system more explicitly, but they do so without ever renouncing the dispositive altogether. The appropriation of these culturally-valued narrative templates therefore plays an important role in the negotiation of the right to speak.

Lastly, the appropriation of narratives of overcoming allows for positive, even prestigious representations of the present, narrating self. Whereas the conversion narrative and, to a lesser degree, the self-made man narrative unequivocally demonize the pre-conversion or pre-success state of the experiencing self, this is not the case with the texts in my corpus. Mental illness pathographies remain strikingly ambiguous in their descriptions of the unsaved subject and madness, especially when compared to the unified subjects and unequivocal rejection of their pre-conversion or pre-self-making states in the older genres. I therefore suggest that the emulation of these genres helps to emphasize the utterly decentered nature of a subject caught in the tension between madness and normalcy. To provide further evidence for this, my analysis now illustrates how authors textually fashion themselves as mad.

CHAPTER TWO

Self-Fashioning as Mad

Authors in my corpus are just as adamant about their mad Otherness as they are about their normalcy and aggressively confront supposedly normal readers with their difference. During the recurrent psychotic episodes that can be managed but not cured, Marya Hornbacher slides back and forth "between the world you know and a world of my own" (*Madness* 201) and concludes "[m]y days will always be different from your days; my idea of stability isn't your idea" (*Madness* 276). Likewise, Lori Schiller acknowledges that—despite her salvation through more effective anti-psychotic medication (247)—there are still occasional hallucinations and "bizarre paralyses" that are "a nasty reminder that I am still a card-carrying member of the 'mentally ill' club" (270). Robert B. Oxnam's alters even go so far as to doubt whether "we could ever learn to be fully human" (232) in the sense of having an integrated, singular self. Statements of this kind textually produce the second half of the authors' double sense of self and thus create one of the central tensions in mental illness pathographies, namely between a self-fashioning as normal *and* as mad. In the following sections, I analyze the stigma-political and literary ways in which authors come out as discredited individuals, create sympathy for their experiencing selves and the mad in general, raise awareness, encourage reform in the way they are seen and treated, and alternately appropriate *and* reject negative *and* positive stigma beliefs to support their changing discursive position on what being mad entails.

Moreover, authors appropriate various narratives, tropes, and discourses that produce contradictory meanings of madness which allows them to respond to multiple, conflicting stigma-political demands. For example, when authors draw upon the trope of the mad genius, it enables calls for the reduction of occupational discrimination, whereas discourses of incapacitation and suffering aid pleas to have a condition taken seriously or to underscore the need for better, more extensive medical and interpersonal assistance. While I do not want to speculate about the degree to which the production of contradictory meanings is a conscious stigma-political strategy, I will analyze how intertextual references and narratives that alternately romanticize, demonize, and pathologize madness destabilize stigma beliefs.

Memoirs in my corpus also throw questions of responsibility and agency in madness into relief through the appropriation of Gothic tropes of seduction, possession, mind control, *doppelgänger*, and monstrosity. Just as the female protagonists of Gothic horror stories and Gothic romances,[1] who have sparked heated academic debates[2] on whether they are damsels in distress, preyed upon by malevolent men and circumscribed by social pressures (cf. Davison 124) or whether they are active, free to explore and to enjoy adventures (cf. Moers 126), experiencing selves in my corpus retain a high degree of ambiguity: Authors fashion their experiencing selves as *both* the victim of a malicious yet seductive madness *and* as a (self-) destructive, monstrous villain. In this manner, memoirs address fears regarding the danger which the mad pose for the rest of society as well as the suffering of those diagnosed with mental disorders. The appropriation of Gothic tropes and the double self-fashioning as victim *and* perpetrator thus produces the meaning of madness as monstrosity *and* as possession or victimization and allows authors to communicate the complexities of their lived experience.

Furthermore, the Gothic mode has long been the locus of negotiations of controversial issues of identity, such as gender roles and transgressive sexualities, and addresses a mix of contemporary and archetypal fears (cf. Reyes, "Introduction" 12–13). By transforming dreaded Others into fantastic or allegorical characters, the Gothic mode allows readers to pleasurably engage with their fears in the safe space of literature. Likewise, memoirs in my corpus use the Gothic mode to address frightening topics such as the loss of self, of one's sense of reality or of control over one's actions without alienating too many readers with the Otherness of experiencing selves.

Since the starting point of this study is the literary reaction to stigma, this chapter is structured around the qualifications and mitigations that accompany the public acceptance of a stigmatized identity and that reduce the social fallout for the speaking subject. Authors in my corpus implicitly and explicitly address common stigma beliefs about the mad when they stress specific attributes in their self-fashioning. When they present themselves as functioning members of society, they reject the notion that persons with mental disorders are helpless or incapacitated, and several authors even draw upon supposedly positive stigma theories to connect madness to creativity or genius. When they depict their mad selves in humorously exaggerated ways, they not only reject the association of madness and dejection—and complicate their own claims to suffering—but also employ humor in aggressive ways that illustrate how stigma-based tropes and humor can be used to reveal the constructedness of these tropes.

Simultaneously, authors in my corpus stress the suffering connected to their conditions and compare their plight to those of other marginalized groups such as Jewish people in attempts to discourage discrimination and lend legitimacy to their stigma-political efforts. However, authors do not simply reject negative stigma beliefs and emphasize positive ones, but they also engage with one of the most pervasive fears—the dangerous mad person—from the point of view of those with lived experience and in a manner that suggests authenticity. Mental illness pathographies therefore constitute complex attempts at self-fashioning within a field of tensions and internal contradictions.

Complicating Madness and Identity Politics

One way in which authors assert their madness is to appropriate, alter, combine, and problematize the approaches of various identity-political movements to promote a "stance of respect, appreciation and affirmation" for their condition (B. Lewis, "Mad" 116).[3] While no author in my corpus mentions identity-political movements connected to madness such as the neurodiversity movement, the Mad Pride movement or any of its splinter groups by name, my selection of memoirs covers the entire scope of stigma-political and epistemological positions that are held in these movements. My corpus includes memoirs such as Kaysen's that are *generally but not completely* rooted in the radical, anti-psychiatry rhetoric of the Mad Pride movement in the 1970s and conceive of the diagnosis of mental illness as a tool of oppression and of madness as a journey toward self-liberation (see Chapter One). My corpus also contains memoirs like Oxnam's or Chase's that *predominantly but not only* understand madness as another way of being that comes with advantages and disadvantages. These memoirs echo the contemporary neurodiversity movement. Lastly, my corpus includes texts such as those by Jamison and Hornbacher that *mostly* adopt the medical framework of the psychiatric dispositive in their efforts for coalition politics, but they remain critical of what they perceive to be excessive pathologization and an enforcement of "psychic conformity in the guise of diagnostic labelling and treatment" (B. Lewis, "Mad" 115–116). My corpus thus contains a wide range of positions, and in this section, I analyze how the acceptance of the label "madness" is communicated in the same nuanced, ambivalent manner as the authors' rejection thereof.

Even though I focus on attempts to reclaim and redefine madness that are similar to disability rights activists' challenges to the meaning of impairment and disability (cf. McWade et. al. 306; B. Lewis, "Mad" 116; Spandler et al.), I wish to stress that there is also a sharp difference to the activities of advocacy groups, namely that no text in my corpus produces a unified definition of madness. By assuming several rhetorical positions and conflicting stances on madness, authors not only express complex attitudes towards their lived experience and avoid the essentialism connected to traditional identity politics (cf. Heyes), but they also destabilize neatly bureaucratized meanings of madness such as those disseminated by the American Psychiatric Association in the *Diagnostic and Statistical Manual of Mental Disorders* (*DSM*). In this manner, they actively contribute to the visibility of diverse conceptions of madness in the public consciousness.

To contextualize the demands for the recognition of mad identities, I provide a quick outline of the identity-political movements that share the authors' focus on madness, namely the Mad Pride and the neurodiversity movement. The Mad Pride movement took shape during the 1970s, alongside the African American civil rights movement, the women's movement, the lesbian and gay movement, and the disability movement (B. Lewis, "Mad" 118). In its current form, the Mad Pride movement, whose name alludes to Black Pride and Gay Pride, is "an international coalition" made up of "consumer/survivor/ex-patient"[4] groups who resist and critique biomedical and clinician-centered approaches to mental health, advocate for alternative and peer-run support during crises, fight for visibility and participation in general culture, and reclaim sanist slurs such as "mad," "crazy" or "nutter" (B. Lewis, "Mad" 115–121). Mad Pride can be linked to the neurodiversity movement[5] since the concept of neurodiversity has come to include mood disorders, schizophrenia, and anxiety disorders, at least in its usage in Disability Studies.[6] The neurodiversity movement originated in the 1990s among individuals diagnosed with autism spectrum disorder. Autism activists were among the first who proposed to "replace a 'disability' or 'illness' paradigm with a 'diversity' perspective" (Armstrong, "Myth" 249), that is, they suggested to understand autism spectrum disorder as a valuable expression of human difference rather than to pathologize it. In this diversity perspective, "[t]he 'Neurologically Different' represent a new addition to the familiar political categories of class/gender/race" (Singer, "Why" 64). Advocacy groups can cite the precedent of the civil rights or women's movement in their calls for more social recognition and rights. The stances that are endorsed by Mad Pride and the neurodiversity movement—and echoed in my corpus—therefore have powerful political implications.

The focus on difference furthermore creates a conceptual framework that considers both strengths and needs for support of "the neurologically different" without defining them only in recourse to their supposed disability (cf. Armstrong "Myth"). Mad Pride and the neurodiversity movement are therefore types of "biocultural activism," that is, they are "located at the interface of bioscience and politics" and "continuously struggl[e] with epistemological issues along with more typical political issues. In short, the people in Mad Pride [and neurodiversity] struggle over both truth and values" regarding the nature of their condition and how those who exhibit it should be treated (B. Lewis, "Mad" 116; my addition). Since authors in my corpus also claim a voice in the debate on truth and values regarding madness, their memoirs are political despite the absence of clearly formulated goals, demands, or platforms.

While neurodiversity and Mad Pride activists proclaim the strengths and challenges associated with their conditions, memoirs in my corpus produce madness as a psychiatric disorder as well as a source of creativity, pleasure, and a way of accessing the sublime. Kay Redfield Jamison, who is diagnosed with bipolar disorder, writes longingly about the intensity of her pre-medication years and the desire to once more experience their "furor and fever" (*Unquiet* 211). The narrating self misses the sublime manic illusions of "gliding through star fields and dancing along the rings of Saturn" (211) and the "absolutely intoxicating states that gave rise to great personal pleasure, an incomparable flow of thoughts, and a ceaseless energy that allowed the translation of new ideas into papers and projects" (5–6). Note how "furor and fever" points to the advantages yet retains the framework of illness: "Furor" evokes the history of thought that connects madness to creativity and passion by referencing the Ancient Greek belief that inspired poets were touched by divine fire—*furor*—and rendered mad (cf. Jamison, *Touched* 50–51; Plato, *Phaedrus*). However, "fever" suggests a mind negatively affected by disease. Jamison repeatedly emphasizes the latter, for example when she states that she "believe[s], without doubt, that manic-depressive illness is a medical illness" (*Unquiet* 102; cf. also 5, 91). As these quotes show, Jamison's memoir simultaneously represents her condition as an impairment *and* as an enabling quality, thereby severely complicating traditional notions of illness.

William Styron, a writer most famous for his novel *Sophie's Choice* (1979), spends many pages in his memoir of depression to negotiate the trope of the mad artist as well as the biomedical understanding of the condition. He expresses a notion similar to Jamison when he writes that "[d]espite depression's eclectic reach, it has been demonstrated with fair convincingness that *artistic types* (especially *poets*) are particularly vulnerable to the *disorder*" (34, emphasis added). The narrating self proposes a scientifically verified connection ("demonstrated") between depression and artistic inclinations, thereby tapping into the Romantic trope of the mad (literary) genius, while also pathologizing it ("disorder"). Both Styron and Jamison thus echo the neurodiversity and Mad Pride movement in that they call for support and the recognition of madness' enabling qualities.

What distinguishes Styron and Jamison from these movements is their embrace of a contradiction. Whereas the neurodiversity movement and many in the Mad Pride movement acknowledge challenges but reject the pathologization of their condition, Jamison and Styron see their madness *both* as an illness and as an enabling feature. They therefore destabilize the term through mutually exclusive productions of meaning which complicates the process of stigmatization.

Jamison, Styron, and several others further support their discursive production of madness as a source of creativity by referring to famous mad artists such as Lord Byron, Robert Lowell, Virginia Woolf, Robert Schumann, Hector Berlioz, Anne Sexton or Sylvia Plath.[7] Bringing up famous mad artists who allegedly shared their disorder and its intellectual or artistic benefits supplies anecdotal evidence that legitimates the authors' romanticization of their condition and allows them to claim cultural capital as well as a prestigious social identity. These references furthermore engender pride of their psychiatric diagnoses and demonstrate the centrality of the mad genius or mad artist trope to positive self-fashioning in my corpus.

Additionally, the prevalence of this trope points to the friction between the narrow medico-psychiatric concept of madness as disorder and other culturally salient beliefs. While the emphatic use of the trope does not delegitimize the psychiatric dispositive and its methods of truth production, it can point to well-established ways of interpreting extremes of thought and emotion differently. In this manner, memoirs in my corpus broaden the scope of meanings attached to madness without undermining their chances for coalition politics.

Other authors in my corpus also stress the advantages of their condition without referencing the mad artist trope. Robert B. Oxnam and Truddi Chase repeatedly claim that *they have been able to survive past trauma and even thrive *because* *they have dissociative identity disorder.[8] Oxnam insists that it helped *them be an empathetic teacher in multicultural contexts (251) and to be more self-aware than people without the condition (230). Chase emphasizes the sense of protection *they received from some alters, the intelligence of others, which helped *them to pass a "four-hour real estate exam in forty minutes" (54), and the creativity of yet others that gained *their artwork spaces in exhibitions. These examples show that the representation of madness as enabling is central to the creation of mutually exclusive meanings and extends by necessity beyond the mad artist trope associated with affective disorders.

Like Mad Pride and the neurodiversity movement, authors in my corpus present their condition as a variant of human difference. The narrated version of Chase's therapist supports *their desire to remain a multiple and states that multiplicity is "*another* form of sanity" (77; emphasis added), thus implying that there are multiple, equivalent ones. By attributing these views to a practicing therapist and university professor, Chase uses his authority to lend credibility to these views. By endorsing a perspective of difference rather than pathology, Chase politicizes *their condition in the same way that race, gender, and sexuality are already politicized. While not made explicit in the memoirs of my corpus, this politicization lends legitimacy to mad peoples' fight for the same sort of protection from oppression and stigmatization which other identity-political movements have won for their members (cf. Heyes).

The memoirs by Chase and Oxnam further support the politicization of *their condition through the rejection of cures (Chase xxvi; Oxnam 260)—which echoes the positions of the neurodiversity and branches of the Mad Pride movement (cf. Sinclair)—as well as *their appropriation of the narrative of self-making. The refusal to integrate most alters by the end of the memoirs supports *their claims that *they experience a non-pathological variant of human difference. While both authors strongly evoke the narrative of self-making through the emphasis on *their resourcefulness, determination, and hard work, *they do not use that narrative template to produce *their condition as a hardship that needs to be overcome. It is only the chaos of unmanaged multiplicity that is a hardship. Well-adjusted multiplicity, by contrast, is represented as enabling and a state of success. In this manner, Chase and Oxnam's memoirs alter a culturally-valued narrative to support their identity-political perspective of difference, which illustrates that no textual feature, trope or narrative structure unequivocally supports either affirmations of normalcy or of madness. Instead, textual features reinforce tensions and contribute to the multivalence of madness as an identity category.

The thesis that no textual feature is tied to the self-fashioning as either normal or mad is supported by Marya Hornbacher's memoir on bipolar disorder. As Chapter One showed, she appropriates the tropes of conversion narratives to express how she was saved by submission to psychiatric treatment and the psychiatric truth of madness as disorder. However, like many Puritan authors of conversion narratives, Hornbacher also conceives of her sinful or mad past as a prerequisite for the relative peace and pleasures of the present (Clark, "Repenting" 58). While reformed sinners express gratefulness for their turbulent past because it brought them to God, Hornbacher insists that her lived experience of madness is a source of personal growth and happiness. She states that her mind may be "strange and imperfect" (*Madness* 279) but that she also based her career and interests on her conditions. She admits, "while I think and feel, like Byron says, a bit too wildly at times, I also delight in the workings of the intellect and imagination … my private reality [of psychosis] is a very lonely place.

But.… I find value in having been to the places I've been" (*Madness* 279; cf. also Jamison, *Unquiet* 218). Hornbacher thus not only exhibits a common reaction to stigmatization when she fashions her condition as "a blessing in disguise" (Goffman, *Stigma* 11), thereby avoiding shame and rejecting assumptions of inferiority inherent to the process of stigmatization, but also produces contradictory meanings of madness. By fashioning her madness as *both* disorder and blessing in disguise, Hornbacher creates a tension even within the textual feature of the conversion template, transcends the unequivocal rejections of pathologization that are voiced by the neurodiversity movement (cf. Sinclair), and conveys complex emotions about her lived experience.

Similarly, Kay Redfield Jamison produces contradictory meanings of madness within the psychiatric framework but uses them in a more expressly political manner. As a practicing psychiatrist and researcher into affective disorders, Jamison collaborated with a Nobel Prize laureate in research on the "manic depressive gene," thereby establishing herself as an authoritative participant in the psychiatric discourse (191–193). However, she also supports discursive positions akin to those of the Mad Pride or neurodiversity movement when she discusses the ethical and social implications of prenatal testing for affective disorders. The narrating self worries whether giving parents the option to abort fetuses with the gene for bipolar disorder could "risk making the world a blander, more homogenized place" because it gets rid of "the risk takers, those restless individuals who join with others in society to propel the arts, business, politics, and science" (194). By insisting that "manic-depressive illness can confer advantages on both the individual and society" (194; emphasis added) Jamison avoids universalist arguments about the value of human difference that are common to traditional advocacy and opts instead for a more neoliberal stance that presents people with mental illness as socially useful. Moreover, by stating that manic-depressive *illness* should therefore be managed, not cured or eradicated, she severely complicates the traditional medical understanding of disease upon which psychiatry operates. In advocating a view of bipolar disorder as enabling difference *and* pathology, Jamison not only complicates the meaning of madness from within the hegemonic psychiatric discourse but also uses her double role as renowned psychiatrist and patient to supply proof of the value of mad individuals for society. Moreover, her concerns about prenatal testing evoke the role that medicine has historically played in rites of purification to eradicate stigmatized individuals such as the eugenics movement (see Introduction), which means that she engages in biocultural activism insofar as she argues over the truth and value of madness.

Many other authors in my corpus also complicate understandings of madness as impairment which are not only widespread but also central to psychiatric definitions of mental disorders. Since at least the seventeenth century, there has been a conflation of incapacitation, idleness, and madness which persists to this day and of which authors are aware (cf. L. Davis 6; Foucault, *Madness* 38–64). Elizabeth Wurtzel claims that "[t]he measure of our mindfulness, the touchstone of our sanity in this society, is our level of productivity, our attention to responsibility, our ability to plain and simple hold down a job" (55). The ability of "just barely going through the motions—showing up at work, paying the bills … [means that] you are still okay or okay enough" (55). Likewise, the American Psychiatric Association (ADA) stressed functioning in their attempts to distinguish mental health from pathology in the *DSM-IV*. The ADA defines "mental disorder" as "(A) a clinically significant behavioral or psychological syndrome or pattern that occurs in an individual [and that] (B) is associated with present distress (e.g., painful symptom) or disability (i.e., *impairment* in one or more important areas of *functioning*)" (7; emphasis added). The latter is defined further as "occupational, academic, social (including interpersonal), and role *functioning*" in an elaboration of the definition by the editorial board of a leading journal of psychiatry and clinical psychology (Stein et al. 1760; emphasis added). Considering this focus on functioning, receiving a psychiatric diagnosis can be read as an adverse judgment on one's ability to be a productive member of society. When authors in my corpus narrate their professional, academic, and social achievements, they fashion themselves as counterexamples to popular and psychiatric assumptions about mad persons' ability to function.[9]

Iterations of personal and occupational achievements furthermore point out that the experiencing self should not be reduced to their madness but that they are defined by other social roles and interests as well. Since every author in my corpus carefully documents their achievements, a few examples shall suffice. Elizabeth Wurtzel states, "[a]t heart, I have always been a coper" (133) and explains that she was able to confine her most severe depressive episodes to her times off work, which, to her mind, was why no one took her suffering seriously enough. Despite her severe depressive episodes, she attended Harvard University, received the Rolling Stone College Journalism Award (151), and boasts, "[m]y editors were mystified by my productivity" (155; cf. also Chase 31). Robert B. Oxnam is similarly focused on *their professional achievements and explains how *their alters made various successes possible. This included going from "the first few words of Chinese-language study in the fall of 1964 to a doctorate in Qing dynasty history in the spring of 1969 (something of a speed record in a difficult field)" (22), accompanying President Bush, Sr., on an Asia trip as an expert or hosting a television show (12). In Truddi Chase's memoir, the written version of an expert on multiple personality disorder tells the written version of Chase's psychiatrist, "[y]our client is a business woman [sic]. Her competence doesn't tie in with the disablement that multiple personality caused people like Eve and Sybil" (103). This passage not only suggests that Chase's experiencing self is so high-functioning that *their case invites a reconsideration of the very definition of *their condition but ascribes the statement to a member of the hegemonic psychiatric discourse as well. As these examples show, authors in my corpus challenge stigma-based, institutionalized, and morally charged beliefs about the incapacitation of the mentally ill by providing "a living model of fully-normal achievement" (Goffman, *Stigma* 25). The descriptions of their professional achievements furthermore enable readers to see textual selves as more complex individuals rather than mad persons only.

Considering that these nuanced concepts of madness are often produced through contradictory attitudes, none of which are clearly privileged, a few comments are in order. Debra Beilke claims that contradictions like these exist because madness exacerbates the ambivalences of the (postmodern) self or the flux of opinions and attitudes (31). However, I suggest that the internal contradictions of texts that alternately conceive of madness as a mental illness, a disposition that comes with advantages and disadvantages, the source and consequence of artistic talent, and a facet of human difference are a function of literature and support stigma management. First, creating a collage of multiple contradictory discursive positions and narratives constitutes a literary representation of the complexities of lived experience. Secondly, while the authors' refusal to restrict themselves to one definition of madness does complicate the formation of advocacy groups and unified political action, it also helps them avoid both the trappings of essentialism that is a feature in traditional identity politics. Consequently, mad individuals are freer in their self-fashioning and can call attention to the difficulty of determining when a person can be deemed mad as well as the need to renegotiate this question in each case anew.

The Humor in Madness

Because stigmatization is frequently tied up with ridicule of the discredited subject, representations of mad experiencing selves as hilariously eccentric or comically incapacitated can be read as a form of self-stigma or as identification with those who discriminate against the mentally ill. However, adapting Berndt Ostendorf's argument on minstrelsy, I suggest that the textual performance of stereotypical roles of madness allows for complex processes of signification and stigma-political maneuvers (Ostendorf

65–94).[10] This section traces these processes with attention to the authors' double sense of self as well as the double audience of the textual performances: those who do not share the experiencing self's stigmatized condition (i.e., Goffman's "normals" or those who consider themselves less blemished) and those who do and whom Goffman calls "the Own" (*Stigma* 5).

Of course, there are significant differences between African American minstrels and authors in my corpus. On the one hand, there is the African American experience of diaspora, slavery, and continuous systemic racism as well as the rather strict limits to artistic expression within which African American minstrels operated. On the other hand, there is the white, (upper-) middle class mad person's experience of symptoms and discrimination yet also the relative freedom of self-fashioning in their memoirs. Despite these differences, I hold that memoirs in my corpus negotiate stigma and do cultural work that is similar in its effects—if not its context—to the subversion of racial stereotypes first used by African American minstrels in the late 1800s.

To better express my claims about the functions of the humorous mode in mental illness pathographies, let me summarize Ostendorf's thoughts on minstrelsy. Ostendorf suggests that minstrelsy played out humorously what nineteenth-century Euro-Americans feared in all seriousness: "the blackening of America" (67). A white minstrel who "acculturated voluntarily to his 'comic' vision of blackness" (67) allowed a white audience to engage with the perceived threat in the safety of an imitation that was itself restricted to highly stereotypical forms. Minstrels furthermore asserted the superiority of white America by defining the exact symbolic space people of color could occupy and by presenting them in accordance with stigma beliefs, namely as childish, foolish, or primitive (70, 74–75). In other words, "minstrel shows articulated the fear of 'difference' by exaggerating it and by fixing or domesticating the difference in a stereotype" (74). Moreover, minstrel performances delegitimized African American people's social or legal demands and thus helped Euro-Americans to avoid pressing questions about the general application of their ideals of liberty and equality (67–73). Lastly, minstrelsy ensured that "the teeth of black culture were pulled and as stereotype it would be safely recognizable by all" (75). After the Civil War, African American artists, to whom most avenues of upward mobility were closed, entered the minstrel business and quickly found they had to "out-minstrel [their] white competitors and out-maneuver [their] audience" to "minimiz[e] the dehumanizing aspects and maximiz[e] the artistic and human potential" (83). They exaggerated the tropes of minstrelsy to such absurd degrees that they could reveal them to be just that: stereotypes (83–84).

Similarly, the use of humor in my corpus bolsters the willingness of normals to engage with an Other. In the style of minstrel shows, memoirs include humorous descriptions of stereotypically mad behavior that depict the Other as lesser and create a pleasant sense of superiority in normals (cf. Berger 7–8). Moreover, these exaggerated, stereotypical depictions reduce the perceived threat of madness by suggesting that mental illness is "safely recognizable by all" (Ostendorf 75) and so outlandish that it does not implicate the reader's state of mind at all. I wish to add to Ostendorf's claims that humorous representations which ascribe incapacitation to supposedly dangerous stigmatized groups—like the mad or people of color—can create pleasure by (temporarily) removing the sense of threat. For this reason, passages that reduce madness to idiosyncrasy, incapacitation or odd but innocent forms of social deviance counterbalance media tropes of the dangerous, unpredictable mad person and can be just as pleasurable to audiences as depictions of people of color as child-like, lazy or dim-witted.

I will analyze these mechanisms by drawing upon a passage from Marya Hornbacher's *Madness: A Bipolar Life*.[11] Even though Hornbacher also describes the suffering caused by her condition, she repeatedly uses humorous clichés in a manner reminiscent of the performances of both white and black artists in minstrel shows. Hornbacher—like all authors in my corpus—fashions herself as both normal and mad so her textual performance of clichéd madness and insouciance has two effects. On the one hand, the narrating self uses humorous acknowledgments of the danger of once again turning mad as a coping mechanism, just as white minstrels jokingly acknowledge the threat of the "blackening of America." Moreover, both Hornbacher and white minstrels represent the Other as harmless, thus enabling normals' pleasurable engagement with them. On the other hand, Hornbacher's textual performance makes fun of supposedly sane peoples' stereotypes of the mad by revealing the strong element of fantasy in those stereotypes through exaggeration, artificiality, and the incorporation of an unrealistically large number of tropes, just as black minstrels did. The humorous mode therefore enables ambiguous modes of reading and writing.

Let me relate one of these incidents as concisely as possible. At one point, Hornbacher's experiencing self undergoes the elevated mood and high energy of hypomania and acts stereotypically, humorously mad. While cleaning her condo, the experiencing self muses that the sound of a vacuum cleaner always put her to sleep when she was a baby and that a clock in a blanket will do as much for a puppy. Finding this funny, she states, "I note out loud, 'Hilarious!' over the roar of the vacuum cleaner. I notice I am talking to myself and turn off the vacuum cleaner so I can hear myself better" (230). The experiencing self then begins and abandons various projects but eventually decides that it is time to do the laundry. She takes her bed-clothes, and

> singing a little laundry song, and I trail through the basement with my quantities of lin-ens, note that my laundry song has taken on a vaguely Baroque sort of air, and note fur-ther that, to my regret, I do not play the harpsichord, though my first husband's mother did, but she was really fucking crazy, and once called me a shrew. "A shrew!" I cry. "Can you *imagine*! Who says *shrew*? [231].

Arriving at the relatively small washing machine, the experiencing self is dismayed to discover that her heavy brocade bedspread will not fit, but then figures that "the washer will, in its eminent wisdom, suck in the bedspread in its chugging, 'obviously' I say, rolling my eyes at my own stupidity" (231). Back upstairs, the experiencing self has a humorously awkward encounter with her neighbor and flees back to the laundry room only to notice that her "bedspread is emerging out of the washer in an enormous coil, burbling over the edges like some kind of disgusting tongue" (232). Trying to wrestle the bedspread from the washer only drenches the experiencing self in water and causes the coil of fabric to twist even higher. Bellowing "I have you now!," she climbs on the washer that is still turned on, grabs the bedspread, hops down, and with "the soaking bedspread over [her] shoulder, lean[s] forward with all [her] weight and begin[s] a long, slow trudge across the basement, looking a little like Titian's Sisyphus" (232). Laboriously shoving the wet bedspread into a dryer that is also too small, she hears it "make a sound of great mechanical distress, *nnnnnnneeeeeeeeeee*" (233) but decides the dryer will be better able to do its job when it is not intimidated by her presence. Back in her apartment, she picks up a hefty book on bipolar dis-order in the hope that it will "surely, somewhere, somehow … explain to me precisely why the *fuck* I am like this" (233). The chapter ends when "the dryer screams in pain, makes a disturbing *chunk* sort of sound, and goes silent" (233).

The incident summarized above depicts the experiencing self's actions in a manner that conforms to the humor-related tropes of madness. The experiencing self is comically unable to perform such basic tasks as doing laundry due to her faulty, absurd logic and personification of machines like the attribution of "eminent wisdom" (231) to the washer. This absurd logic is also present when she turns off the vacuum cleaner to hear her-self speak. Hornbacher's experiencing self furthermore has a grand time talking to herself and singing songs, which is another very noticeable trope of madness but also speaks to her child-like innocence. Lastly, there is humor to the experiencing self's ignorance of the extremity of her own madness, which is visible when she calls her former mother-in-law "really fucking crazy" for using the word "shrew." The comic impact of these tropes is strengthened by the elements of slapstick or the farce,[12] such as experiencing self's frantic actions, exaggerated movements, and reactions like moving frequently between locations (from her apartment to the laundry room, back upstairs, downstairs and up again), struggling to fit an item into a container that is too small, jumping on the washer, wrestling with the wet, moving coil of a bedspread, and laboriously trudging through the laundry room in an attempt to pull the fabric out of the machine. All of this is emphasized by a show of affects that is greater than socially allowed and includes swearing, bellowing, and riotously laughing at one's thoughts. Additionally, as in slapstick, the experiencing self's actions have violent consequences, yet ultimately do not incur tragic results for any character with whom readers can sympathize. Just as Wile E. Coyote falls off cliffs and is shown flattened, the personified dryer dies in a humorously loud and dramatic manner. Because of these textual features, readers can enjoy Hornbacher's performance as unperturbedly as white audiences enjoyed minstrel shows.

However, the passage from Hornbacher's memoir is also markedly constructed and performative and thus subverts as well as contains stereotypical views of the mad. One hint towards the constructedness of the passage is in the reference to Titian's painting of Sisyphus, that is, to the oil painting of a myth.[13] Like the mythological figure in the painting, the experiencing self is an artful representation of a commonly recognized figure that supports meaning-making—a function shared by clichés or stereotypes. The experiencing self which readers encounter is thus twice removed not only from the historical author but also from the complexity and humanity of real-life mad persons. While the passage gains some of its humor from the way it suggests we are watching someone being happily, unselfconsciously mad, it also has a distinctly theatrical quality.[14] When the experiencing self talks to herself in short soliloquies that reveal her absurd logic, uses comically exaggerated movements in her attempts to free the bedspread from the washer, and sings Baroque songs about a mundane task, these actions are geared towards an audience ready to laugh at the antics of a stereotyped madwoman. However, just as African American minstrel performers mocked uninformed stereotypes of white minstrels and their audience in their exaggerated performance of these stereotypes, this passage implicitly mocks those who believe in clichés about the mentally ill.

The rhetorical device of humor also has several other functions in shame and stigma management. For those who suffer from any (stigmatized) hardship, the use of humor can create a sense of emotional distance that helps avoid feeling the full force of negative affects connected to mental illness. As Sigmund Freud suggested, "the essence of humour [sic] is that one spares oneself the affects to which the situation would naturally give rise" ("Humour" 162). Freud further states that humor allows the person who uses it the illusion of being invulnerable against the unpleasant conditions of the real and even offers a certain dignity that results from the emotional distance the speaker creates with their humorous remark. Humor is also relevant to stigma politics in memoirs as the humorous mode produces a sense of optimism about the fate of protagonists as well as a shared moment of respite from having to acknowledge the suffering connected to mental disorders (cf. Berger 13). Moreover, studies have shown that people perceive stigmatized individuals who use humor as more relatable and feel less need for social distance, which is particularly important in the self-fashioning of groups to whom stigma beliefs of dangerousness and incurability are attached (Corrigan et al. "Does").

However, the use of complex modes of writing such as humor can also be a hazard to stigma-politics. While the exaggeration of the trope of the insouciant mad person can reveal the constructedness of this trope without resorting to the moralizing tone of traditional advocacy work, it can also affirm stereotypes about the humorous helplessness of the mad and do so with all the authority of lived experience. This suggests that life writing does not make traditional advocacy work obsolete but can supplement it by (sometimes) destabilizing stereotypes about madness.

Humor is used in my corpus to perform complex stigma-political maneuvers, to create distance between oneself and emotionally draining, shameful experiences, to present experiencing selves in a positive, unthreatening light, and to depict madness as a source of humor. Authors thus add yet another layer of meaning to madness, thereby creating an ever more complex notion of their condition. The appropriation of African American forms of stigma negotiation through minstrelsy furthermore speaks to the similarities authors in my corpus perceive between the discrimination they experience and that of other historically marginalized groups. These implicit claims of similarity serve to lend legitimacy to the authors' calls for reduced stigmatization and furthermore shame those who continue the marginalization of the mad by equating sanism with racism and anti-Semitism—a mechanism I explore below. Lastly, I propose that it also serves as a change of pace or comic relief from the many other passages that depict the experiencing self's suffering in detail and with graphic language. It is these parts of my corpus that I turn to now.

Madness as Suffering

A key stigma-political strategy common to autobiographical accounts is to evoke compassion or the desire for social change, and like many other marginalized groups, authors in my corpus elaborate extensively on the suffering that is connected to their supposed blemish. According to Martha Nussbaum, compassion arises when we think "that someone else is suffering in some way that is important or nontrivial" (142–143), when that person is not to blame for their state, when the suffering person is like us, and "has possibilities in life that are similar" (144)—in short, when the elements of "*seriousness*," "*nonfault*," and "*similar possibilities*" are present (142, 143, 144). Since I already discussed how authors textually produce their similarities to supposedly normal readers in Chapter One, this section focuses on how authors stress their lack of responsibility and the seriousness of their suffering. As this suffering is not only linked to the authors' condition or the side effects of their treatment but also to discriminatory behavior, texts also confront normals with the ways their actions contribute to the suffering and impairment connected to madness.

An emphasis on suffering is central to several textual elements and therefore resurfaces at different points in this project, but in this section, I focus on how testimony to suffering creates a sense of urgency to the authors' fight against discrimination and presents the impairment attributed to madness as the result of marginalization. Spectacular accounts of misery and emotional appeals not only encourage social reform—and thus place mental illness pathographies in the tradition of eighteenth- and nineteenth-century patient protest literature (Scull, *Madness* 232–242)—but also charge the discourse emotionally. Authors in my corpus achieve this in three ways: First, through attention-grabbing comparisons of the experiencing self's suffering to that of victims of the Holocaust. Secondly, authors describe the painful and degrading treatment experiencing selves received in mental hospitals. Lastly, they relate what Goffman calls "atrocity tales" (*Stigma* 25), i.e., accounts of extreme mistreatment at the hands of normals who harbor stigma beliefs against the mad.

Suffering is also central to the stigma-political efforts of contemporary disability activists. These activists resist "individualizing and medicalizing approaches[15] and embrace the social model of disability by reframing disability as a social restriction and oppression rather than simply a medical problem … [and] call attention to the fact that much of the suffering of different bodies comes from social exclusion, isolation, and lack of opportunity" (Lewis, "Mad" 116). While there is still some debate whether applying the social model of disability to mental disorders is appropriate or desirable (cf. Penson), this model allows me to focus on the social experience of madness and to continue the debate started at the beginning of this chapter about the nature of madness. While I previously analyzed how authors complicate the current understanding of madness as disorder by stressing the advantages their conditions bring, this part considers how impairment and distress—which are central to the individualizing and medicalizing psychiatric understanding of mental illness (cf. *DSM V* 20)—are (also) socially produced.

Kristina Morgan's *Mind Without a Home: A Memoir of Schizophrenia* (2013) narrates one of the most severe cases of discrimination in my corpus, namely the loss of her job as an English teacher at a high school when she revealed her diagnosis to the assistant principal. The narrating self stresses the element of "*nonfault*" (Nussbaum 143), thereby creating empathy and politicizing her victimization. Morgan begins the account of losing her job by establishing that her condition was carefully managed and that she was a capable, responsible, and popular teacher (K. Morgan 187, 190–191). In this manner, she immediately contradicts stigma beliefs that individuals with schizophrenia cannot handle stressful jobs such as teaching or that they are not safe to take care of children. Moreover, Morgan keeps descriptions of her symptoms to a minimum in this passage, stressing instead her qualifications and her multiple safeguards, thereby fashioning herself primarily as someone who is barred from doing the job they consider their calling and presenting the justification for her removal as unfounded.

The narrating self continues emphasizing the experiencing self's rational behavior but also contrasts it with her employer's reaction of fear and discrimination. One day, the experiencing self informed the assistant principal about her condition and explained that she "was getting signals from other realities" and needed to check whether she should take a day off by asking someone other than her students whether they were real (188). The assistant principal was frightened by this confession, sent the experiencing self to a psychiatrist for evaluation, and finally fired her. The narrating self wonders why neither her boss nor the psychiatrist could see "my calls to crisis as ensuring nothing would happen by doing a reality check as I was taught to do" (190). She then muses, "how much different is this than taking insulin so you ensure … that you don't end up in a diabetic coma on the floor?" (190). Note how Morgan emphasizes the element of nonfault by explaining that the experiencing self acted in the most responsible manner she knew. Also, note how the narrating self attempts to move away from stigma beliefs about the alleged dangerousness of persons with psychotic disorders by comparing her condition with one that is potentially incapacitating but not associated with violence at all. Morgan further establishes her lack of fault and politicizes the loss of her job when she states three times on one page that she is "discriminated against" (191), i.e., that she lost her job not because of what she did or failed to do but because of who she is. This impression is cemented through three repetitions of the assistant principal's words who said as much herself: "You are a great teacher, Kristina, but you are also a schizophrenic and because of that we fear our students are not safe with you" (189; cf. also 188, 191). By contrasting her experiencing self's attempts to be a responsible teacher with the assistant principal's explicitly stigma-based attitude, Morgan's memoir presents a cut-and-dried case of structural discrimination of herself as a mad person: The assistant principal drew on "established and legitimized category systems, concepts, stereotypes, judgement principles, generalized strategies, and societal norms" as well as "established rules and regulations, procedures[, and] role definitions" (Burns 152) within her institution—such as sending the experiencing self to a psychiatrist for evaluation—to Other Morgan's experiencing self and to rob her of opportunities and social participation. The realization that discrimination of this sort is possible, despite legal protections such as the *Americans with Disabilities Act* (1990), can create outrage and compassion among readers.

Attempting to increase these feelings further, Morgan stresses the seriousness of her suffering (cf. Nussbaum 142–143) by establishing both how much she loved teaching and how desperate she was when she was laid off. She states that she minded neither the long hours nor the relatively low pay and that she would even trade a decade of her life for a classroom filled with students (187). She furthermore relates how her experiencing self was mortified by being told that she was not safe to be around students and states, "I thought I would die on the spot. Had I a gun, I would have" (189). The experiencing self's condition subsequently worsened, she was hospitalized, and it took her a year to recover from the emotional turmoil caused by this incident. In this way, Morgan's account of these events also illustrates how stigma beliefs and sanism can cause significant distress and even impair a stigmatized person's functioning due to the emotional and psychic fallout that results from discrimination.

Whereas Morgan insists that the assistant principal overreacted due to fear about the experiencing self's potential for violence, other authors narrate incidents where normals were unsympathetic or incredulous regarding the seriousness of their condition. These reactions classify as "microaggressions," i.e., "brief and commonplace daily verbal, behavioral or environmental indignities, whether intentional or unintentional, that communicate hostile, derogatory, or negative … slights or insults" (Sue et al. 271; cf. also Campbell and Manning). Although the concept comes from the field of race studies, I suggest that it also applies to situations where contempt for the supposed weakness of an individual with mental illnesses is communicated verbally or nonverbally. Truddi Chase recalls how the experiencing self's best friend—who is, in fact, the only friend ever mentioned in the memoir—downplayed *their suffering and suggested that *they could overcome *their problems with willpower alone. The friend tells Chase's experiencing self, "they're only mood swings! You are not sick, you haven't multiple personalities" and that *they could get *their life back on track if *they put "that multiple business" out of *their head (Chase 257). Marya Hornbacher observes similar reactions to patients on the closed ward by their visitors who think that patients perpetuate their condition through willfulness or weakness and resent them for it: "Their voices, when they speak, are accusing, or sarcastic. Some of them have for months been telling their person to snap out of it, to cheer up, to get herself together, to stop feeling sorry for herself" (*Madness* 190). While neither Hornbacher nor Chase specify their emotional responses to the delegitimization of the suffering caused by madness, they include harrowing descriptions of their lived experience throughout their memoirs. It is therefore a safe guess that disbelief and hostility cause additional misery, desperation or anger, increase a sense of loneliness, and lower self-esteem. In this manner, memoirs in my corpus hint at the negative emotional fallout of microaggressions but do not lecture or moralize.

Considering that mental disorders do not have objectively verifiable symptoms like cancer, AIDS or strokes, persons with mental disorders need to convey the severity of their suffering in other ways. In my corpus, one of the most attention-grabbing ways to establish that being mad means suffering and to reject responsibility for that suffering is the deployment of the Holocaust as a metaphor and the appropriation of victim status through direct comparisons to concentration camp inmates. Cherry Boone-O'Neill claims that even in the early stages of her eating disorder her mother found the experiencing self's body to be "frighteningly reminiscent of the photographs of the survivors of Auschwitz" (53) and told her that she looked "like a concentration-camp victim" (54). Likewise, Marya Hornbacher's mother thought that her eating-disordered daughter "looked like an escapee from Auschwitz" (*Wasted* 175), and Mark Vonnegut claims that, during one psychotic episode, his experiencing self "looked like pictures of refugees from Hitler's concentration camps" (118) due to his persistent food refusal (he thought it was poisoned during his floridly psychotic phases). These statements are an example of the "Americanization of the Holocaust,"[16] in which the Holocaust is reductively metaphorized and appropriated to express personal anguish such as that connected to extreme emaciation. However, I suggest that these comparisons are not evoked "with an inflammatory casualness" (Flanzbaum, "Americanization" 96–97) but instead contribute to the conceptualization of madness and perform crucial stigma-political work.

Leaving aside the question whether such comparisons are appropriate, the use of the Holocaust as metaphor by Hornbacher, Boone-O'Neill, and Vonnegut suggests that since the horrors of incarceration in a concentration camp and those of madness inscribe themselves onto the body in a similar manner, the experience may also be similarly horrifying. The feature that prompts the comparison in those three cases is the extreme emaciation of the experiencing selves' bodies, but other attributes connected to victims of the Holocaust are evoked as well. The "total institution" (cf. Goffman, *Asylum* xiii–46) of the concentration camp reduced inmates to such an extreme state of bodily decrepitude and existential disregard that all human potentialities were lost and only the biological fact of life remained. As they describe it, the three authors' madness created a similarly closed system of intra-psychic torture that robbed their experiencing selves of the ability to exist beyond the limits of biological survival. In other words, just like structures and practices in concentration camps sought to deprive inmates of all prerequisites for life beyond mere existence, madness prevented authors in my corpus from forming meaningful relationships, developing as a person, and retaining a sense of self (cf. Vonnegut 23; Hornbacher, *Wasted* 10; Boone-O'Neill 62, 73; Goffman, *Asylum* 6–51).

Oxnam's therapist makes a similar claim when he tells the experiencing selves that the abuse-generated system of multiple personalities makes sense "in the way that a concentration camp makes sense. It was a closed system" (157). I therefore propose that one reason for invoking this comparison is to establish the suffering of madness and the way it destroys both body and mind of those that experience it. This is particularly important in conditions that are seen as phases in adolescent development such as eating disorders (cf. Hornbacher, *Wasted* 5–6; Boone-O'Neill 162–163) or those that are so strongly connected to stigma beliefs about dangerousness that public discourse tends to ignore the internal suffering it causes, which is the case with schizophrenia and, to a lesser extent, dissociative identity disorder.

The desire to have her condition taken seriously is also a major theme of Elizabeth Wurtzel's memoir of depression, *Prozac Nation,* and informs her references to the Holocaust. When she was already attending Harvard University, she suffered an emotional breakdown and tells a friend that she will just do some homework since "work always makes me feel better … '*Arbeit macht frei*,' I added, realizing that Timothy wasn't Jewish and probably wouldn't get my morbid reference to Auschwitz" (199; cf. also 341).[17] In this quote, Wurtzel, who addresses her Jewish identity at length in her memoir, refers to the inscription on the gate to the Auschwitz concentration camp. By assuming the cynically mocking stance of those who oversaw the extermination through labor that was practiced at Auschwitz and simultaneously pointing to her Jewish identity, Wurtzel assumes the subject position of both torturer and victim, and thus communicates two features of her lived experience. First, the passage implies that her depressed mind pursues her destruction with as much sadism and efficiency as Nazis did with the Jewish people. This double subject position illustrates how her self-fashioning as mad is characterized by a constant tension between identification with her depression and the externalization and personification of her condition—a theme also expressed in various metaphors taken from the genre of Gothic horror (see below). Secondly, her words hyperbolically suggest that she preferred working herself to death over having to face the barrage of negative thoughts that caused her breakdown. This reference to the Holocaust therefore not only establishes the severity of her suffering but also provides insight into the complex internal mechanisms that make depression so hard to bear.

The identification with Jewish people during the Holocaust performs an additional stigma-political function, namely, to shift the mode of writing from confessional to testimonial. The authors quoted above do *confess* to being so mad that they nearly starved themselves to death or tortured themselves in cruel and unremitting ways, that is, they scrutinize and implicate themselves with these admissions of madness (cf. Radstone 169). However, "in the post–Holocaust world, where the most recognizable feature of Jewish identity became victimhood" (Flanzbaum, "Americanization" 32), identification with Jewish people has become a way to express personal anguish or a sense of being victimized by destructive societal forces, as was common practice in the mid-century literary movement called confessional poetry (cf. Gross 201–203, 222–223).[18] By assuming the subject position of the general cultural trope of "the Jew," authors change the communicative intent from *confessing* their misdeeds to bearing witness, i.e., *testifying* to environments that fostered the development of mental illnesses as well as to the internal havoc wrought by a madness that is personified to varying degrees. In other words, authors in my corpus move away from a stance that frames their madness as a transgression and towards one that depicts it as suffering with "*nonfault*" (cf. Nussbaum 144).

Moreover, the identification with Jewish victims of the Holocaust is a plea to reduce the discrimination against people with mental illnesses. Anti-Semitism became much less socially acceptable as the atrocities of the Holocaust were collectively processed in the mid–1950s. Texts in my corpus may fashion discrimination against the mad as similarly unacceptable by stating that their suffering is comparable and that they are thus as undeserving of stigmatization as Jewish people.

The treatment in mental hospitals is another source of suffering and victimization for the experiencing selves in my corpus. According to Erving Goffman, mental hospitals, like concentration camps, are a type of "total institutions," i.e., "forcing houses for changing persons" that radically destabilize the inmate's sense of self through "a series of abasements, degradations, humiliations, and profanations of self" (*Asylums* 12, 14).

Although most narrating selves acknowledge the necessity of confinement for their well-being, all of them also feel that their stay at mental hospitals entailed unnecessary chicanery of the kind which Goffman discusses in *Asylums*. This included the imposition of a rigid structure of the day's activities and constant supervision (cf. Hornbacher, *Madness*; Schiller and Bennett; Smola), systems of rewards and punishments that coerce patients into obeying apparently arbitrary rules (Vonnegut; Kaysen; Beers; Hornbacher, *Wasted*), and objectifying admission procedures that include confiscating personal possession and medically examining new patients (Hornbacher, *Wasted*; Kaysen; K. Morgan). In more extreme cases, it included stripping the inmate of their usual appearance through cutting of hair and beard (Vonnegut), as well as removing the most fundamental sense of autonomy through forced medication, forced feeding, placement in soft cells or other forms of physical restraint, brutal treatment, and many other humiliations (Beers; Kaysen; Schiller and Bennett; Goffman, *Asylums* 14–51).

Since the ways in which patients in mental hospitals are exposed to disciplinary power, the dehumanizing medical gaze, and "profanations of self" (Goffman, *Asylums* 14) have been discussed extensively in Michel Foucault's *Psychiatric Power* and *Discipline and Punish: The Birth of the Prison* and, of course, in Goffman's *Asylums*, I will not discuss these mechanisms in more detail. Instead, I wish to point out that some authors state that their condition was "aggravated and perpetuated by the stupidity of those in authority" (Beers 66; cf. also Kaysen 47; Hornbacher, *Madness* 240–241). In this manner, some authors in my corpus not only protest their helplessness but also provide further support for the social model of madness which exists in a tension with the medical model they also subscribe to. Additionally, these expressions of discontent about this treatment call attention to the fact that coercive methods are still common practice in mental hospitals despite advances by activists and legal reforms.[19] By decrying their maltreatment and victimization, authors in my corpus suggest that another effect of madness is a fundamental vulnerability—even as privileged, white, cisgender, able-bodied, middle-class subjects. The authors' awareness of this vulnerability also explains the extensive rhetorical efforts authors make towards engaging psychiatrists in a dialogue about the conceptualization of mental illness and its treatment, which Chapter Three discusses.

As this section showed, authors in my corpus produce their identity as mad through the suffering it entails. They not only illustrate particularly painful mechanisms of their condition but also show how much distress is caused by normals who delegitimize or relativize their condition or by the institutions meant to aid in the recovery from madness. In case of the latter two aspects, authors implicitly support the social model of disability and thus create yet another tension between mutually contradictory meanings—in this case between the medical model that conceives of madness as a disorder with concrete, observable symptoms and the social model in which the impairment attributed to mental illness is not exclusively caused by the symptoms of madness but also the result of coercion and discriminatory social practices. Madness is thus inextricably linked to a fundamental vulnerability to maltreatment. Memoirs of mental illness, then, can also function as a platform for authors to express their outrage, call for social change, and raise awareness for the struggles of the mad.

Madness and Gothic Horror

However, authors also severely complicate their self-fashioning as vulnerable subjects through the multiple meanings of madness which they produce by appropriating the Gothic mode and tropes of horror fiction.[20] Authors in my corpus communicate the fear that frequently accompanies psychotic symptoms by describing them as apparitions or else they evoke the gloom and obsessive thoughts of depression through imagery of Gothic landscapes and dungeons. In other cases, the appropriations convey the horror at finding oneself internally divided or possessed by forces beyond one's control. Intertextual references to and appropriations of the Gothic mode are very common in my corpus, probably because the Gothic mode focuses on similar conflicts and themes. These themes include "the legacies of the past and its burdens on the present; the radically provisional or divided nature of the self; the construction of peoples or individuals as monstrous or 'other'; the preoccupation with bodies that are modified, grotesque or diseased" (Spooner 8), death, insanity, perversion, and obsessive desire (Spooner 21). Following Halberstam, I define the Gothic mode as "a technology of subjectivity, one which produces the deviant subjectivities opposite which the normal, the healthy, and the pure can be known," yet which also dissolves "boundaries between good and evil, health and perversion, … truth and deception, inside and outside … and threaten[s] the integrity of the narrative itself" (2). Its "rhetorical style and narrative structure [are] designed to produce fear and desire within the reader" (Halberstam 2). This fear "emanates from a vertiginous excess of meaning … a rhetorical extravagance that produces, quite simply, too much" (Halberstam 2). The Gothic mode in all its complexities therefore offers itself to the life writing of Othered subjectivities and their multilayered, even contradictory textual self-fashioning.

While all memoirs in my corpus acknowledge the experiencing self's madness and translate it into figurative language, they also differ in the way they position madness in relation to the self. There is a spectrum that ranges from the complete externalization of madness, which threatens an essentially normal self, to the complete internalization or self-fashioning as a mad Other. The production of madness as horror can therefore support opposing types of self-fashioning which illustrates the presence of tensions on all textual levels. Moreover, the Gothic mode and horror tropes are uniquely suited to communicate the processes of identity construction that result from the experience of madness. They can convey the horror, terror, and occasional pleasurable thrill connected to mental disorders but also negotiate the separation and identity of the experiencing self and madness in a complex manner which helps to reinforce the central tension between normalcy and madness that runs through my corpus.

No author restricts themselves to either the externalization or internalization of madness, which speaks to the ambivalent, changing relationship between their disorder and their (experiencing) self but also reinforces their postmodern emphasis on multifaceted identities. The greatest degree of externalization exists in passages that fashion the experiencing self's madness as a malevolent personified entity which pursues the experiencing self and thus evokes the classic Gothic escape narrative. Just as the protagonists of Gothic romances are threatened by villainous men or supernatural entities, experiencing selves are terrorized by their madness, which not only establishes the radical distinction between self and madness but also reinforces claims to victimization (see above).

Other passages make the distinction between madness and self progressively more difficult. In some cases, narrating selves acknowledge the experiencing self's attraction to a personified madness and shape the account like a seduction narrative with a "dangerous lover" (Lutz ix). In yet other cases, narrating selves concede a blurring of boundaries between the experiencing selves and madness. This blurring is generally expressed through the tropes of possession or *doppelgängers*. While madness is conceptually a discrete entity, it is also closely connected to the experiencing self. It has either entered their mind or is linked to the self through forms of identity and opposition in the *doppelgänger* trope. Lastly, my corpus comprises passages that depict the transformation of the experiencing self into a monster and that acknowledge the experiencing self's mad Otherness. The Gothic mode and the ambivalence and contradictions on which it thrives therefore enable authors to negotiate complex questions of identity and separateness of a person and their madness. In this manner, authors not only fashion themselves in a suspenseful manner but can also claim a voice in the debate on whether madness is an illness one can catch and treat or whether it is an integral part of one's personality. By presenting themselves as *both* vulnerable to an externalized, personified madness *and* as the source of horror which stigma theories deem them to be, authors in my corpus can convey the complexities of what it means to be mad on an intra-psychic and a social level.

Moreover, the tropes of Gothic and horror fiction enable a debate about responsibility for one's mad Otherness. Like Dr. Jekyll despaired at the recognition of his previously repressed self—Mr. Hyde—authors in my corpus are horrified by their destructive behavior during acute episodes of madness. Narrating this experience by drawing explicitly and implicitly on horror tropes or popular Gothic texts such as Stevenson's *Dr. Jekyll and Mr. Hyde* (1886) helps authors to simultaneously accept and reject responsibility for behavior in times of acute mental crises which has a strong impact on the creation of sympathy (cf. Nussbaum 143). These intertextual references furthermore comment on the stigma theory that conflates madness with badness, while the markedly fantastic nature of horror tropes removes the negotiation to the space of literature where the reader can safely engage with fearful topics such as the dangerous mad person or the experience of going mad.

The Gothic mode furthermore enables the pleasurable consumption of threatening Others and can therefore address focal points of cultural anxiety. Many popular Gothic romances and horror stories address fear-inducing or controversial subjects by creating metaphorical monsters around them. For example, Mary Shelley's *Frankenstein* (1823) expresses unease about rapid scientific advancements, and Ira Levin's *Rosemary's Baby* (1967) reflects the debate about female reproductive rights (cf. Murphy 144–145). Similarly, authors in my corpus make intertextual references to *Dr. Jekyll and Mr. Hyde*, introduce witches, monsters, *doppelgänger,* and the theme of possession into their texts to temporarily remove their story to a genre in which the examination of fear-inducing topics is acceptable or even thrilling. However, the very appropriation of Gothic tropes suggests that they acknowledge the potential monstrosity of the mad person which creates a tension to the subject position of the victim.

On the one hand, the representation of lived experience through metaphorical monsters is an attempt to establish a clear distinction between a familiar, normal self and an intrusive madness and is therefore a continuation of the kinds of stigma and shame management discussed in Chapter One: A core self remains untainted by madness which is externalized into Gothic entities that absorb the shame and the blame. On the other hand, the appropriation of the Gothic mode is a defense against the fear reaction prompted by the uncanny experience of finding that one has become an Other for the people around one.[21] In this manner, drawing upon Gothic tropes can function both as a shield against stigma-based discrimination as well as an expression of the fear that comes from the realization that one has indeed turned mad.

Because of the genre conventions of life writing, such as the use of the realist mode, and stigma theories about a mad person's inability to distinguish reality from delusion, the appropriation of Gothic tropes can also have adverse stigma-political effects (cf. Wood 2–3). Descriptions of malevolent entities that pursue innocent protagonists may convince supposedly normal readers to reduce discrimination of the mentally ill as they already suffer enough. Conversely, it can render the experiencing or even the narrating self uncanny and increase the desire for social distance. According to Freud, a living person is perceived as uncanny "when we ascribe evil motives to him … [and] attribute to these intentions capacity to achieve their aim in virtue of certain special powers" ("Uncanny" 231). Those two elements are supplied by well-established stigma theories. The dangerous mad person who lives in their own reality is a popular trope of horror and enjoys ever-increasing popularity since the 1950s (Murphy 150). Moreover, animal strength and/or supernatural cunning have been attributed to the mad for several hundred years (Foucault, *Madness* 70–79). Mental illness pathographies that use the Gothic mode for self-fashioning may therefore both reinforce *and* challenge beliefs about the dangerousness of the mad, which speaks to the ambivalence of literature but also to the advantages and problems of using literary texts in stigma and shame management.

A more persistent fear reaction than the one created by the mediated encounter with the mindscape of a mad person may derive from the dissolution of boundaries between the concepts of normalcy and madness. Both the identification with the experiencing or narrating self (cf. Chapter One) and the uncanny nature of madness contribute to this effect. Freud claimed that the layperson sees in epilepsy and madness "the workings of forces hitherto unsuspected in his fellow-man but which at the same time he is dimly aware of in a remote corner of his own being" ("Uncanny" 231). To read about the insanity of persons who have presented themselves as relatable and, in many respects, normal can therefore create the more or less pleasurable dread of considering one's own vulnerability to mental disorders and destabilize clear distinctions between sanity and madness in a lasting fashion.

To continue the line of inquiry begun in the section on suffering, I turn to Gothic tropes of victimization and vulnerability first. Few authors consistently fashion themselves as Gothic protagonists or shape their narratives in the form of Gothic romances. However, almost all writers in my corpus use tropes from the (European) Gothic tradition to describe their lived experience of madness in terms of a persistent sense of unease or threat through various supernatural entities and thereby create a Gothic narrative of threat and seduction.

Threat, Seduction, and Externalized Madness

Gothic narratives of threat and seduction reinforce the central tension in self-fashioning as they both acknowledge the experiencing selves' madness and insist on their essential normalcy. Clifford Beers expresses this tension between the lived experience of madness and the emphatic self-fashioning as normal when he emulates the literature of horror to communicate the experiencing self's fear during his psychotic states. Confined to a hospital after a suicide attempt, his room "soon became a chamber of torture" (11), filled with the sound of "[g]hostly rappings on the wall and ceiling" (11). At night, handwriting appeared on his bed sheets (15), "[h]uman bodies, dismembered and gory," were visible on the ceiling, and the experiencing self firmly "believed there was some one [sic] who at fall of night secreted himself under my bed" (16). The narrating self is quick to normalize these perceptions or at least the experiencing self's fear of them by stating that "[h]andwriting on the wall has ever struck terror to the hearts of even sane men" (15) and that dread about a man under the bed "in itself was not peculiar, as sane persons at one time or another are troubled by the same notion" (16). In this manner, he not only produces madness as horror but also fashions himself as (emotionally) normal.

However, Beers' self-fashioning as normal only works if one accepts these apparitions as the reality they would be within the framework of horror fiction. Yet, the narrating self does not acknowledge the distinction between the Gothic trope of writing on the wall and the relative absence thereof in what we call reality. By insisting that anyone would share his fear reaction, Beers' blurs the boundaries between literary tropes and the world of "sane men" which speaks to the experiencing self's conviction in the truth value of his delusions and therefore communicates a central aspect of his lived experience. At the same time, the narrating self's inability to tell reality and delusion apart raises questions about the reliability of Beers' account and can confirm stigma beliefs about life writing by the mad.

Whereas Beers appropriates Gothic tropes only occasionally, other authors fully develop inner Gothic landscapes. Robert B. Oxnam, for example, metaphorizes the complexities of *their experience of living with dissociative identity disorder through intertextual references to the shadowy, ancient castle in Bram Stoker's *Dracula* (1897) and the labyrinthine architecture of Horace Walpole's *The Castle of Otranto* (1764): A significant portion of the memoir takes place in Oxnam's inner landscape, which is (initially) dominated by two humid medieval castles which are full of secret passages and trap doors, like *Otranto*. Moreover, one of the castles is "perpetually shrouded in fog, day and night, and neither sun nor moon revealed more than its ominous outline" (Oxnam 125) and thus recalls the inability of Stoker's protagonist to get a good look at the castle of Count Dracula. The trap doors, secret passages, and the perpetual fog convey the mystery and uncertainty that come with the repression of traumatic memories as well as Oxnam's confusion about the workings of *their mind. Since Oxnam's castles, and especially its dungeon, are used to hold various alters captive (cf. both *Otranto* and *Dracula*), the twofold effects of dissociative identity disorder also become clear through this extended metaphor: On the one hand, the walls of the castle—like the mental disorder—provide (psychic) protection against outside attackers. On the other hand, both disorder and castle are rigid structures that can become a place of confinement, stopping the experiencing selves from interacting meaningfully with the outside world or *their alters (cf. also Philips, Introduction xiv). Lastly, the castle metaphor complicates the self-fashioning as either normal or mad to a greater degree than was the case in Beers' use of Gothic and horror tropes because it presents madness as a larger structure that exists *separately* from various alters yet also *within* the experiencing selves.

Another way in which memoirs acknowledge the textual selves' madness but insist on a core of normalcy is by fashioning experiencing selves as victims of menacing entities much like the heroines of Gothic horror stories. Several authors describe their conditions as "a demon" or "demons" (Styron 42; Boone-O'Neill 93; Wurtzel 283) and Marya Hornbacher fashions her bipolar disorder as a monster which holds her between its teeth and "thrashe[s] [her] back and forth" (*Madness* 153) during psychotic episodes. Since demons generally have supernatural powers and Hornbacher's monster must be much larger than the experiencing self to hold her in its teeth, this imagery simultaneously contradicts stigma beliefs that the mad could pull themselves together and externalizes the monstrosity and evilness attributed to the mad. By representing their madness as powerful entities, authors thus express their sense of helplessness and lay claim to a victimized normal self which creates tensions with narrative templates of self-making.

In a multifaceted appropriation of the Gothic mode, authors also convey that their condition was at times intensely pleasurable. As J. Jack Halberstam put it, the Gothic evokes "fear of and desire for the other, fear of and desire for the possibly latent perversity lurking within the reader herself" (13). Simultaneously, these pleasures are marked as deviant and fixed in the elsewhere of an aberrant Otherness which needs to be expelled. Contemporary readers may thus enjoy memoirs that detail the deviant pleasures of madness just as Victorians could devour Gothic novels "without regarding such material as debased" (Halberstam 13). Rendered safe for consumption through their vilification of madness, memoirs represent its seductive side, i.e., those attributes which made experiencing selves want to stay mad. In other words, memoirs in my corpus also depict normal experiencing selves that are seduced by madness.

Some female authors in my corpus represent the seductive attributes of madness through images of captivity and descriptions of intense bodily or sexual pleasure.[22] Although they rarely personify their disorder to the degree that allows for a coherent Gothic narrative of threat and seduction, which Deborah Lutz calls the "dangerous lover romance" (ix), their imagery constitutes an appropriation of tropes from popular, female-coded romance genres which communicates the desire, pleasure, and thrill contained in the authors' experience. According to Deborah Lutz, the "dangerous lover" is darkly erotic, mysterious, "in rebellious exile from comfortable everyday living" (ix), and "a tragic hero whose main energy comes from villainous actions, self-destructive impulses, or character flaws" (29). He is the romantic "subject who lives imprisoned in the blighted landscape of his own mind" (ix). Lutz cites Emily Brontë's Heathcliff (*Wuthering Heights* [1847]) and Charlotte Brontë's Mr. Rochester (*Jane Eyre* [1847]) but also the titular characters in Bram Stoker's *Dracula* and E.M. Hull's *The Sheik* (1919) as (Victorian) Gothic and Modern incarnations of the dangerous lover. By emulating aspects of popular narratives marked by violence, rough seduction, and immoderation which "tend to repeat again and again to the point of supersaturation of meaning" (Lutz 7), authors furthermore convey the all-consuming drama, intense sensations, excess, and repetitiveness that also make certain forms of madness so appealing.[23] Although the most explicit examples are from texts about eating disorders, I supplement my analysis with passages from other memoirs to illustrate that this trope expresses the (erotic) appeal of several kinds of madness. The representation of madness as both pleasurable and horrifying creates yet another tension and illustrates that the complexity of lived experience cannot be reduced to singular, unified narratives and selves.

The first similarity between dangerous lover romances and some mental illness pathographies is that both conflate the figures of lover and enemy into one complex entity, who subsequently threatens, seduces, and comforts the protagonist or experiencing self, although usually in opposite sequence. Whereas the dangerous lover narrative tends to begin with a mysterious stranger who poses a vaguely or explicitly sexual threat to the heroine, it usually ends with him as an utterly devoted and erotically alluring lover (Modleski 45). Narratives in my corpus generally begin with the experiencing self's infatuation but quickly turn dark when the experiencing selves find out that their madness *qua* lover is not only comforting and erotic but also destructive. Marya Hornbacher illustrates this when she states that an eating disorder is "so very seductive. It is so reassuring, so all-consuming, so entertaining. At first." (*Wasted* 64). By depicting mental illnesses as dangerous lovers, authors in my corpus retain the Gothic gesture of marking the monster as both perversely desirable and as that which must be reformed or expelled.

Representations of madness as a lover tend to focus on desire and emotional or physical intimacy. Marianne Apostolides' memoir evokes intense longing and the physical act of taking in the object of desire when she explains that "it [food] was my lover. I had to devour it" (75). She is even a little relieved when she splits up with her live-in boyfriend because she "could binge again … make love to the food" (104) without having to hide her actions. Musing about her obsession with her eating disorder that lasted more than a decade, Marya Hornbacher states, "You will never find a lover so careful, so attentive, so unconditionally present and concerned only with you" (*Wasted* 125). While she does not describe it in the same glowing terms, Elizabeth Wurtzel also claims a personal and exclusive connection to her depressive disorder, which is implicitly personified through the term "relationship": "it started to seem like the most intimate relationship I'd ever have would be with depression" (353). In all of these examples, authors show that their madness is not only an intrusive Other—as cancer or lupus are regularly depicted in pathographies of somatic illness (cf. Hawkins, *Reconstructing* 61–77)—but that they have an intense connection to an entity that both *is* and *is not* them. They use imagery from the semantic field of love and relationships to access the lover's discourse which includes the desire to lose the boundaries between oneself and the object of affection, to be engulfed or annihilated in the Other (Barthes 11). Likening their madness to a lover therefore communicates the appeal of certain mental disorders as a coping mechanism, asks the reader to understand why the experiencing selves lost themselves so completely in them, and why they struggled to renounce their lover/madness. Moreover, it exemplifies the desire to *simultaneously* keep the disorder conceptually separate from a core self and to merge with it.

In other passages, authors convey the abandon, passion, and fulfillment they found in madness by describing their condition in erotic terms. For example, Marianne Apostolides' representations of binging and self-induced vomiting at times evoke orgasm: "As the wave of food moved through my body, I would surge, body arching…. My belly would contract hard, my back would curve like a frightened cat's…. My heart would be beating fast" (75–76; cf. also Jamison, *Unquiet* 67, 123; Boone-O'Neill 95). In this quote, the movement of food is rhythmic like waves and thereby evokes intercourse. The wave of food furthermore causes movements associated with the force and abandon of orgasm: surging, arching, contracting. In this manner, Apostolides conveys the intense satisfaction she derived from vomiting—a bodily function most people experience as highly unpleasant—to illustrate that her lived experience of madness was also characterized by sensuality and carnality.

Marya Hornbacher makes the sexual implications of starving, binging, and purging even more explicit when she states that she and other individuals with eating disorders desired "food *qua* lover" and recalls how she saw Jane, an eating-disordered friend, "doing something to an apple with her mouth that was positively erotic … her tongue on the wet, white flesh" (*Wasted* 150). When asked about it, Jane replied, "I'm making love to it" and the narrating self comments that in eating disorders, "food becomes the object of your desire. You either prefer the desperate hunger of unfed passion, or the battering cycle of food moving in and out and in and out of your body in a rhythm that you never want to end" (*Wasted* 150). Note how she reinforces the "near-pornographic sexual violence" (Lutz 6) that characterizes her relationship to the dangerous lover/madness when she envisions the repeated penetration by and ejection of the object of her desire as a "battering," whereas Jane's erotic encounter with the apple appears to be more careful, attentive. Hornbacher thus reinforces the double attraction of the madness of eating disorders as passion and comfort. The lover metaphor in *Wasted* and the other memoirs quoted above furthermore illustrates that madness can evoke the full range of responses a person may have toward a lover and thus creates additional, more nuanced meanings of the term.

Furthermore, metaphors of intercourse and orgasm simultaneously externalize madness and accept it as a part of oneself, thereby contributing to one of the central tensions in my corpus. Metaphors of intercourse evoke the penetration of bodily boundaries and thus comment on the experiencing selves' sense of distinction from and unity with their madness. Metaphors of orgasm have a similar effect, because "[t]he petit mort, the little death of orgasm, brings sex into the realm of danger. Orgasm leads to the possibility of self-dissolution in ecstasy and sublimity" (Lutz 40). Following Roland Barthes, I want to add that, conceptually, love and sex not only dissolve the self in ecstasy but also allow for lovers to be engulfed or annihilated in the object of their desire (11), in this case, personified madness. This extended metaphor enables several authors in my corpus to fashion their lived experience as the story of a normal self that was seduced by the dangerous lover madness. That narrative of seduction and loss of self, in turn, helps authors to bear the shame connected to their most transgressive, illness-related behavior.

True to the complexities of the Gothic mode, authors in my corpus increasingly blur the lines between an innocent (read: normal) experiencing self and an externalized madness when they metaphorize their lived experience as a story of possession, mind-control or *doppelgänger*. While I am aware that an entity that violently enters a subject and takes control is conceptually separate from a look-alike yet distinct self, both of these tropes have been connected to madness and illustrate the progressing dissolution of the boundaries between self and Other so well that I will discuss them together (cf. Bär 22–25). All these tropes can be recuperated into the traditional Gothic escape narrative that features an external villain, yet they also revolve around protagonists and their mirror images as they commit acts they would not normally carry out. They thus raise questions about the boundaries between self and Other as well as the responsibility for actions while mad.

Gerald Bär's comprehensive overview of research on the *doppelgänger* suggests that this literary motif speaks to the inability to conceive of the self as a coherent entity that incorporates good as well as bad aspects (2–69). Facing a *doppelgänger* is uncanny and a popular trope in the Gothic mode because previously repressed aspects of one's personality are externalized into an Other but also recognized to belong to oneself (cf. Freud, "Uncanny"). Authors in my corpus frequently draw upon the trope of the *doppelgänger* to simultaneously disavow and accept their madness and thus fashion themselves as both mad and not mad.

Marya Hornbacher in fact mixes the tropes of *doppelgänger* and possession to illustrate this complication of boundaries between self and Other as well as the double self-fashioning. In *Madness*, the narrating self explains that she changes from "calm" to "raging" as quickly and completely as "flipping a switch" (56):

> Julian and I are going along, having a perfectly lovely evening, and then it's dark and I am screaming … turning over the glass-topped coffee table, ripping the bathroom sink out of the wall…. The rages always come at night. They control my voice, my hands, I scream and throw myself against the walls…. *Slow down!* I am screaming at myself, *Marya, slow down*!
> And the madness screams back, I won't!
> It slides under my skin, borrowing my body without asking: my hands are its hands, and its hands are filled with an otherworldly strength. Its hands feel the need to lash out, to hit something…. Half in abject terror, half in awe, I watch [*Madness* 56–57].

The passage above narrates Hornbacher's lived experience of madness as a Gothic horror story of possession by a personified, destructive madness, thereby externalizing blame and responsibility. When "a perfectly lovely evening" devolves without explanation or transition into a dark scene of destruction, Hornbacher's experiencing self is depicted as the unsuspecting victim and madness as an unpredictable aggressor who can exert complete control over the experiencing self's actions and intrude into her body in a physical manner ("slides under my skin"). Possessed by madness,

Hornbacher's experiencing self becomes indiscriminately aggressive ("need to … hit *something*"), supernaturally strong, and a threat to those around her. Since madness also controls her voice, the experiencing self is unable to communicate her suffering coherently and can only throw herself against walls, screaming. The literary and antiquated expression "abject terror" further accentuates the Gothic mode and evokes the trope of the victim who is so horrified she can do nothing but watch. In this passage, Hornbacher presents her madness as monstrous or intrusive while simultaneously laying claim to a normal, yet helpless self, thereby managing shame and blame for her actions during psychotic episodes through externalization.

However, the passage does not maintain the distinction between a rational core self and a distinct, personified madness. In the line "I am screaming at myself, *Marya, slow down!* And the madness screams back, I won't," the narrating self does not produce two distinct entities ("screaming at *myself*"), and the response suggests that madness is interpellated by the experiencing self's name. This implies that the experiencing self and madness are the same, that madness may feel foreign, but is part of the self. At the same time, the expression "screams back" refers to an exchange between two different entities, however metaphorical, thus also evoking the trope of the *doppelgänger*. For this reason, all assumptions about madness, all productions of meaning are immediately destabilized because their opposite is also true. Moreover, this dissolution of boundaries between self and Other, or sane and mad self, further ties this account to the Gothic mode (Anolik 5), and implicitly identifies the loss of boundaries as one of the key features of madness.

In a similarly Gothic fashion, Kristina Morgan's memoir of schizophrenia describes the experiencing self's behavior in a manner that is reminiscent of the symptoms of possession in Blatty's *The Exorcist*, i.e., uttering obscenities and thrashing about. The narrating self recalls that during one hospitalization "[t]he air pushes me to act out. My mouth does not stop saying *fuck*. My body bangs itself into walls" (xvii). Note how being pushed around by air speaks to the experiencing self's loss of control during episodes of acute psychosis as well as the perceived omnipresence and intangibility of the threat. Yet, despite the effects on the experiencing self that evoke an iconic portrayal of possession, Morgan's personification of her mouth and body do not produce a foreign, malevolent presence but rather root the deviant behavior in the experiencing self's body and thus suggests a greater acceptance of responsibility for acts of madness than Hornbacher's more traditional narrative of possession. This reveals that apparently similar tropes can be used to make very nuanced claims about agency and the positioning of the self towards madness.

In all examples discussed above, "the potential for horror lies in the manner in which the subject may be expelled out of, lose control over, or even be consciously imprisoned in their bodies" (Foley 230) by the radical Otherness of madness. Yet, even though these examples depict the experiencing selves as helpless, normal victims of their supernatural foes—and thus reject the ascription of badness—the passages also implicitly present the mad as untamable, uncanny Others, thereby reinforcing stigma beliefs. This representation supports one of my key observations, which is that the rejection of any stigma belief comes at the price of reinforcing another one. When they deflect responsibility for mad behavior onto malevolent personified disorders, they fight the association of madness and badness but at the same time lose their claim to agency and to control over their disorders.

Once narratives draw upon Gothic tropes, clear distinctions between a normal, victimized self and a monstrous Other become impossible. I therefore suggest that the reliance on Gothic tropes, which is so prevalent in my corpus, utterly destabilizes not only the concepts of madness and normalcy but also commonsense notions of self and Other, victim and perpetrator, seduction and force. The process of stigmatization, which requires these types of clear distinction, is complicated and tensions are thrown into relief.

The Body, Monstrosity, and Otherness

The matter becomes even more complicated when authors also rely on Gothic tropes of the monstrous body to produce deeply ambiguous acknowledgments of the experiencing self's mad Otherness. Texts in my corpus transpose the Otherness of mental illnesses onto the body, which is represented as horrifying and mysterious. The tendency to metaphorize deviant mental processes as transgressive corporality not only mirrors past and contemporary tropes of the Gothic mode and therefore places itself emphatically in the tradition of that genre but can also mask the shame associated with the stigma of madness (cf. Spooner 63; Reyes, "Obsessed"). Because Cartesian dualism and religious asceticism value the mind over the body and these traditions of thought still influence contemporary notions of selfhood, the mind is more readily associated with the self than the body (cf. Spandler and Anderson 20). Madness that inscribes itself onto the body thus allows for a greater degree of externalization than madness that affects the mind. Moreover, displacing abstract negotiations about normalcy and madness or self and Other onto the body makes these negotiations more concrete and tangible.

Authors tend to express these negotiations through intertextual references to one of the most famous stories in which the body signified the state of the soul it contained, Robert Louis Stevenson's *Doctor Jekyll and*

Mister Hyde (1886). Furthermore, narrating selves direct a "medical gaze" (cf. Foucault, *Birth* 165) to bodily symptoms and the Otherness they represent, so memoirs in my corpus also evoke the nineteenth-century literary trend Royce Mahawatte calls "Victorian horror" (79). Mahawatte claims that the "rise of medical and pseudo-scientific epistemologies contributed to the institutionalization of the body as a source of horror" (79). The body of Victorian horror—and in many horror texts since—is unstable, in pain, dead, undead, and "somehow confusing, disturbing, or at least medically inscrutable…. It is a body that at times wants to cannibalise, or one that is snatched and cannibalised by forces around it" (Mahawatte 79). The most famous example of this literary trend is, of course, Stevenson's above-cited novella, but Mahawatte also analyzes the medical casebook genre, most notably Samuel Warren's *Passages from a Diary of a Late Physician* (1830–37). Warren's serial narrative is about the work of a gentleman doctor and the medical cases he encounters. Patients thrash about on their deathbeds, grind their teeth, and froth at the mouth while their conditions are not only described in medical terms but additionally *imagined* as demonic possession or harpies that pierce vital organs with their fangs. As Mahawatte points out, "Warren's work is acutely empirical, and it is down to the imagery and literary allusions in the prose to create a terrifying parallel world clearly aimed at readers familiar with Gothic literature" (83). Much like the memoirs in my corpus that repeatedly reference the psychiatric discourse in their accounts of their mental disorders, Victorian horror's blend of empiricism and fantastic imagery increases the sense of authenticity that make the symptoms of body and mind all the more horrifying.

A further similarity between memoirs in my corpus and Victorian horror is that conditions are rendered more concrete in the reader's imagination by describing them both in terms of observable symptoms and through established tropes of imaginative writing—a tension that is mirrored in the oppositional mechanisms of truth production employed by authors in my corpus (cf. Chapters Three and Four). While displaying their Otherness on the stage of the body suggests greater acceptance of the experiencing self's condition than representations of madness as possession or *doppelgängers*, the Cartesian split between body and mind is still so well-established in Western culture that displacements of madness onto the body symbolically contain madness: "I am a 'normal' person inside an Othered body." The admission of monstrous, mad Otherness that manifests on the body therefore always also allows for a self-fashioning as normal.

Although they hardly depict *their experiencing selves as monstrous, Truddi Chase and Jane Phillips, who are diagnosed with dissociative identity disorder, present *their bodies in line with the tropes of Victorian horror as medically inscrutable. Truddi Chase's experiencing selves have "headaches with no pain" (30) and never get drunk because there are so many alters that each one only gets one drink (307). Likewise, Jane Phillips' experiencing self feels no pain when *their mouth and facial tissues are severely inflamed because individual alters absorb the sensation (72–74). The experiencing selves' physicians cannot explain *their exceptional imperviousness to pain and the effects of alcohol which produces *their madness as vaguely supernatural. Moreover, it hints at the experiencing selves' desensitization to pain after years of horrific physical, emotional, and sexual abuse at the hands of family members, thereby presenting *their madness as a response to trauma rather than, say, the result of sinful behavior or neurobiological predispositions, i.e., a personal or biological flaw. The self-fashioning as resistant to pain and alcohol therefore Others the experiencing selves but also rejects responsibility for that Otherness.

Chase's memoir furthermore emulates the Victorian horror trope of mysterious bodily transformations. The narrated version of Chase's therapist witnesses rapid, horrifying changes in his patient's manner and even in *their physical appearance. For example, *their cheekbones rise higher in *their face (25) or submerge so *their face appears softer and rounder (39–40). *Their eyes change from "pale green and slanted" to grey and oval (29) and then again to "nothing more than eye sockets, really, and a deep, burnt-sienna colour, as if rotted" (105), and again to an "unusual apple-green colour"—all of which frightens *their therapist (208, 41). Not only do these transformations emphasize the presence of individualized, full-fledged personalities within one body by making them more tangible, but they also add to the mystery and Gothic mood of the memoir which is further strengthened by the fact that Chase's therapist, a trained professional, is scared. Through the appropriation of these tropes, Chase acknowledges that (*their type of) madness remains a source of fear and mystery despite rapid scientific advances.

While Chase's face reflects a frighteningly fragmented subjectivity, *their appearance does not symbolically communicate that the experiencing self is depraved or evil. Robert L. Stevenson's Edward Hyde is a prime example of the latter. Hyde is "ape-like" in his fury as well as "pale and dwarfish; he gave an impression of deformity without any namable malformation … the man seems hardly human! Something troglodytic" (30, 23)—the latter referring to a degraded, primitive, or brutal person who lives in seclusion or underground. This description of Hyde's body speaks to his function as the embodiment of Dr. Jekyll's repressed primal drives ("troglodytic" as in primitive), his (moral) degeneration[24] ("dwarfish," deformed), as well as the fact that he tended to stay hidden behind the polite, cultured façade of Jekyll, i.e., that he remained underground or in seclusion. That his mere sight arouses hatred and the impression of deformity suggests that the perverseness of his nature "transpires through and transfigures" the body (Stevenson 23). Mr. Hyde's horrifying body symbolizes his monstrosity and can be read as an expression of nineteenth-century fears about the decline of Western civilization and the corrupting influence of urban life. This example illustrates how the Gothic mode can negotiate contemporary fears and why authors in my corpus draw upon it to address the fearful aspects of madness.

Comparably, Marya Hornbacher uses depictions of a monstrous body to signify unease with contemporary beauty standards. When the experiencing self is at a weight of only seventy pounds, she receives a new college roommate whose soft, radiant, "gold-rosy" skin, shiny hair, and alluring "tits and ass" (*Wasted* 266) lead Hornbacher's narrating self to describe her experiencing self's appearance in a particularly harsh, ghoulish, and graphic fashion:

> Where my breasts had been … there were now only small brown-button nipples stretched over a rib cage, skin sunken inward between each bone. Where my derriere had been, there was nothing at all, a straight line from the nape of my neck to my legs, ending in a tiny bone in the center of the bow of pelvic bones, which jutted out fore and aft in an odd flat sweep. My face was the strangest, cheeks sunken so far deep that you could see all of my teeth through the skin, throat taut and concave below my chin, eyes seeming to move farther and farther back into my head with each day. I looked like a monster, most of my hair gone, my skin the gray color of rotten meat [*Wasted* 266].

This passage is a confrontation with a body that has been turned grotesque[25] and monstrous by the extreme cruelty that is directed against the self and the (female) body in eating disorders. Through sustained self-starvation, Hornbacher's experiencing self had forced her body to cannibalize itself to perform a minimum of vital functions. The result is a body that is rendered alien and shaped by absences—of breasts, butt, hair—and the withdrawal of flesh into concavities—between the ribs, along the throat and the cheeks, and eyes that recede into the head. By contrasting her romantic and crudely erotic longing for the roommate with her own body that is devoid of any feminine fleshiness, she replays a cultural dynamic that simultaneously idealizes or fetishizes women while also exhibiting an extreme form of misogyny through its unrealistic standards of thinness. At the same time, the passage presents a body that is the result of a perverse obsession with (a lack of) consumption and a grotesque exaggeration of current beauty standards, as Hornbacher herself repeatedly points out (cf. *Wasted* 6–7, 16–17, 117–118, 129). The excerpt quoted above therefore condenses various contemporary societal ills—misogyny, dangerous beauty standards, and a cruel disdain for the unruly body—into one grotesquely exaggerated body in a fashion that is both uncanny and Gothic (cf. also Halberstam 3).

Moreover, the passage uses the Gothic mode to establish that madness is horrifying and to recreate particularly shocking aspects of Hornbacher's lived experience for the reader. The passage presents a living body whose shape is alien and feels wrong, just as the "degenerated" body of Mr. Hyde and the fragmented body of Frankenstein's monster did to onlookers. Like these famous Gothic monsters, the monstrous body of the experiencing self invites readers to imagine the harmful impact of a powerful force on the body, but in this case, it is not science unmoored from morality but madness. When Hornbacher's narrating self describes a body that has no flesh, only "a straight line from the nape of my neck to my legs," she evokes a body that lacks a prominent feature of the human shape and forces readers to consider the extremity of the transformation that the experiencing self forced upon her body—a profoundly unsettling experience. Hornbacher increases the sense of "wrongness" when she presents her mostly hairless, skeletal body whose skin has "the gray color of rotten meat," i.e., a body that looks as if it should be dead but is not, and thus evokes several monsters, namely the animated skeleton, the mummy, and the zombie. All these abject[26] creatures are uncanny because they fail to obey the boundaries between life and death, threaten our ontological assumptions, and furthermore exhibit "a Gothic sensibility in the morbid fascination with death and decay" (Cherry et al. 2). It is only from the vantage point of her monstrous, uncanny, anorexic body that disrupts the most basic notions of the categories right and wrong that the extent of the experiencing self's madness can become clear. Her madness was such that she perceived her normal-weight if prematurely developed body as so unacceptable that years of sustained starvation and the slow mutation into a skeletal zombie seemed preferable: After an extremely early onset of puberty at the age of nine, the narrating self recalls, "My body was wrong—breasts poking through my shirt, butt jutting, all curvaceous and terribly wrong. Everything was wrong" (Hornbacher, *Wasted* 44). By describing her body as monstrous, Hornbacher not only implicitly acknowledges the experiencing self's madness but also recreates the horror the casual observer must have felt at her sight and allows the reader a glimpse of the body-related horror of her madness.

The sexualization of the monstrous body compounds this horror and the pervasive Gothic mood of *Wasted*. Despite her disavowal of sexual feelings, the narrating self presents the experiencing self's naked body in graphic descriptions that focus on erotically coded body parts like nipples, the site of previously "bouncing" breasts (*Wasted* 266), butt, hips, throat, hair, and face. The erotic undertones are strengthened by the narrating self's musings on the roommate's attractive physique which also focuses on the appeal of the woman's breasts, behind, and hair. These similarities force the reader to consider the experiencing self as a sexual being, to imagine the sexual consumption of a body that is as excessive in its rejection and devouring of food as it is of sexual partners (*Wasted* 18, 52–53, 74–78, 95). The similarities furthermore speak to the symbolic interchangeability of eating, sex, looking, and other forms of consumption which are both identified as key aspects of her lived experience of mental disorders by Marya Hornbacher and feature prominently in canonical Gothic texts in the construction of the threat of the monster (cf. Halberstam 2–17). As Hornbacher puts it, even the agents or relations of consumption are suddenly destabilized and made strange: "It was as if people could *see*, just by the very presence of my breasts, that I was bad and sexual and needy. I shrank back from my body as if it were going to devour me" (53). In this manner, the text evokes a very Gothic, eroticized sense of threat that recreates the conflation of several modes of consumption for the reader as well as the unease around them that is an important catalyst to Hornbacher's madness.

However, the emaciated, monstrous body of the experiencing self not only symbolically communicates aspects of her madness but also overshadows shameful mechanisms of the eating disorder. Etymologically, the monster is a thing to be exhibited and looked at (Foucault, *Madness* 70), and the narrating self uses the spectacle of the experiencing self's physical monstrosity to both draw attention away from the way her madness requires other people to feed on and her attempts to replay this behavior in her relationship to the reader.[27] An eating disorder is not only an attempt to create a sense of control in a situation that feels disorienting, a mode of self-destruction or the effect of a dangerous delusion, but it is also an aggressive form of self-assertion. Eating disorders are an insistence on one's will in the face of the will of others who insist that one *must* eat and proffer food. And lastly, it is an attempt to secure an identity through ascetic practices and the marking of the boundaries of the self through the process of abjecting (cf. Kristeva 2–3; see Chapter Four). For these mechanisms to work, there must be others who see and oppose the eating disordered person's refusal of food. As Virginia Burrus points out, "ascetic practice is inherently performative. Indeed, asceticism, like martyrdom, seems to require a spectator" (25). Hornbacher's experiencing self finds this audience in her parents, lovers, friends, and roommates, whom she aggressively exposes to the sight of her wasting body while rejecting their food and care. The spectacular exposure of her naked and emaciated body not only (temporarily) distracts the reader from considering the effect of Hornbacher's self-destruction on her loved ones but also *demands* the same kind of attention and helpless response from the reader: "you look terrible, you must eat." A body turned monstrous from a sustained lack of consumption therefore serves as a diversion from a monstrous self that consumed others and now attempts to consume the reader as well.[28] In this manner, the passage from *Wasted* reflects both the repressive aspects of the Gothic mode which "figure human difference as monstrosity" (Anolik 2) and its progressive aspects because it allows us to recognize the monster's subjective perspective and the emotional pain of having a body that feels wrong.

Other authors in my corpus also address the sense of their own monstrosity and Otherness but still fix it in a fictionalized elsewhere, that is, beyond the normal, core self they also claim for themselves. However, the unstable nature of the Gothic monster also enables readings of the experiencing self's transformations into a vicious or inscrutable creature that not only convey the dread of realizing that one has lost control over oneself but communicates other mechanisms of madness.

Kay Redfield Jamison, who for years rejected pharmacological treatment of her bipolar disorder even though she is a trained psychiatrist herself, uses parallels to Robert Louis Stevenson's *Dr. Jekyll and Mister Hyde* to describe the textual selves' stances towards their condition. Through these references, she removes her illness narrative to the realm of the fantastic, thus enabling readers to consume her memoir with the "pleasurable fear" (Sedgwick vi) associated with the Gothic mode and shielding herself from shame for these incidents. Like Henry Jekyll, who washes his hands of Hyde's evil deeds (Stevenson 75–76, 84), Jamison's memoir conveys a deep aversion to linking acts committed during psychotic breaks to her textual selves. The narrating self explains, "I had to try and reconcile my notion of myself as a reasonably quiet-spoken and highly disciplined person, one at least generally sensitive to the moods and feelings of others, with an enraged, utterly insane, and abusive woman who lost access to all control or reason" (*Unquiet* 121). Note how Jamison ties the attributes of discipline and general sensitivity firmly to herself through the repeated use of the first-person possessive pronoun ("*my* notion of *my*self"). The psychotic counterpart, by contrast, is lost in the generalities of the indefinite article and absolutes that suggest snap judgments rather than careful analyzes of character: "*an … utterly* insane, and abusive woman who lost access to *all* control or reason." Although the textual selves, like Henry Jekyll, eventually attempt the "difficult reconciliation of totally divergent notions of oneself" (*Unquiet* 120; cf. Stevenson 86), the extended intertextual reference to Stevenson's novella communicates the abject terror of finding oneself capable of previously unthinkable actions—like verbally abusing a partner or smashing furniture—and the difficulty of coming to terms with them.

An explicit intertextual reference to Stevenson's novella furthermore allows Jamison to both express her horrified awareness of her Otherness and to reframe one of her most destructive actions within the logic of Stevenson's text. While she does not describe any bodily changes visible to outside observers, she expresses her tumultuous inner life as a disturbed sense of embodiment: "my body is uninhabitable. It is raging and weeping and full of destruction and wild energy gone amok. In the mirror, I see a creature I don't know but must live and share my mind with. I understand why Jekyll killed himself before Hyde had taken over completely" (114). In this passage, which immediately precedes the description of her attempted suicide by overdosing on lithium, i.e., her medication for bipolar disorder, Jamison not only references Jekyll and Hyde explicitly but also emulates the expressions of Henry Jekyll's account of the late stages of his (ab)use of the drug that transformed him into Edward Hyde. Jekyll is unable to remain in his body without the help of the mysterious drug ("uninhabitable"), finds himself "*raging* and freezing with the passions of Hyde" (85; emphasis added), feels his body to be "not strong enough to contain the *raging energies* of life" (86; emphasis added), and is terrified because "[h]e had now seen the full deformity of that *creature who shared with him some of the phenomena of consciousness*" (86; emphasis added). Like him, Jamison experiences the horror of an acute estrangement from herself ("a *creature* I don't know") and an inhospitable body that seems to have acquired a mind of its own ("*It* is raging"). By empathizing with a remorseful Jekyll, who could not bear to become a person that is "wholly evil" (Stevenson 74), the narrating self appropriates the stigma-based trope of the evil mad person. In this manner, Jamison effectively reframes one of her most destructive actions—her suicide attempt—as an act of (moral) self-preservation that is comprehensible to those familiar with the story of Jekyll and Hyde. In other words, she fashions her experiencing self as so out of control and aggressive that she can recuperate another act of madness—attempting suicide—as the behavior of her relatively reasonable self who tries to expel its monstrous Otherness. The intertextual references to Stevenson's novella therefore enable complex negotiations of the boundaries of self and Other, madness and sanity as well as the question of responsibility for one's actions during periods of madness.

This intertextual reference expresses another key aspect of Jamison's illness experience, that is, the addictive potential of states that ultimately prove destructive and the experiencing self's inability to take medication as prescribed despite severe consequences. Henry Jekyll marveled at the odd sensations he experienced when he transformed into Edward Hyde: "There was something strange in my sensations, something indescribably new and, from its very novelty, incredibly sweet. I felt younger, lighter, happier in body; within, I was conscious of a heady recklessness, a current of disordered sensual images running like a mill race in my fancy, a solution of the bonds of obligation" (Stevenson 72). In the beginning, he immensely enjoyed escaping into the carefree life of Mr. Hyde but eventually became terrified when Hyde's deeds grew more violent, and he could no longer control the transformation. Similarly, Jamison explains that "my manias [...]

were absolutely intoxicating states that gave rise to great personal pleasure, an incomparable flow of thoughts, and a ceaseless energy" (*Unquiet* 5–6). She felt like "[she] could do anything, that no task was too difficult" (36) and "almost everything was done to excess" (42). On top of that, "sensuality is pervasive and the desire to seduce and be seduced irresistible. Feelings of ease, intensity, power, well-being, financial omnipotence, and euphoria pervade one's marrow" (67). The desire to experience these intoxicating states explains Jekyll's inability to stop taking his mysterious draught and Jamison's reluctance to take the mood stabilizer lithium as prescribed, despite her knowledge of the severe effects that result from her failure to do so. The similarities to Stevenson's novella illustrate the highly pleasurable as well as the horrifying aspects of Jamison's lived experience of madness, thereby creating another textual tension between the horror and pleasure of mental disorders and an ambiguous representation of the self in madness.

Lori Schiller's account of schizophrenia, *The Quiet Room* (1994), includes a similarly ambiguous depiction of a mad experiencing self in the Gothic mode. Schiller's experiencing self was much more incapacitated by her condition than many other authors in my corpus and accordingly, much of the memoir focuses on her multiple and extended stays in mental hospitals and assisted living facilities during the 1980s. One of the most prominent symptoms of the experiencing self's madness is hearing fear-inducing, malevolent voices that threaten her with rape and hell. When the experiencing self responds to her fear by acting out, male attendants on the closed ward overpower and forcibly strip her for a procedure called cold-wet-packing. Cold-wet-packing is a form of restraint for patients in acute, violent mental crises who are not sufficiently stopped from hurting themselves or others by temporary solitary confinement, tranquilizing shots or two-point restraints. In this procedure, attendants wrap patients firmly in sheets soaked in ice water, and protocol demands that the procedure lasts at least two hours (Schiller and Bennett 153–154). Schiller explains that "[t]he idea behind cold wet packs was to chill the patient thoroughly. As the body struggled to warm itself, it would use energy. And as the person tired from the effort to get warm, he or she would calm down, and, it was hoped, fall asleep" (153).[29] What makes the depiction of these events so ambivalent is that Schiller sandwiches the textual production of the experiencing self as excessively violent between two passages that evoke innocent Gothic heroines who are victimized by malevolent entities (cf. Kungl 170–171). Through this arrangement of descriptions in the narrative, Schiller complicates the distinction between victim and aggressor and effectively humanizes her experiencing self at its most monstrous.

Like many Gothic horror stories, Schiller's memoir includes detailed descriptions of an (intrapsychic) soundscape that is dominated by "demonic, atonal or muffled voices" (Foley 219), which convey the super-natural threat to the innocent protagonist. Even though Schiller's expe-riencing self is in the relative safety of a modern psych ward, she is the only one who can hear these voices and is therefore as alone in the face of the haunting as any Gothic heroine in a mysterious castle. Among other sounds, the experiencing self hears "a single witchlike Voice that screeched and cackled in derision," "a horrendous crowd, an appalling cheering sec-tion that had suddenly turned into a riot" as well as a male voice who spoke to her "in low, gravelly tones, hoarse and husky, a true demon from hell" (150). She adds, "The sounds of that inferno *filled my ears, filled my head, began to consume my whole body*" (151; emphasis added). As in stories of possession, the experiencing self's ears, head, and body are taken over ("filled") by madness until the self is no more ("consumed"), thus com-pounding the impression of victimization through tropes of possession. In this passage, as in other manifestations of the Gothic soundscape, "[t]he voice appears consistently ... as an excessive, untamable object" (Foley 228), an "assault upon the senses" (Foley 229), a patchwork of voices that "remains disembodied, and ultimately outside the quotidian" (Foley 229). The same is the case in Schiller's account because the cacophonous assault of multiple voices remains untamable and horrifying until the last chapters of her memoir, which speaks to the utterly disturbing nature of the expe-riencing self's madness and marks her as an innocent victim similar to the protagonists in (modern) Gothic horror stories.

To convey the utter horror of the haunting and demonic posses-sion, Schiller's memoir intensifies the Gothic mode by a twofold blurring of boundaries, namely between experiencing and narrating self as well as between hallucination and reality. When interpellated by the voices to come to hell with them, the narrating self states,

> I screamed. I tried to run. Nowhere to go. Tried to hide. Nowhere to go. Nowhere safe. They're everywhere. A chair. A window. Must break away. Must break. Must punch. And I punched, and I kicked, and I flailed. The shrieking, the tormented, the buzzer sounding, running feet. Cries and shouts. They're coming! They're coming! I can't stop them! I can't stop them!
> I must break something. I must hurt something. I must hurt someone. I must hurt myself [152].

Note how the repetitions, many exclamation points, the simple, paratac-tic syntax, and the incomplete staccato sentences convey an overwhelmed mind that is reduced to the most primal reactions—flight and fight. The narration only implies causal relationships ("A chair. A window. Must break away ... the buzzer sounding, running feet") and assumes an agi-tated quality that mirrors the almost preverbal panic of the experiencing self. This shift in narrating style constitutes the first blurring of boundaries:

the experiencing self's panic affects the tone of narration itself. The second blurring is in the loss of distinction between different referents of "they," that is, Schiller's disembodied tormentors and the mental healthcare professionals on the psych ward who come running when she starts acting out. By no longer distinguishing between these referents, the text suggests that the visions of hell in the experiencing self's mind have now seeped into her physical environment and dissolved the line between hallucination and reality. The dissolution between these two states, i.e., the confirmation of deep-seated assumptions about the physical reality of one's fantasies, is utterly uncanny (Freud, "Uncanny" 234). That Schiller was subject to this uncanny experience whenever she was floridly psychotic speaks to the truly horrifying nature of her lived experience. These two instances of blurred boundaries therefore suggest the boundless horror of madness and further position the experiencing self as the innocent victim.

However, this self-fashioning as the victim is complicated because the passage quoted above also presents the experiencing self (and possibly the narrating self who emulates the experiencing self's state of mind through the changes in the narrating voice) as a dangerous mad person, striking out mindlessly at foes neither seen nor understood by onlookers. Whereas earlier passages in the memoir produce a delusional yet understandably terrified self through an inconspicuous syntax and a wider range of vocabulary, the limited vocabulary and short sentences in "[m]ust break away. Must break. Must punch" (152) suggest a mind focused solely on inflicting damage and devoid of logical thought. The passage thus produces the meaning of madness as destructiveness and animalism as is suggested by the near-loss of language and the reduction to primal reactions.

Schiller renders her experiencing self even more fear-inducing when she insists that she had "superhuman energy, superhuman strength. I literally punched a hole in the wall.... I was beyond even the Quiet Room" (152–153): tranquilizing shots no longer calmed her in this state, and she remained a danger to herself even in a locked room. As the experiencing self had broken three geriatric chairs used for restraint through struggling before, the staff knew "from experience ... that only cold-wet-packing would do for [her] now" and called for "reinforcements" (153) from other wards. However, in her agitation, the experiencing self could temporarily "fight off a whole Quiet Room full of men" (153), which further supports her claim about superhuman strength. Even though the inner turmoil of the experiencing self is well-established, the events present her as uncanny. She possesses both "evil motives"—she wants to hurt others—and the "capacity to achieve their [here: her] aim in virtue of certain special powers" (Freud, "Uncanny" 13), i.e., her unusual strength. Because of this presentation as uncanny and dangerous, Schiller confirms the stigma trope of the dangerous mad person and complicates the self-fashioning as the victim in a horror story through an acknowledgment of her Otherness and monstrosity.

However, this self-fashioning as a dangerous mad person is immediately destabilized again. The text casts her in the position of victim when it evokes the subgenre of asylum horror movies, sensation fiction as well as patient protest literature through its depiction of force used against patients, humiliating medical practices, and the threat of sexual abuse (cf. Hermsen 157–169, Scull, *Madness* 232–242).[30] As Schiller explains,

> [t]he big burly attendants looked to me just like the horrid rapists of my Voices' hell…. Big strong men held me down while unseen hands stripped off my clothing. Off came my high-tops. Off came my favorite blue sweatshirt with the green frog on it. Off came my only pair of jeans that fit. Off came my socks one after the other. How was I going to cause any problems by keeping my little socks on my little feet? And then finally off came my bra. My undies were all that stood between me and the rape that my imagination had fabricated [153].

In this passage, Schiller destabilizes the self-fashioning as a monster with superhuman strength by stressing both the physical superiority of the male aggressors as well as the vulnerability and innocence of the experiencing self. First, she describes the male attendants by repeating the adjective "big" in combination with "strong" or its synonym ("burly"), whereas her experiencing self is rendered small and helpless through a rhetorical question about the potential danger of allowing her to keep her "little socks" on her "little feet." The passage further stresses the experiencing self's vulnerability by stating that she was wearing a sweatshirt with a frog on it, i.e., an item more likely worn by young girls than women in their twenties. Likewise, the word choice "undies" is more frequently used by children or persons who feel that the more mature term "underwear" is indecent, thereby compounding Schiller's self-fashioning as diminutive, which creates a great tension to the self-fashioning as a dangerous, aggressive mad person on the same page.

Moreover, the passage communicates Schiller's sense of victimization by hinting that the "big, strong attendants" who strip her of her clothing are a sexual threat, thereby once more evoking the genre of asylum horror and sensation fiction. First, the passage conjures a sexual threat by comparing the attendants to the rapists in hell which the experiencing self hallucinated about. Secondly, the scene is highly uncomfortable as it lingers on the removal of every piece of clothing and enforces a reduced reading pace by isolating each item in individual sentence rather than simply enumerating or summarizing them. Additionally, the narrating self explicitly addresses both the bodily and emotional effects of the procedure when she states that, after cold-wet-packing, her experiencing self would be "embarrassed, degraded and demeaned by the whole process" (55). By evoking the spectacle of (sexual) abuse in asylum horror movies, Schiller points to the horrific quality of her experiencing self's experience and the suffering that her treatment on the psych ward entailed. After showcasing her own mad monstrosity, Schiller endows her experiencing self with the fundamentally human capacity for shame and suffering again. In this manner, she blurs the lines between victim and aggressor, human and monster in a fundamentally Gothic fashion that complicates stigma beliefs about the aggressiveness and animality of the mad and which gestures towards the challenges of responding appropriately and humanely to persons in the midst of a mental crisis.

Truddi Chase's memoir of dissociative identity disorder, *When Rabbit Howls* (1990), uses horror tropes to illustrate the threat of the loss of self in madness and to present a deeply ambiguous stance on her experiencing selves' monstrosity. Chase also evokes the trope of possession when the written version of *their therapist describes the switches between the distinct personalities, rapid changes of *their voices, and the "audio chimera" (Foley 229) that results. Chase's voice ranges from childlike over young adult to adult woman (41), includes nonhuman sounds like when one of Chase's selves "howled like some demented animal" (53), and at times the voice is itself multiple: "A low, howling sob began, mingled with a soft, childish weeping, as if she were crying two sets of tears" (32). The multiplicity and nonhumanity of voices are utterly horrifying because they evoke the demonic ventriloquism, which forms a major part of the soundscape of modern Gothic and horror. Moreover, Chase's voice(s) speak to the fragmentation and dehumanization that resulted from years of emotional, physical, and sexual abuse and are thus shocking because they illustrate the extent of Chase's traumatization. The sheer force of the trauma has shattered the "intimate kernel of subjectivity" (Dolar 15) and removed *their voice from its position "at the axis of our social bonds" (Dolar 15) by exposing the excessive, untamable, animalistic parts that the "communicating subject has learned to suppress" (Foley 229). Freed from the ties of subjectivity and the restrictions that apply to socialized, communicating subjects, Chase's experiencing selves are "mysterious and unknowable, as inhuman as any ghost or monster lurking in the darkness" (Anolik, Introduction 2). At the same time, the narrator and the written version of Chase's therapist, who frequently functions as a focalizer, continuously remind readers that these are effects of the severe abuse that Chase experienced. If readers indeed take Chase's shattered subjectivity as evidence of *their monstrosity—and there is the real possibility that they could—the text ensures that readers at least know that Chase's horrifying Otherness stems neither from an innate badness, which would mark *them as a creature of a different ontological order, nor from bad choices on *their part but that *they were turned into the being *they are by a third party. The memoir therefore balances representations of Chase's Otherness with rejections of blame, which not only adds to a thrilling reading experience but also performs stigma-political functions.

The Gothic mode and particularly its use of the uncanny contributes significantly to the production of a conflicted identity caught between the poles of normalcy and madness. Not only does the Gothic mode famously establish *and* subvert self—Other, human—inhuman, known—unknown, good—evil, and healthy—pathological binaries but it also stresses the impermanence of conditions and selves.

Moreover, the Gothic mode draws attention to the absence of reliable, clearly circumscribed meanings of madness, which references to psychiatric diagnoses throw into relief. In the words of J. Jack Halberstam, "[w]ithin Gothic novels ... multiple interpretations are embedded in the text and part of the experience of horror comes from the realization that meaning itself runs riot" and that there is "a vertiginous excess of meaning" (2) which breaks down conceptual walls and counteracts the impulse to produce knowledge by creating conceptual categories. This excess of meaning is particularly disturbing in accounts that also feature detailed and systematic discussions of madness as mental disorder as well as lists of symptoms and preconditions for certain psychiatric diagnoses (see Chapter Three). As Terry Castle points out, "the Freudian uncanny is a function of *enlightenment*: it is that which confronts us, paradoxically, after a certain *light* has been cast" (7). In this context, the *Diagnostic and Statistical Manual* (*DSM*) with its clear delineations of individual disorders derives from the "distinctly eighteenth-century impulse to systematize and regulate, to bureaucratize the world of knowledge" (Castle 9). Without such a highly developed system of knowledge and categorizations of mental illness, the unknown mechanics and unexplained pathologies of the human mind would still be fear-inducing but not be quite so uncanny; Madness—like the supernatural—would fit more "comfortably in a world which is based upon superstition and magical thinking" (Anolik 1). The Gothic mode therefore stresses the unstable and unknown aspects of madness which the psychiatric discourse tends to obscure.

These instabilities and ambiguities contribute to the pleasurable thrill associated with the Gothic mode, its commercial success, and the undermining of the stigmatization process. Readers may not only playfully question the interplay of sanity and madness in their own minds but can also confront a spectacularly horrifying Other in the safe space of literature. Through the extensive adoption of the Gothic mode, memoirs thus simultaneously undermine the process of stigmatization, which depends on clear distinctions and binaries, but also commodify the experiencing selves' Otherness and create an intense, pleasurable reading experience.

Of course, postmodernist thought challenges notions of stable identities and unified selves for all individuals, not just those who lay conflicting claims to the attribute of madness.[31] In the postmodern moment, "the solid and stable modern self loses its footing and becomes fluid, liminal and protean selfhood … this selfhood is a continuous process that is constituted through the multiple and sometimes self-contradictory relationships in which one participates" (Gottschalk 21). As the previous two chapters showed, the tensions in self-fashioning in mental illness pathographies reflect postmodernist assumptions about selfhood. However, I do not propose that the conditions discussed in the memoirs of my corpus are "individual expressions of sociocultural trends in the postmodern moment" (Gottschalk 24) or that the destabilization of (illness) identity is a conscious stigma-political strategy on the part of the authors. Instead, madness is described (and read) through the conceptual patterns that are culturally available. In other words, the postmodern moment and its conceptualizations of selfhood undermine totalizing notions of madness—and consequently the process of stigmatization—in manners that were not possible when modern notions of the self as stable were dominant.

The previous two chapters also showed that the textual tension in my corpus between normalcy and madness *cannot* be understood as a strain between two clearly defined, stable attributes. Instead, it is a continual oscillation between claims to two labels with shifting, context-dependent, vast webs of meaning that were historically thought to be mutually exclusive. These variable and even contradictory meanings of madness—and their supposed negation normalcy—are based on multiple pervasive stigma theories, the denotations authors ascribe to the terms based on their lived experience, and their desire for stigma management as well as the knowledge produced by the psychiatric discourse. In short, normal and mad signify highly variable things to different people. In reference to Stuart Hall, I therefore claim that madness is a "floating signifier," much like race and gender (Hall 5). In Hall's words, floating signifiers "gain their meaning, not because of what they contain in their essence but in the shifting relations of difference, which they establish with other concepts and ideas in a signifying field" through the constant loss, appropriation, and contraction of new ones and "the endless process of being constantly re-signified, made to mean something different in different cultures, in different historical formations, at different moments of time" (8). The active destabilization of the meaning of madness through claims to mutually exclusive labels then opens up the possibility to also consider madness beyond essentializing (neuro)biologisms and in terms of performativity.

However, authors in my corpus do not simply reject psychiatric knowledge and neurobiological explanations of their condition. They also actively "inhabit and authenticate" (Fee 10) that discourse and draw on it for meaning-making and stigma management. Moreover, they contrast objective, psychiatric methods of truth production with subjective, literary ways to create the personal truth of the lived experience of madness. Analogously to the previous analysis, the second part of this project therefore considers the interplay of these two means of truth production.

PART II

Objective and Subjective Truth

In this part of the project, I turn to the second tension in mental illness pathographies which—like the tension in self-fashioning discussed above—remains unresolved. The second tension exists between the artistic, subjective truth of lived experience that is produced through literary means and the psychiatric truth of madness as mental disorders which the psychiatric dispositive presents as scientific and objective. Authors in my corpus produce both the supposedly objective psychiatric truth by referencing specialist literature or reproducing parts of their patient file and the subjective truth of their personal madness using confession and a markedly self-referential, literary mode of writing. In this manner, texts in my corpus create even more meanings of madness, for example that it is a medical disorder, abjection, or trauma. The tension between these methods of truth production therefore has a paradoxical effect. These two methods authenticate the authors' claims about madness but since these methods also add more meanings of madness, they further semantically destabilize the very claims they make. Moreover, this tension between the modes of truth production mirrors the double sense of self as both normal and mad since objective truth requires normalcy in the form of rationality whereas subjective truth is expressed through literary means that evoke the *furor* of mad artist.

I hold that the appropriation of these methods enables authors in my corpus to manage stigma, shame, and intimacy, empowers them to claim a voice in the conceptualization of madness, and can function as an overture to coalition politics with members of the psychiatric dispositive. Moreover, they help communicate the extreme states of mind and allow memoirs of madness to function as "vicarious support groups" (Hawkins, *Reconstructing* xi) that give concrete advice to their Own and present a mode of meaning-making. Lastly, methods of objective and subjective truth production authenticate spectacular stories of madness and thus increase the reading pleasure and voyeuristic appeal. Subjective and objective methods of truth production therefore contribute to stigma-political work and the (commercial) appeal of mental illness pathographies.

In Chapter Three, I explore how texts negotiate the psychiatric discourse that produces madness as a collection of mental disorders. Unlike many (scholar-)activists, most authors in my corpus do not *primarily* critique the psychiatric discourse for contributing to "the subtle imposition of systems of meaning that legitimize and thus solidify structures of inequality" (J. Lee 106) or the disqualification of the mad as "legitimate knowers at a structural level through various institutional processes and practices" (Liegghio 123). Instead, texts in my corpus also embrace the psychiatric discourse and show that "socially meaningful identities are produced through a new reflexive engagement with clinical understandings of depression [here: 'madness']" (Fee 12). Texts in my corpus therefore engage the dominant discourse of psychiatry in a pragmatic rather than ideological manner.

In Chapter Four, I discuss how mental illness pathographies produce "forms of truth that are felt rather than proven by evidence" (Cvetkovich 77). Authors in my corpus authenticate these truths through confession, which is "one of the West's most highly valued techniques for producing truth" (Foucault, *Sexuality* 58; cf. also C. Mills). However, the artistic rendition of a subjective, felt truth does not exist in opposition to or in isolation from the psychiatric, objective truth. By combining psychiatric knowledge with distinctly literary features such as experimental narrative structures, unusual imagery, and idiosyncratic language, texts in my corpus enable readings of these literary features as personal, artistic representations of the states which the psychiatric dispositive describes in general, codified terms. Mental illness memoirs thus "inhabit and authenticate" (Fee 10) the psychiatric discourse while also destabilizing binaries between objective truth and subjective truth. As in the rest of this study, I provide examples from several works in my corpus to show the prevalence of the tropes as well as analyses taken from Marya Hornbacher's *Madness* to show the presence of contradictory meanings within a single text.

Chapter Three

Producing
Objective Truth

The successful appropriation and deployment of the psychiatric discourse is no easy feat. Historically, the supposedly objective, medico-scientific truth of madness is the domain of those we now call psychiatrists. As Michel Foucault explains, psychiatrists decide on the processes of rarefication that determine not only the forms of thought and techniques that give access to truth but also the progressions of selection, qualification, and specialization a subject must undergo to "have access to a truth that science posits as universal" (*Psychiatric* 247). Moreover, since the institutionalization of what we now call psychiatry in the late eighteenth and early nineteenth century, mad doctors, as they were called then, have worked towards the constitution of their profession as a mental *analogon* of medicine, i.e., science. They have produced a clinical, classificatory discourse which defines madness as several distinct mental illnesses, each with its unique combination of symptoms. They have observed developments, deduced prognostics, and standardized diagnostic criteria. To find and speak the truth of madness, they have striven to develop "the instruments required to discover it, the categories necessary to think it, and an adequate language for formulating it in propositions" (Foucault, *Psychiatric* 236). In short, they use the rhetoric and technologies that are linked to scientific practice for the construction of a supposedly objective truth and claim that only their methods can disprove their findings (cf. Foucault, *Psychiatric* 133–134, 236; B. Lewis, *Moving* 61–79, 97–120). Psychiatry therefore establishes and protects its discursive dominance by insisting on rarefication, scientific methods, and a technical language.

More recently, the psychiatric dispositive has fashioned its truth claims as atheoretical. Bradley Lewis found in his analysis of contemporary psychiatric discourse that prominent discursive agents present the descriptive approach to the diagnosis of mental disorders that is practiced from the *DSM III* onwards as "unvarnished by theory" (Wyatt 2018), simply because the lists of symptoms required for the diagnosis make no claims about etiology. Moreover, Lewis points out, the rhetoric surrounding technological advances like neuroimaging techniques fashions the measuring of brain activity as "a direct window on the brain" (Andreasen and Black viii) that allows researchers to immediately observe mental processes and emotions. Although I am highly critical of how prominent psychiatrists like Wyatt, Andreasen, and Black pave over the assumptions about the connection between blood flow in the brain and, say, aggressiveness or deny the theoretical basis of a framework that understands madness as quasi-medical disorders, I use the phrase "objective truth" in reference to psychiatric concepts. I do so because of psychiatry's self-fashioning as atheoretical and objective, because the myth of objective science is one of the most prevalent beliefs in Western societies, and because authors in my corpus also perpetuate psychiatry's self-fashioning when it supports their stigma-political strategies.

The attribute "mad," by contrast, has long been conflated with a loss of reason, the erosion of intellect, and "a flawed or disordered way of seeing, perceiving, judging, and thus, knowing" (Liegghio 123). The mad are therefore by definition excluded from legitimate discourse and are vulnerable to being silenced or marginalized. According to Maria Liegghio, when mad individuals share thoughts and feelings in institutional psychiatric contexts, these "details are reinterpreted and re-storied into professionalized formulations. In the professionalized and institutionalized descriptions, the person, their experiences, and the details of their lives become subjugated, disqualified, and ultimately, unrecognizable" (124). There is a marked power imbalance between the mad and the psychiatric dispositive, and through psychiatrization, "the *DSM* categories become the social texts that speak for, on behalf of, and in place of the individual" (Liegghio 125). In this view, the psychiatric discourse poses a threat to mad people's "social positions as legitimate knowers" (Liegghio 125).

Despite their marginalized speaking position within it, authors in my corpus draw upon the psychiatric discourse extensively. In some cases, authors present psychiatric truth claims about the diagnosis and day-to-day management of their conditions and include explanations of different diagnostic categories, psychotropic medication, and different forms of therapy. Here, the appropriation of the psychiatric discourse empowers their Own with knowledge. In other cases, authors present their independent study of textbooks or research and apply psychological and psychiatric concepts to their experience and self-observations, thus imitating the diagnostic process. The narrating self in Marya Hornbacher's *Wasted*, for example, frequently considers her lived experience through the lens of psychiatric truth: She classifies the experiencing self's tendency to perceive her actions from an outside perspective as "objectifying consciousness" (14) and applies the term "triangulation" to her enmeshed family relations (24). Hornbacher and authors like her use the psychiatric discourse in the meaning-making process and tie diverse aspects of their lived experience together into coherent narratives of mental disorders. In yet other cases, narrating selves use a combination of their knowledge of the psychiatric discourse and their experience to criticize therapists and psychiatrists that interact with the experiencing selves or to make general claims, e.g., about the relationship between depression and alcohol withdrawal as William Styron does (41). In these instances, authors use their knowledge of the psychiatric discourse to legitimate their claiming of a voice in the discursive construction of madness and to point to flaws in its treatment. The widespread and varied appropriation of psychiatric truth suggests that authors in my corpus do not perceive the psychiatric discourse as disempowering—quite the contrary!

I emphatically exclude discussions about the potential for containment and subversion of this discursive strategy. As my previous analysis has shown, texts in my corpus eschew binary oppositions in favor of contradictions and ambiguity. This tendency suggests that there will be ample textual evidence that texts contain *and* subvert psychiatric dominance of the discourse on madness at the same time.

To address the diverse effects that the appropriation of the psychiatric discourse can have, I structure the following analysis according to the three groups of potential readers of mental illness pathographies: Those who share the experiencing self's condition and whom Erving Goffman calls "the Own," those who do not, i.e., "normals," and psychiatrists. Goffman suggested that the third category of persons interacting with stigmatized individuals are "the wise," that is, those who do not bear the particular stigma but are "privy to the secret life of the stigmatized individual" (*Stigma* 28). He suggests that family members, friends or romantic partners of stigmatized individuals are often "wise," as are outcasts of a different kind (28–30). While psychiatrists may know much about the "secret life" of the mad, they are not as closely associated with their patients as the groups in Goffman's examples, and there exists a significant power differential between the mad and psychiatrists, especially in the closed systems of mental hospitals. Rather than counting psychiatrists towards "the wise," I keep them as a distinct audience. However, the structuring of my analysis according to readership does not mean that all effects are exclusive to the groups. Even though I discuss, say, the voyeuristic pleasures of getting to see personal or medico-psychiatric documents in the section on normals, this does not mean that the Own or psychiatrists are immune to these pleasures. The organization according to the memoirs' addressee therefore follows the demand for a structured analysis rather than the absence of effects of mechanisms on all three groups.

Writing for "the Own": Literacy and Meaning-Making

In the address of the Own, memoirs in my corpus not only reveal the similarities between mental illness pathographies and other didactic genres such as conversion narratives and self-help books but can also function as a "vicarious support group, offering some guidance in the bewildering and often frightening terrain of serious illness" (Hawkins, *Reconstructing* xi). Narrating selves supply their Own with "tricks of the trade" (Goffman, *Stigma* 20), that is, concrete advice on how to live with their stigmatized condition. This advice includes strategies on how to manage a condition as well as long lists of treatment centers and further literature in the memoirs' appendixes. Narrating selves also empower their Own in the interaction with members of the psychiatric dispositive by explaining technical terms and concepts and implicitly encourage their Own to use psychiatric knowledge for meaning-making and a reduction in self-stigmatization. Narrating selves therefore offer mediated access to the psychiatric discourse and fashion themselves as well-informed and competent patients.

To present themselves as reliable sources of information, narrating selves foster trust among their Own in several ways. In passages explicitly addressed to the Own, narrating selves use the second-person singular pronoun to create the atmosphere of a friendly conversation, acknowledge possible concerns, and generally stress kinship and commonalities (Vonnegut 207–209; Hornbacher, *Madness* 265). Marianne Apostolides provides the most explicit examples of this when she discusses treatment options in a reassuring tone in the chapter titled "Advice to Girls and Women Experiencing an Eating Disorder" (156–167). She states, "if you feel uncertain or threatened by the thought of living without your eating disorder—I want you to know that I respect your position, because I have been there, too" (156; cf. also Hornbacher, *Madness* 265). Apostolides' use of the present perfect not only suggests that she has successfully overcome her reluctance towards therapy and that readers may grow out of it as well, but the anticipation of fears assures her Own that "there are sympathetic others who are ready to adopt his [the stigmatized person's] standpoint in the world and to share with him the feeling that he is human and 'essentially' normal in spite of appearances and in spite of his own self-doubts" (Goffman, *Stigma* 30). Furthermore, passages like the one quoted above reassure the Own that they are normal in the sense that there are others like them and thus stress the relative, relational nature of categories such as normal, thereby discouraging self-stigma.

Before they disperse psychiatric truth claims about their condition, authors in my corpus generally stress the nature and limits of their knowledge. At the beginning of her memoir on living with anorexia and bulimia, Hornbacher's narrating self states, "I am not a doctor or a professor or an expert or a pundit. I'm a writer. I have no college degree and I never graduated from high school. I do research. I read. I talk to people. I look around. I think. Those aren't qualifications enough. My only qualification, in the end, is this: I live it" (*Wasted* 7–8). After admitting that she possesses neither formal (doctor, professor) nor informal (expert, pundit) types of qualification, Hornbacher emphasizes her practice of various established methods of academic knowledge acquisition. Rather than connecting those methods with commas and thus allowing the reader to speed through the list, the full stop after each simple, paratactic sentence forces the reader to consider each item. The premium, however, is placed on her lived experience, the immediacy of which is suggested by the present tense. Moreover, the confession about the limits of her knowledge creates the impression of honesty, while the narrating self's use of scientific methods such as a review of research, observation ("I look around"), and interviews ("I talk to people") as well as her first-hand experience fashion her as someone with access to the objective, scientific as well as the subjective truth of her condition. According to this self-fashioning, the narrating self is doubly qualified to make truth claims about her type of madness which undermines psychiatrists' role as the sole dispensers of truth claims on the subject.

When authors in my corpus provide mediated access to the psychiatric discourse, they empower their Own through knowledge and help them to engage mental healthcare professionals on a more equal level, e.g., by explaining diagnostic terms and psychiatric concepts. Some narrating selves further encourage self-confidence among their Own through a critical engagement with the hegemonic psychiatric discourse. Marianne Apostolides, for example, explains in her introductory chapter that "[a]n eating disorder is not a disease, it is a set of behaviors that has no known specific cause. In clinical-psychology-speak, that means it is a 'syndrome' with no known 'primary etiology'" (xiii). This passage not only uses inverted commas to mark clinical terms as the language of an Other but also privileges the layman's description over the psychiatric idiom by defining eating disorders without recourse to clinical terminology first and only then translating it. She implicitly criticizes the power imbalance created through this technical language and stresses her allegiance to her Own by referring to the psychiatric discourse as "clinical-psychology-speak," which evokes the Orwellian concept of "Newspeak," an invented language that obscures and distorts the meaning of words to secure ideological and political control. Some authors like Apostolides therefore alert their readers to the power imbalances that the psychiatric dispositive creates –among other things – through its use of technical language and empower them with knowledge about the psychiatric idiom.

Even texts which do not exhibit the highly critical stance of Apostolides' memoir show that using the language of psychiatry does not unequivocally pathologize textual selves. In an epigraph, Kristina Morgan supplies an annotated definition of schizophrenia which she adapted from the fifth edition of the *Diagnostic and Statistical Manual of Mental Disorders* (*DSM-V*). Morgan privileges the psychiatric idiom by using technical terms first and then explaining them in brackets, e.g., "disorganized speech (e.g., frequent derailment and incoherence) … and other negative symptoms (e.g., diminished emotional expression and reduced drive)" (xiii). She does not explain other terms such as "lifetime prevalence" or "catatonic behavior" (xiii) at all, which shows the extent to which Morgan has naturalized psychiatric terms in her speech or writing and continues negotiations of the normal-mad tension. Embracing "[t]he language of psychiatry, which is a monologue of reason *about* madness" (Foucault, *Madness* x–xi) destabilizes absolute textual identities as normal or mad, even in memoirs that frequently fashion textual selves as mad, e.g., by allowing the "disorganized speech" that characterizes acute schizophrenic episodes to intrude into the narration (see Chapter Four). This contradiction shows that the psychiatric discourse can produce the textual selves' normalcy *as well as* their pathologized Otherness and "allows modes of interpretation and renderings of knowledge that collapse naturalized dichotomies between subject and object and knower and known" (Fee 4).

Narrating selves in my corpus not only empower readers with literacy in the psychiatric idiom but also counsel them on treatment options. They provide overviews of the kinds of therapy that are available (Hornbacher, *Madness* 217, 240–241) and list possible side effects of medication (Jamison, *Unquiet* 92–93; Hornbacher, *Madness* 275; Schiller and Bennett 225–227). Frequently, authors couple this information with recommendations for specific forms of treatment, as does Apostolides when she insists that "[n]ot everyone with an eating disorder needs to be on anti-depressants; I suggest you first try individual psychotherapy alone" (162). She then briefly explains the neurochemical effects of a class of antidepressants, namely "selective serotonin reuptake inhibitors (SSRI)" (163; cf. also Wurtzel 297–299), states that they have fewer side effects than older classes, and finally contradicts the assumption that antidepressants are addictive (161–163). Here, the narrating self claims the authority to disseminate knowledge and advice on psychotropic treatment and thereby mirrors the modes of empowerment that were practiced in the women's rights movement. Members of the latter sought to become knowledgeable about their bodies, especially reproductive health, so they did not need to rely on the male-dominated medical establishment and could assist other women (cf. Jurecic 8). This related attempt to emancipate their Own through psychiatric knowledge suggests that mental illness pathographies not only perform cultural work such as producing the meanings of madness and normalcy but are also sites of empowerment and biopolitical negotiations.

Empowered by their knowledge about the psychiatric discourse, narrating selves also present cautionary tales about psychiatric malpractice and thereby encourage their Own to be more critical of individual practitioners than the authors' experiencing selves were. While some memoirs do express outrage about incompetent treatment, texts in my corpus do not fit Anne Hunsaker Hawkins' definition of "angry pathographies" (*Reconstructing* 4), a type of illness narrative that denounces dehumanizing or inept treatment and signals "a striking lack of confidence" and a "cultural discontent with traditional medicine" as a whole (*Reconstructing* 5). By contrast, texts in my corpus generally express trust, even faith in psychiatry and its methods of truth production. In fact, most of the textual selves' anger stems from their firm belief in psychiatry and the individual psychiatrists' failure to compose treatment plans according to the truths produced in this field.

William Styron's memoir of depression provides a salient example of this when the narrating self stresses that he did "fairly extensive reading" (7) of "weight[y] professional works including the psychiatrists' bible, *DSM*" (6) and directly criticizes "an insouciant doctor" (48) with less substantial knowledge of psychiatric truth claims. The doctor had prescribed strong tranquilizers and told Styron's experiencing self that he could take it "as casually as aspirin" (48). Styron later learns that "[f]or some time now, many experts in psychopharmacology have warned that the benzodiazepine family of tranquilizers, of which Halcion is one (Valium and Ativan are others), is capable of depressing mood and even precipitating a major depression" (48). He then adds that the "*Physicians' Desk Reference*, the pharmacological bible" (48) recommends a much lower dosage and duration of use than his doctor ordered and generally cautions against the prescription of benzodiazepines to patients of the experiencing self's age (48). Returning to the subject later in the narrative, Styron adds that "[m]uch evidence has accumulated recently that indicts Halcion (whose chemical name is triazolam) as a causative factor in producing suicidal obsession" (71) and muses that his psychiatrist had apparently not read the warnings in the *Physicians' Desk Reference* (71).[1] As suicidal obsessions were one of the most painful symptoms of Styron's depression and eventually grew to a point where the experiencing self had to be hospitalized, this information implies that the experiencing self's condition may have been aggravated by incompetent treatment.

The passages quoted above also illustrate Styron's self-fashioning as a self-taught expert on depression as well as the didactic intent of his memoir. Styron bases his criticism of the doctor on his independent review of authoritative psychiatric and medical texts. Through referencing his sources, Styron makes sure that his criticism cannot be delegitimized as the mere opinion of a discredited individual and that the doctor failed to meet the standards of his profession. Moreover, the passages demonstrate Styron's faith in the psychiatric discourse through his repeated comparisons of diagnostic and pharmacological manuals to the bible. The simile suggests that doctors have the moral obligation to be well-versed in these texts and to follow their "commandments" closely. Through this cautionary tale and the inclusion of both brand and chemical names of medication which his Own may encounter, Styron empowers readers to seek responsible treatment. In this respect, Styron's memoir fulfills functions Erving Goffman attributed to advocacy and self-help groups by stigmatized individuals, i.e., protecting the Own against victimization by "fraudulent servers" who peddle ineffective cures (*Stigma* 9). Styron's self-fashioning as a particularly well-informed patient therefore not only supports his criticism of his doctor but encourages his Own to also place their faith in the psychiatric discourse but to remain critical of individual practitioners.

Even though Marya Hornbacher relates very similar instances of malpractice (*Madness* 110, 240), she retains her faith in psychiatric truth. Recalling the moment when the experiencing self was diagnosed with bipolar disorder, the narrating self states,

> all that time I've felt as if I am spinning away from the real world ... off in my own aimless orbit—all of it, over. Suddenly the solar system snaps into place, and at its center is this sun; I have a word. *Bipolar.* Now it will be better. Now it has a name, and if it has a name, it's a real thing, not merely my imagination gone wild. If it has a name, if it isn't merely an utter failure on my part, if it's a disease, *bipolar disorder*, then it has an answer. Then it has a cure. At least it has something that *should help* [*Madness* 67; cf. also Boone-O'Neill 80].

This passage not only shows Hornbacher's allegiance to the cultural myth of the invincibility of modern medicine ("if it's a disease ... [t]hen it has a cure") but also reveals the psychiatric discourse's potential for meaning-making. By using an extended metaphor and turning her newly acquired diagnostic label into the center of her life-as-solar-system, she both makes her condition the organizing force that subjects all other life events to its gravitational pull and suggests that this new understanding is nothing short of a Copernican Revolution in her personal way of interpreting her being in the world. The passage further emphasizes the singular position which both her condition and her diagnosis have in her life by isolating the term "Bipolar" in its own sentence, whose full stop marks the finality of its truth. Hornbacher thus uses the psychiatric discourse for "formulation," i.e., she draws upon it for an interpretive framework with which she makes sense of the disorienting experience of madness (cf. Kleinman 48–49; Lifton 367).

Mark Vonnegut also reveals how he used his psychiatric diagnosis for meaning-making. Vonnegut's experiencing self first became floridly psychotic when he was living with a couple of friends in an autonomous commune in the Canadian wilderness in the early 1970s. According to the narrating self, the experiencing self and all of his friends at that time espoused the concepts of madness that were propagated by the anti-psychiatry movement: "'Schizophrenia is a sane response to an insane society.' 'Mental illness is a myth.' The Sanskrit word for crazy means touched by the gods" (111; cf. also 131). This meant that the experiencing self tried to understand his condition as a spiritual journey and was lovingly but inadequately cared for by friends and gurus. Only after the experiencing self stops to make sense completely do his friends take him to a mental hospital. Here, after almost two hundred pages that describe the psychological turmoil, extensive philosophical and spiritual internal debates about the possible roots and implications of his extreme states of mind, Mark Vonnegut's narrating self presents the experiencing self's psychiatric diagnosis in a simple, straightforward language: "What I had was schizophrenia. It was probably genetic. It was biochemical. It was curable" (186). These four sentences produce a clearly delineated meaning of Vonnegut's condition as a genetically transmitted, biochemical, psychiatric disorder. The shortness of the sentences stands in great contrast to the rambling, complex grammatical constructions that characterized the narration during the experiencing self's psychotic states and therefore suggests clarity of vision that supersedes the previous confusion. Moreover, the short, paratactical sentences impose a high level of control on the speed with which information is disseminated and mirror the way the psychiatric discourse brings Vonnegut's madness under control conceptually. Lastly, the passage quoted above provides hope for a cure and manages the sense of shame and self-stigma by conceiving of madness "more as a matter of biochemistry than of psyche, and thereby depersonalizing it" (L. Zimmerman 469). This understanding of schizophrenia can, then, "cut much of the pain and frustration for you and your friends" because "[n]o one's to blame" (Vonnegut 211; cf. also Cvetkovich 16). Vonnegut's memoir therefore draws upon the psychiatric discourse to impose order on the chaos that is life in madness and to produce the "*nonfault*" (Nussbaum 143) of those who are diagnosed with it, which is central to the development of compassion.

Likewise, the passage that describes Hornbacher's reaction to her diagnosis reveals how the psychiatric understanding of madness as mental disorders can be used to contradict common stigma theories. Hornbacher's experiencing self reasons that if her condition has a diagnostic label, it is "a real thing, not merely my imagination going wild … it isn't merely an utter failure on my part" (67; cf. also Apostolides 90). The status as a quasi-medical condition counteracts two of the most dominant stigma beliefs about madness, namely that patients are malingering ("my imagination going wild") and that their condition is the result of sin, poor character or the lack of willpower ("an utter failure on my part"). Moreover, the psychiatric discourse legitimizes the patients' lived experience of madness, even in the absence of objective evidence of affliction such as x-rays of broken bones, elevated body temperature or the measurable presence of a virus in the bloodstream. Consequently, patients can claim that a "mental illness is just like diabetes; it's something you have to take medication for and *that's okay*" (Hornbacher, *Madness* 154). Official psychiatric diagnoses thus medicalize extreme states of mind and transgressive behavior and therefore enable the mad to claim patient status, access socially sanctioned and subsidized forms of treatment, and to manage shame and blame.[2]

However, embracing the psychiatric understanding of madness as an illness like any other—and equating it with diabetes in particular—also has its downsides. Marya Hornbacher had to find out the hard way that metaphorizing her condition as diabetes is "a strikingly simplistic understanding of what having bipolar means" (154). It prevented her from becoming more active in the management of her condition because this stance allowed Hornbacher's experiencing self to ignore how intimately her mental illness is tied up with her moods, behavior, and thoughts. Diabetes is frequently understood as a condition one *has* rather than a crucial factor in how one *is*, perceives or relates to the world. In Hornbacher's case, this had disastrous effects on the experiencing self's health and life (69–70).

Nevertheless, a narrow neurobiological understanding that conceives of mental disorders in terms of imbalanced neurotransmitters—akin to the imbalanced blood sugar and insulin levels of diabetes—*seems to* reject stigma-based implications about the person who lives with the disorder, which is why, in the late 1990s and early 2000s, many advocacy groups and mental healthcare professionals endorsed this position as a way to reduce stigma (Corrigan and Watson). However, this conceptualization of madness has proven ineffective in reducing stigma (Corrigan and Watson; Morrall "Fear"), probably because it neglected the significant stigma that is attached to diabetes and assumptions about the diabetic's responsibility for their condition (Browne et al.). Moreover, it has conceptual flaws: As Maria Liegghio points out, "madness/mental illness does not occupy the same cultural, political, or even medical space as diabetes" (240). Marya Hornbacher's rejection of a simplistic medicalization of madness thus foreshadows developments in stigma politics. While I don't mean to suggest that Hornbacher was a forerunner to advocacy groups, it does speak to the extent to which the author absorbed the stigma-political strategies of her day, and by extension the centrality stigma has in her memoir *Madness: A Bipolar Life*.

Additionally, "align[ing] mental illness with cultural concepts of disease" (Liegghio 240) such as diabetes entails the transfer of widely accepted responses to disease that left Hornbacher's experiencing self feeling powerless: "[w]e typically defer to professional/expert authority over diagnoses and treatment, and we accept certain forms of segregation and state intervention—medical, social, institutional—as both legitimate and necessary" (Liegghio 240). In some cases, recovery is possible, "but only if the illness is effectively reigned in, decoded, and worked upon by professionals" (Liegghio 240). This conceptualization legitimizes the biopolitical control of transgressive individuals and robs those labelled mentally ill of their agency—something Hornbacher's experiencing self was keenly aware of. After the initial relief passed, the experiencing self felt that receiving a psychiatric diagnosis confirmed that her state of mind was worse than she thought and that she had no control over her behavior or mental health: "All that time I wasn't crazy; I was, in fact, *crazy*. It's hopeless. I'm hopeless. *Bipolar disorder. Manic depression*. I'm sick. It's true. It isn't going to go away. All my life, I've thought that if I just worked hard enough, it would" (67). As this quote shows, the equation of mental illnesses with illnesses of the body, which the psychiatric dispositive attempts, can have detrimental effects on patients such as a perceived loss of agency, hopelessness or, conversely, a stance of not taking it seriously enough. These negative emotional responses stand in great contrast to the joy which the experiencing self expressed at being presented with a mode of making sense of her emotionally turbulent life and reveals a rather conflicted stance towards the understanding of madness as mental illness.

In the passage quoted above, these conflicts and tensions are exacerbated through allusions to the complicated relationship between a vernacular understanding of madness as "being crazy" and the understanding of madness as clinical mental disorder. Whereas the former suggests eccentric, transgressive, or aggravating behavior for which the "crazy person" is judged, the latter evokes a person so seriously "disordered" that only medical specialists can handle them, as the connection via italicization of "*crazy*," "*Bipolar disorder. Manic depression*" emphasizes. The repetition of "crazy" and its double reference to a vernacular and a medical context also suggests that the vernacular and the medico-psychiatric discourse are not as separated as the psychiatric self-fashioning as producers of an independent, objective truth would have it (cf. B. Lewis, *Moving* 38–60). This means that these discourses mutually influence each other and that stigma beliefs affect mental healthcare professionals and their conceptualization of madness. Moreover, the speed with which Hornbacher's experiencing self relinquishes colloquial interpretations and adopts medicalized, yet stigma-laden readings of her moods and behavior demonstrates the discursive authority of the psychiatric discourse. The text thus also depicts the psychiatric dispositive as a tool of disempowerment and its various diagnostic terms for madness as labels that express stigma beliefs and discredit transgressive individuals who experience distress. By acting out the effects of the social and cultural domination imposed by the psychiatric dispositive on the experiencing self's understanding of herself, Hornbacher implicitly includes anti-psychiatric criticism in her memoir and problematizes psychiatry's self-fashioning as an objective, quasi-medical science.[3]

Despite their conflicted stance towards psychiatric understandings of madness, authors in my corpus still rely heavily on its truth claims and enable their Own to access its benefits—such as meaning-making or stigma- and shame management—by educating their Own about the forms their disorder can take. Usually, this knowledge is woven into the narrative, i.e., symptoms are pointed out as such when they occur in the experiencing self. Some texts like Marya Hornbacher's *Madness: A Bipolar Life* and Kay Redfield Jamison's *An Unquiet Mind* even include long dialogic sections that relate the diagnostic process, including the psychiatrist's questions regarding symptoms, a family history of mental disorders, or family dynamics. These dialogues not only convey the experiencing selves' sense of reassurance at finding a supposedly rational, medico-psychiatric explanation but also structure the dissemination of psychiatric knowledge to the reader. Readers may then find similarities between the experiencing selves' answers and their own lived experience, independently conclude that they have the same condition, and seek psychiatric treatment as needed.

The last function, which the psychiatric discourse fulfills for the Own, is related to the management of intimacy and "disclosure etiquette" (Goffman, *Stigma* 117), i.e., recommended ways to reveal one's status as a discredited individual to normals. In autobiographies by stigmatized individuals, Goffman suggests, the voluntary disclosure of one's blemish constitutes "the final, mature, well-adjusted phase [of learning to live with a stigmatized attribute]—a state of grace" (*Stigma* 102). Yet, many authors "remain acutely and painfully aware of how difficult it is to understand these behaviors [being 'physically assaultive' or 'screaming insanely at the top of one's lungs'], much less explain them to others" (Jamison, *Unquiet* 120). The clearly defined, dispassionate language of clinical psychiatry can make coming out as mad via life writing less excruciatingly intimate: Instead of having to find words that reflect their personal lived experience, authors use the abstract language of psychiatry to narrate the workings of their mind. This use of clinical terminology thus serves as a model for the Own regarding the manner and language in which to disclose their condition (cf. Goffman, *Stigma* 115–117). Additionally, specific diagnostic labels contribute to a reduction in fear, both for the stigmatized person and those around them because medico-psychiatric labels suggest that the problem has been identified by an expert and can now be treated.

As this section showed, the appropriation of the psychiatric discourse has multiple effects and authors implicitly encourage their Own to draw upon it for the management of stigma and shame and to make sense of the disorienting experience of madness. Moreover, psychiatric knowledge empowers the mad in their interaction with mental healthcare professionals, protects them from victimization by enabling them to spot malpractice, and provides them with a language that helps them disclose their condition in a concise, dispassionate manner that meets the demands of disclosure etiquette. In other words, they fulfill similar functions as those that Erving Goffman ascribed to support groups for stigmatized individuals (*Stigma* 17–22). Narrating selves fashion themselves as sympathetic to a less experienced stigmatized individual, provide moral support and effectively function as a guide to "the kingdom of the sick" (Sonntag, "Illness" 3). Memoirs in my corpus therefore use the experience of stigmatization and pathologization as a point of connection to their Own while also schooling them in a pragmatic engagement with that discourse to access its benefits.

Moreover, when narrating selves present themselves as doubly authenticated by their lived experience and their research, they attempt to transcend the binary opposition between patient and medical expert and illustrate how the psychiatric discourse shapes the experience of affliction and wellbeing. As Dwight Fee points out, "[t]he dissemination of expert knowledge predictably brings intense efforts to refine the understanding of the condition by both the subject and the expert, expanding both professionalized and personalized discourses of illness and their intimate reciprocity" (12). Authors in my corpus therefore claim a voice in the knowledge production on their conditions and signal their willingness to cooperate with the psychiatric dispositive.

This chapter therefore illustrates that psychiatrization not only imposes biopolitical control but can also help the mad to make the experience of madness psychologically livable, thus simultaneously empowering and disempowering them. These conflicting effects already demonstrate that, for severely discredited individuals like the mad, no discourse, argument, or mode of self-fashioning can unambiguously reduce the adverse effects of stigma. Any attempt to manage the stigma simultaneously empowers and disempowers the discredited individual. Despite the catch-22 situation of never being able to contest a stigma belief without endorsing another one, authors in my corpus are very concerned with a variety of stigma-political tasks like increasing knowledge about the mad among those that do not share the author's condition. To authenticate their truth claims about the mad as well as their own identity claims, authors in my corpus draw upon the psychiatric discourse as well as other established methods of truth production, which is what I turn to now.

Writing for "Normals": Reliability and Voyeuristic Pleasures

The second audience, which mental illness pathographies have, are those who do not share the author's condition, i.e., normals. Normals generally have significantly less contact with the mad than mental healthcare professionals, frequently depend on portrayals in popular culture and news media for knowledge about madness and the mad, and are consequently more likely to hold stigma beliefs (cf. Wahl, *Media* 56–87; Cross, *Mediating*). Since many stigma theories associate madness with incoherence, dissolution of meaning, and unreliability as a narrator of one's life story (Wood 1–2), appropriations of the supposedly objective psychiatric discourse can support the impression of reliability and thus the author's claims. Moreover, truth claims from the psychiatric discourse that contradict common stigma beliefs have more discursive weight than similar statements by discredited persons and therefore constitute a valuable stigma-political tool.

To further create the impression of truthfulness, authors in my corpus draw upon a variety of culturally valued methods of truth production beyond those of the psychiatric dispositive. Among those methods are journalistic interviews with witnesses, the inclusion of expert testimony and authenticating documents as well as academic methods of research and referencing. The latter includes situating one's claims within the academic discourse by assuming a position relative to previous research, the use of technical terms, employing established systems of reference, and making one's point in a formal and impersonal way. Authors, then, perform reliability and trustworthiness for normal readers, thereby demonstrating that madness need not entail cognitive impairment or unreliability. These methods furthermore provide multiple perspectives on the textual selves' condition and authenticate memoirs in my corpus, that is, they prove that the authors have lived experience of the condition they claim for themselves and support the narrating self's version of events. In this sense, they continue the negotiation of who has the right to make truth claims about madness and support authors' claims to that right.

Moreover, the various methods of truth production—especially the inclusion of authenticating documents—can enhance reading pleasure. They assure readers that the spectacular stories of madness are true and furthermore create the thrill of getting to see personal or confidential documents such as facsimiles of official medico-administrative papers like admission or discharge forms, patient files, but also photos and excerpts of personal letters or diaries. Especially medico-administrative documents cater to voyeurism and simultaneously reduce fear by demonstrating that madness can be documented and bureaucratized, that it is "knowable" and, therefore, potentially "masterable" (L. Zimmerman 472).

Reliance on the psychiatric discourse can furthermore curtail normals' insecurities about the mad and proper modes of address. As Goffman points out, "'mixed contacts'—i.e., the moments when stigmatized and 'normal' individuals are in the same 'social situation'" (*Stigma* 12)—can be a source of great unease for both stigmatized individuals and normals (16–18). Mental illness pathographies can reduce this unease because literacy in the supposedly neutral and precise discourse of psychiatry can provide normals with confidence in the political correctness of their utterances. Simultaneously, references to the psychiatric understanding of madness as mental illness conceptionally brings madness under control, provides ready interpretations of being transgressive as pathology, and reduces fear about the mad.

Lastly, the production of an objective truth about madness also has didactic functions. Based on their experience and research, some authors supply advice on the interaction with mad individuals that is specifically addressed to normals with mentally disordered family members, friends or students. Marianne Apostolides, for example, includes chapters targeted towards these groups where she attempts to explain the eating disordered mindset and to function as a mediator (148–155). Even when texts do not make this didactic function explicit, memoirs by (ex-)patients are appealing to normals as they promise "an intimate engagement with and potential knowledge about the addicted [here: mad] subject, as well as the hope that recovery is possible" (Smith and Watson 148). The effects of objective truth on normals are therefore as diverse as the effects on the Own.

A fairly common way to produce the objective truth of one's madness is the inclusion of expert testimony, that is, passages where authorities on madness attest to the historical author's identity as a mad person and the memoir's authenticity. Since the cultural and political force of memoirs by marginalized subjects depends on the belief in their authenticity (cf. Couser, *Memoir* 79–107), a third of the authors discussed in this project grant their therapist or psychiatrist the first or last word in prefaces, introductions or the afterword. The validation of (illness-related) truth claims through a licensed therapist or medical doctor can influence the reader's perception of the narrative's relevance and increase interest by marking it as a true story.

Mental illness pathographies share this practice of framing the subjective experience of a discredited person with testimony by esteemed witnesses with other types of life writing, e.g., slave narratives. The following comparative analysis does not attempt to equate the lived experience of (former) slaves and the mentally ill but seeks to point out general mechanisms of stigmatization that can affect the behavior of even the most benevolent normals. For example, slave narratives generally included prefaces by prominent white abolitionists who vouched for the discredited subject. In the case of Frederick Douglass, Wendell Phillips and William Lloyd Garrison assure the reader that the narrative is "essentially true in all its statements" (Garrison viii) and that they put "the most entire confidence in its truth, candor, and sincerity" (W. Phillips xvi). While these statements corroborate Douglass' account, the mere presence of these guarantees reveals the extent of the discredit and even perpetuates it. Using witnesses who do not share the author's stigma to establish the truth of an account is therefore a double-edged sword.

In a similarly problematic fashion, mental healthcare professionals and abolitionists emphatically affirm the discredited subject's humanity and thus call attention to the severity of the stigma. In his preface, William Lloyd Garrison refers to slaves as "brothers" and "human beings" twenty-four times in the space of ten short pages. With a similar impetus, Lori Schiller's psychiatrist emphasizes that *The Quiet Room* is "a story not just of mental illness but of a human being" (Doller, Foreword xiii). The emphasis of the marginalized subject's humanity shows that abolitionists and mental healthcare professionals are aware of the need to vouch for the discredited subject whose very humanity is in question, an act which simultaneously subverts and contains stigma beliefs.

Moreover, testimony by esteemed or expert witnesses shows that stigma beliefs are so deep-seated that even the most well-meaning normals may hold them. William Lloyd Garrison cites the case of a white man who was transformed into an unintelligible brute when he was forced into slavery. Though he admits that this was an "extraordinary case of mental deterioration, it proves at least that the white slave can sink as low in the scale of humanity as the black one" (viii), thus suggesting that life in bondage does, in fact, detract from the humanity of a person. Similarly, Jane Doller denies the human quality of empathy and a basic psychological wholeness to the mentally ill when she explains that the experience of schizophrenia is like "liv[ing] with a broken brain … [and that] the thing that has broken is the person's ability to relate to another person" ("Chapter 25" 235). In this way, the radical Otherness of the discredited subject is reinforced amidst claims to the contrary, thus exemplifying the complexities and inner contradictions inherent in anti-stigma efforts by normals.

A central aspect of these stigma-political efforts is the creation of sympathy. To accomplish this feat, abolitionists and mental healthcare professionals emphatically confirm the accuracy of descriptions of "the many sufferings he [here: the marginalized subject] has endured" (Garrison iii). Just as Garrison bemoans "the privations, sufferings and horrors" (vii) which Frederick Douglass and fellow slaves were subjected to, Dr. Jeffrey Smith states that his patients with dissociative identity disorder experienced "the most terrible things that could be done to a child" (262). Similarly, Dr. Jane Doller calls living with schizophrenia "worse than the worst experience of solitary confinement" ("Chapter 25" 235). Mental healthcare professionals who frame memoirs in my corpus therefore support the production of madness as suffering but also increase voyeuristic pleasures by vouching for the reality of the spectacular misery that texts in my corpus describe.

Abolitionists and mental healthcare practitioners further produce the truthfulness of the life writing in question when they confess to the strong emotions the texts aroused in them. Dr. Jeffrey Smith admits that he sometimes finds himself shying away from his patients' testimonies, just as William Lloyd Garrison proclaims that he perused Douglass' narrative with "a tearful eye, a heaving breast, an afflicted spirit" and was "filled with an unutterable abhorrence of slavery and all its abettors" (viii). Abolitionists and therapists therefore use confession to further contribute to the impression of truthfulness while simultaneously fashioning themselves as sympathetic to marginalized subjects, and implicitly prescribing these emotional responses to readers.

Psychiatrists and therapists are not the only witnesses that authors draw upon to create the impression of truthfulness. Cherry Boone-O'Neill's memoir includes several short passages from her husband's diary (132–149), which document his desperation about Cherry's dramatically low weight, as well as letters from her parents that confirm her salvation (166–177). While the excerpts from the diary intrude into the narrative proper but individually do not even take up an entire page, the letters appear after the end of Boone-O'Neill's narration. Through this clear separation and their affirmation of claims made earlier by the narrating self, these texts support and supplement Boone-O'Neill's account rather than supplanting it. Moreover, both diaries and letters are perceived as highly personal documents and therefore increase the impression of authenticity as well as voyeuristic reading pleasures.

Lori Schiller's account of schizophrenia, by contrast, repeatedly turns over the narration to the historical author's family and friends. Schiller explains that, "in the interest of accuracy" she and her co-author Amanda Bennett "interviewed as many people involved with my life, my illness and my treatment as possible" (viii). Moreover, she states that her condition and some of the treatment have caused memory loss, so she yielded the narration of these times to people with clearer recollections of them (vii). As a result, Schiller's family and friends narrate a full third of the memoir, even such dramatic events as Lori's first suicide attempt (M. Schiller 39–50). In this show of transparency, Schiller and Bennett attempt to defuse concerns about the compatibility of amnesia, psychosis, and life writing and produce the impression of reliability through witness testimony and their candor about Schiller's limitations. However, despite emphasizing that the account concerns her lived experience through the three first-person singular possessive pronouns ("my life, my illness, my treatment"), Schiller ultimately endorses the devaluation of narratives that reflect the sense of fragmentation, uncertainty, and instability of perception that can be a part of the experience of severe mental illness.

Marya Hornbacher, a journalist by training, uses witness testimony to emphasize her adherence to journalistic methods of truth production. She includes interviews she conducted with her parents about various aspects of their family life, particularly their perspective on events when she was very sick or too young to remember. The passages mark verbatim quotes as such and notes the parents' pauses, laughter, and sighs as well as Hornbacher's interjections and follow-up questions (*Wasted* 34–35, 256, 259). By following journalistic standards of transparency, Hornbacher invites a mode of reading that is associated with texts that strive for objectivity and reliability. Additionally, the journalistic mode enables Hornbacher to manage the intimacy and shame that is connected to writing about one's stigmatized condition.

Marya Hornbacher further contributes to the impression of reliability by ostentatiously adhering to the conventions of academic writing and referencing. Although several narrating selves in my corpus cite research to back up truth claims about their mental illness, *Wasted* is the most striking example of this reliance on academic sources for support. Whereas other authors only obscurely refer to "objective evidence" (Vonnegut 208, 211) and "studies" Vonnegut (208; cf. also Phillips 35, 55; Wurtzel 377), Hornbacher's memoir provides careful references in footnotes and a lengthy bibliography. This bibliography begins with the caveat, "the articles in scholarly, medical, and psychiatric journals consulted for this book would be too numerous to cite and they are of such varying degrees of relevance and specialization I elected to include only book-length texts in this bibliography" (291). She then directs readers to the *International Journal of Eating Disorders* for more exhaustive research on "both the medical and psychological aspects of eating disorders" (291). In addition to providing transparency about her editorial choices, the caveat also contributes to Hornbacher's self-fashioning as an authority on eating disorders: She presents herself as an expert whose knowledge in multiple privileged discourses—scholarly, medical, psychiatric, and psychological—is so specialized that a complete list of her sources would be of little interest to a lay audience. Despite this omission, her bibliography lists more than ninety titles and includes a wide variety of texts, some by canonical thinkers in the fields of cultural studies, sociology or philosophy such as Pierre Bourdieu, Susanne Bordo, Judith Butler, Michel Foucault, and George Herbert Mead, others are more specialized like monographs on *The Religious Significance of Food to Medieval Women* or *Ideals of Feminine Beauty from the Victorian Era to the Jazz Age* (291–296). Through her specific references and the inclusion of canonical and specialized texts, Hornbacher claims cultural capital and enlists the discursive weight of academic, medical, psychiatric, and psychological research to support her truth claims.

Through this adherence to the academic mode, *Wasted* demands to be read as an ambitious, interdisciplinary contribution to the discourse on eating disorders. She constantly compares her lived experience to psychiatric research, looks at it through the lens of feminist and cultural theory, or likens it to religious practices and literary representations of eating, hunger, and femininity. In this manner, Hornbacher attempts to shed light on the complex phenomenon of eating disorders and simultaneously rejects the lowbrow status of life writing—at least in her case. By referencing valued discourses, Hornbacher and authors like her supply themselves with the discursive weight of privileged discursive agents to challenge myths about their condition and support their truth production on madness.

Kay Redfield Jamison is the only author in my corpus who does not need to rely on witness testimony or academic references to support her truth claims because she is already authenticated by being a researcher of mood disorders and a clinical psychiatrist. Her double role as patient and psychiatrist is established in the front matter, which proclaims that she is a "Professor of Psychiatry at John [*sic*] Hopkins University School of Medicine" and the "recipient of numerous national and international scientific awards." Jamison continually establishes her double authority on bipolar disorder because *An Unquiet Mind* not only charts her evolving condition but also traces her academic career in such detail that the memoir is equal parts pathography and CV. Among other things, the memoir describes her first job as a lab assistant at a psychology department (47), her coursework in clinical psychology (58), an internship at the UCLA Neuropsychiatric

Institute (59), her dissertation, dedicates an entire chapter to the tenure process (124–135), plus another one to her collaboration with Nobel Prize winner James Watson on research about the "manic-depressive gene" (185–198). Based on these scientific credentials and her social capital, Jamison not only proves that madness need not entail complete incapacitation but also destabilizes the patient—psychiatrist or normal—mad binary and makes her truth claims from a position of authority.

References to the objective truth of psychiatry not only encourage the impression of reliability but also provide support against stigma beliefs. The psychiatric understanding of madness as a collection of mental disorders enables authors to produce the meaning of madness as pathology rather than dangerousness (Styron 46), sinfulness (Vonnegut 132), weak will and malingering (Hornbacher, *Madness* 190; Styron 32; Phillips 81) or a cry for attention (Hornbacher, *Wasted* 5). The inclusion of psychiatric truth therefore continues negotiations about the meaning(s) of madness and lends much needed discursive weight to discredited individuals who wish to remove assumptions of nonseriousness or attributions of blame for their condition.

To establish the seriousness of mental disorders, narrating selves produce madness as a medical condition by linking madness to the body or by equating mental and bodily disorders in terms of suffering and treatability. Frequently, texts lay the groundwork for this comparison through detailed explanations of neurochemical, i.e., bodily, processes of psychiatric conditions or by pointing to their genetic basis (Jamison, *Unquiet* 185–198). As William Styron put it,

> never let it be doubted that depression, in its extreme form, is madness. The madness results from an aberrant biochemical process…. It has been established with reasonable certainty … that such madness is chemically induced amid the neurotransmitters of the brain, probably as the result of systemic stress, which for unknown reasons causes a depletion of the chemicals norepinephrine and serotonin, and the increase of a hormone, cortisol [46].

In this quote, Styron's use of the highly evocative term madness and its immediate semantic reduction to "an aberrant biochemical process" embraces the medicalizing framework of psychiatric truth. Moreover, Styron appropriates the discursive weight and technical language of psychiatric truth claims when he elaborates on the suspected causes of depression by using the names of neurotransmitters and hormones without providing further information. Authors therefore tap into the psychiatric discourse's self-fashioning as the mental *analogon* of medicine as well as its medicalizing truth claims to access the benefits of the patient status, namely treatment, care, and sympathy.

Mark Vonnegut illustrates this mechanism when he states, "[m]ost diseases can be separated from one's self and seen as foreign intruding entities. Colds, ulcers, flu, and cancer are things we get. Schizophrenic [here: mad] is something we are. It affects the things we most identify with as making us what we are" (ix). While Vonnegut's claim about the non-essentializing treatment of persons with bodily illnesses is somewhat naïve—as Susan Sonntag points out, metaphorical thinking around bodily illness saw cancer as the result of "the repression of violent [or sexual] feelings" (22) or tuberculosis as "a disease of the soul" (17)—his statement does imply that a supposedly more neutral psychiatric view of mental disorders as conditions with roots in the body could undermine the essentializing beliefs about madness and ultimately reduce (self-)stigma.

To encourage a less essentializing view of mad persons and to make complex claims about the relationship between the condition and the self, authors produce madness as a medical condition by using imagery of bodily illness, most notably cancer, infections, and diabetes. Cherry Boone-O'Neill claims that depression is an "emotional and psychological cancer" (47), a sentiment which is echoed by William Styron (7, 32) and Mark Vonnegut (207). The cancer metaphor evokes the potentially fatal course of the condition, the unpleasant side effects of treatment, and the loss of vitality and strength as the mood disorder metastasizes and spreads until it affects all aspects of life. The metaphor further implies that regular if unpleasant states like sadness, exhaustion, and hopelessness grow abnormally or that they feel as limitless as cancer cells' potential for division. Also comparing her depression to cancer, Elizabeth Wurtzel roots the "tumorous mass" (21) of depression entirely in the body when she states that it is a "thing that your own *body* has produced [and that it] is actually trying to kill you" (21; emphasis added). Through these metaphors, narrating selves access the cultural narratives of suffering that surround cancer as well as the empathy they evoke. Moreover, they continue negotiations of the question whether madness is a part of the self or an Other, since cancer is an abnormal development of regular bodily processes like cell division, but cultural narratives also frequently represent it as a foreign, intrusive entity (Hawkins, *Reconstructing* 61–77). In this manner, authors extend the medicalized framework of psychiatry with metaphors of cancer to contribute to the textual tension that exists between depictions of madness as an intrusion into a normal self and representations of the self as blemished, diseased, or mad.

Whereas the psychiatric discourse provides many truth claims about the genetic or neurochemical etiology of mood or psychotic disorders which link these conditions to the body, this is not (always) the case for eating disorders. The research, which Marianne Apostolides and Marya Hornbacher cite, conceives of eating disorders as learned behavior that develops predominantly in families with problematic relationships to food and is a response to cultural, psychosocial, and intrapsychic stress (Hornbacher, *Wasted* 22–25; Apostolides xiii, 1–4, 127). In response to these truth claims, Hornbacher and Apostolides produce the meaning of their madness as pathology through metaphors and similes of infections, i.e., the invasion of an organism by pathogenic agents and the reactions to these agents or the toxins they produce. Unlike metaphors of cancer which are highly ambiguous on whether cancer belongs to the self or whether it is an Other, imagery of infection more readily externalizes the sources for mental disorders and attributes them to pathogenic cultural and psychosocial factors. According to Apostolides and Hornbacher, the "deadly contradictions" (Hornbacher, *Wasted* 6) which revolve around contemporary gender roles or a person's desire for intimacy *and* independence "begin to split a person in two. Body and mind fall apart from each other, and it is in this fissure that an eating disorder … may *fester* and thrive" (*Wasted* 6; emphasis added) until it "infect[s] every part of your life" (Apostolides 24). By conceiving of their conditions as infections, Apostolides and Hornbacher externalize their causes, thereby managing stigma and shame. Moreover, their imagery incorporates psychiatric and psychological truth claims as it highlights the importance of pathogenic environments and implies that eating disorders spread through contact, thus alluding to their status as learned behavior. This imagery furthermore shows that psychiatric objective truth and literary modes of expressing a personal truth are interconnected rather than separate in mental illness pathographies.

Beyond the methods discussed above, authors also include personal documents like diaries, photographs or excerpts from confidential medico-administrative files to simultaneously supply supposedly objective proof of the reality and severity of the experiencing self's condition and to create the thrilling reading experience that arguably helps to make mental illness pathographies the popular commodity they are today. These documents not only authenticate the objective truth of identity claims by authors and give insight into the workings of the psychiatric dispositive but also add to and legitimize the more salacious aspects of mental illness pathographies.

The inclusion of excerpts from diaries as practiced by several authors in my corpus (Phillips 122–125; Schiller and Bennett 200, 205; Hornbacher, *Wasted* 204, 211) promises a more immediate access to the mindset of a mad person than a retrospective description by the narrating self could provide. Almost regardless of the entries' actual content—let alone the inevitable editorial decision on which excerpts to include—marking a text as written without the intention of ever showing it to others encourages expectations of a more intimate and truthful text, i.e., one less concerned with issues of self-fashioning, but which instead chronicles the author's madness as it unfolds.

Moreover, an impression of objectivity arises because the diary is a confessional genre. Since the Middle Ages, Western societies have relied on confession as the main ritual of truth production about the speaking subject. However, the truth of the subject is never revealed by the confessant's discourse alone but remains "incomplete [and] blind to itself" (Foucault, *Sexuality* 66) until it is deciphered by the listening authority. Post-enlightenment medicine, especially psychiatry, brought about "a clinical codification of the inducement to speak … [thereby] reinscribing the procedure of confession in a field of scientifically acceptable observations" (Foucault, *Sexuality* 65). In other words, confession could be used to arrive at a truth about the speaking subject, and this truth had a scientifically validated status. Diary excerpts by mad persons place the reader in the position of the psychiatrist-confessor and thereby promise access to the objective truth of the mad subject.

The dynamics of confessionalism also give rise to the intense sense of power and pleasure connected to receiving (and making) confessions (Foucault, *Sexuality* 44–45). However, because of confession's status as a method of truth production, spectacular confessions of madness are also framed as necessary to arrive at the truth of the speaking subject rather than mere voyeuristic thrills. Confessionalism therefore not only produces the objective truth of madness but also protects authors and readers from charges of sensationalism, thus legitimizing the inclusion of salacious personal details.

Similarly, photographs contribute to reading pleasure and the impression of truthfulness because they are frequently read as objective representations that are not skewed by the subject's exaggerations, mitigations or selective memory. In Cherry Boone-O'Neill's memoir, the photographs simultaneously document her increasing emaciation, subsequent return to health, and appeal to voyeurism and sensationalism. Whereas most of the pictures included in *Starving for Attention* were taken during her performances with the Pat Boone Family or during promotional photoshoots, others create the impression of a glimpse beyond her carefully constructed celebrity persona. Two photos show her severely underweight and apparently oblivious that her picture is taken. In these photos, Cherry Boone-O'Neill is alone at a picnic table, gnawing a bone—"scavenging the remainders of a turkey carcass" (88) as she calls it in the caption—and staring into space. Her t-shirt exposes her skeletal arms, and because of her low body fat, her hands and shins are covered in protruding veins. Severe malnutrition has reduced her hair to thin wisps. The pictures are highly symbolic as they document not only Boone-O'Neill's habit of limiting her food intake to the scraps left over by her family but also visualize her attempt to make do with the bare minimum of food, body, and self. The turkey bones echo Boone-O'Neill's grotesquely skeletal corporality and highlight the devastating effects which her madness had on her body. The photographs therefore verify the narrating self's statements about the extent of the experiencing self's emaciation and legitimize Boone-O'Neill's claiming of a voice as a person with lived experience of madness.

Moreover, the photographs create voyeuristic pleasures as they *seem to* record the quasi-sexual debasement of the experiencing self. Boone-O'Neill's gnawing on the bones and her choice to call her eating behavior "scavenging" continues her memoir's motif of equating eating with animalism. Throughout her account, she descents on other people's leftovers "like a vulture" (41), and when her husband catches her on the floor, stealing scraps of meat from her dog's bowl, she feels as if she had been caught "in an animalistic orgy" (95). The latter quote also exemplifies her conflation of eating, animalism, and untrammeled sexuality which leads to self-condemnation for "whoring after food" (100). This conflation of themes and the depiction of animalistic behavior, then, frame the inclusion of this photograph as a visual confession of Boone-O'Neill's debasement and foster the impression that they depict her during an action she only engaged in secretly and which she considered shameful. The pictures therefore presume to afford an intimate and authentic glance into the world of a mad person, an impression that is strengthened by the subject's apparent oblivion to being photographed. In these ways, the pictures both authenticate and spectacularize Boone-O'Neill's mental illness pathography.

Another technique that creates the impression of objective truth about the mad subject is the inclusion of medico-administrative documents. For example, a nursing note that is reproduced in Lori Schiller's memoir states that "[a]t 8 p m [sic] patient [Schiller] had episode of severe auditory hallucinations coupled with intense psychomotor agitation: She was writhing, forcefully grimacing, holding her hands to her ears, shaking her feet repeatedly, and seemed nearly oblivious to external stimuli. This episode lasted about ten minutes" (Schiller and Bennett 75). The nursing note has the appearance of objectivity because it is composed in a formal, technical language, includes measurable information like the time and duration of the experiencing self's symptoms, and combines them with both detailed descriptions and a translation into the technical terms of the psychiatric discourse ("psychomotor agitation"). The document therefore emulates the methods associated with the production of scientific, objective truth and corroborates the narrating self's statements about the suffering connected to her condition.

Other medico-administrative documents included in memoirs of my corpus also appeal to voyeuristic pleasures through their use of technical language. Nursing notes and other parts of patient files never explain technical terms such as "depersonalization" (Kaysen 103) or "mixed personality features" (Hornbacher, *Wasted* 178). This lack of explanation shows that these documents were intended for mental healthcare professionals only and therefore afford readers a glimpse into the inner working of mental hospitals and the mad subject. Memoirs further compound the sense of seeing classified information through remarks that the historical authors— that is, the very subjects labeled, measured, and described in these forms and notes—had to go to great lengths or even hire a lawyer to obtain them (Hornbacher, *Wasted* 3; Kaysen 150; Schiller and Bennett vii–x). What is more, these documents present madness as the domain of specialized doctors and thereby further stress its meaning as pathology.

Additionally, the inclusion of medico-administrative documents testifies to the extent to which biographical data is "fed into the administrative machinery" (Goffman, *Asylums* 16) and how admission to a mental hospital frequently entails a "violation of one's informational preserve regarding self … [as] facts about the inmates …—especially discreditable facts—are collected and recorded in a dossier available to staff" (Goffman, *Asylums* 23–24). Schiller's memoir supplies parts of her patient file which includes her date of birth, sex, race, religion, marital status, economic status, current living situation, and usual employment (73; cf. also Kaysen 3). Susanna Kaysen even includes a facsimile of handwritten nursing notes which describe in detail how a nurse walked in on Kaysen performing fellatio on her boyfriend (63). The aggressively self-revelatory nature of this inclusion makes it appear "as though one of Charcot's[4] female patients ha[d] taken charge of her own theater of hysteria and transformed the humiliation of being an exhibit [here: subjected to extensive surveillance] into an empowering exhibitionism" (Reynolds and Press 262). Embedded in Kaysen's general critique of the constant surveillance in McLean hospital (54–57), the carefully composed record of Kaysen's behavior transcends its status as evidence of her deviance but instead reveals the extent of disciplinary power in a "total institution" (Goffman, *Asylums* xiiv).[5] Kaysen and Schiller thus expose the inner workings of mental hospitals in a manner that mirrors the institution's violation of the patients' informational preserve with its supposedly objective documentation: Memoirs simply include rather than annotate excerpts from patient files which reveal intimate moments and bodily minutiae just as the medico-administrative documents report rather than comment on symptoms and behavior. The inclusion of these documents therefore produces the reality of surveillance in mental hospitals which is a central aspect of Kaysen's and Schiller's lived experience.

The inclusion of confessional or medico-administrative documents therefore obscures the fictionality inherent in life writing by suggesting access to a less mediated or more objective perspective on the author's lived experience. I suggest that it constitutes an intertextual variation of what Elizabeth Gregory calls the *"reality trope"* in confessional poetry, in itself "a variation on the sincerity claims that poets have long employed to convince readers that their work deserves attention. They claim to speak from the 'real' rather than just the sincere" (35–36). These documents support the authors' claiming of a voice as a person with lived experience and create the thrilling impression of reading a true story. Simultaneously, medico-administrative documents legitimize the description of the more spectacular aspects of mental illness pathographies such as those connected to sexual behavior. Because of the documents' origin in the psychiatric dispositive, even reports on female patients performing fellatio are marked as relevant to the diagnostic process and therefore not only reveal the disciplinary nature of the psychiatric dispositive but also reframe prurient interest through their supposed educational value.

Authenticating documents like photographs or excerpts from patient files, also produce further meanings of madness. While medico-psychiatric documents that tie madness to the body present it as a medical condition, the inclusion of voyeuristic photographs and the confidential nature of medico-psychiatric documents paradoxically reproduce madness as a condition that is not to be talked about. Because the inclusion of confidential documents simultaneously creates a strong sense of learning forbiddingly intimate truths of mad individuals and of witnessing the exhibitionist disclosure of the truths, memoirs in my corpus create a tension between the poles public and private. In this manner, they mirror the tension that exists between medicalizing views of madness that understand it as the private matter of an individual that warrants doctor-patient confidentiality and the social model of madness that sees the condition as a reaction to insane environments and which should therefore be discussed to achieve social change. This illustrates the ever more complex network of tensions and meanings that is created through multiple textual elements.

Writing for Psychiatrists: Self-Specification and Case Histories

Unlike normals and the Own, mental healthcare professionals already possess—and in some cases produce—knowledge of the psychiatric truth of madness. Moreover, psychiatrists have undergone the "ritual process of apprenticeship and evaluation" (B. Lewis, *Moving* 43) that legitimates their position as speakers in the discourse of psychiatry and inserted them into a "fellowship of discourse" whose function is to preserve and reproduce discourse "in order that it should circulate within a closed community [and] according to strict regulations" (Foucault, *Discourse* 225). Psychiatrists and therapists are therefore invested in "maintaining and integrating the social status and social function of the discourse" through the exclusion of those who have not entered it through the same processes. For this reason, gaining the right to speak authoritatively to psychiatrists about madness as mental disorders—not to mention producing multiple alternate meanings of the condition—is more difficult for authors in my corpus than claiming a voice on the subject in the address of the Own or normals.

Due to the opposition of "reason and folly"—as madness was called in the Middle Ages—Western society possesses a "principle of exclusion" from the right to speak (Foucault, *Discourse* 216): The mad are disqualified generally from participation in legitimate discourses as their "words are null and void, without truth or significance, worthless as evidence" (Foucault, *Discourse* 216) and even in psychiatry—a discipline that relies on patient reports in the absence of objective tests—the mad person's perspective "is not included until the psychiatric observer processes it" (B. Lewis, *Moving* 50). For this reason, more radical advocacy groups and scholar-activists affiliated with them understand the appropriation of psychiatric labels and concepts as a form of tacit acceptance of the discursive hegemony of psychiatry and the oppression of the mad (cf. Spandler et al.; LeFrançois et al.).

Contrary to some advocacy groups and scholar-activists, I do not think that the appropriation of the psychiatric discourse in memoirs demonstrates a tendency to "accept the medical category of depression [here: 'mental disorders'] … as if it weren't a construction at all but a transparent and transcendental truth—a final knowledge" (L. Zimmerman 477). Instead, the medico-psychiatric interpretation of madness as a collection of mental disorders is one of the many meanings that texts in my corpus produce and which exists in an unresolved tension with other meanings. In this line of thought, I do not reduce the appropriation of psychiatric truth to matters of subversion and containment but can instead consider the nuanced forms of meaning-making and calls for coalition politics that ultimately attempt to insert the perspectives of those labelled mentally disordered into the psychiatric discourse about them.

To engage mental healthcare professionals in a dialogue about the conceptualization of madness as mental disorders, authors present themselves as literate in the psychiatric discourse to enter a dialogue on a more equal footing and to demonstrate that their goals are reformative rather than revolutionary. William Styron, for example, does the latter when he precedes his criticism of inadequate research in psychopharmacology with acknowledgments of psychiatry's efforts and successes. He states that "[p]sychiatry must be given due credit for its continuing struggle to treat depression pharmacologically" (54; cf. also Oxnam 168). Medications, he writes, "have proved invaluable" (54), as have other "continually evolving psychiatric strategies" (55), such as cognitive behavioral therapy. In these quotes, Styron not only depicts psychiatry as a dynamic, innovative field ("continually evolving") that has yielded verifiable results ("*proved* invaluable"; emphasis added), but the term "struggle" also suggests strenuous efforts and personal involvement on the part of researchers and doctors. In this manner, the narrating self evokes two of "midcentury America's favorite cultural myths: that of the medical encounter as comforting and reassuring … and that of medical science as invincible in its march to eradicate disease" (Hawkins, *Reconstructing* 5). Embracing this myth may be particularly effective in the current cultural climate which favors less positive depictions of doctors and medicine on television (Chory-Assad and Tamborini). Styron thus cushions his criticism in praise and establishes common ground through a shared appreciation of the medico-psychiatric dispositive, thereby fashioning himself as a reformer and keeping lines of communication open.

Clifford Beers' memoir and his career as the founder and chairman of the Mental Hygiene Movement demonstrate the efficacy of striking a conciliatory note in attempts to encourage reform in the institutional care of the mad. The narrating self stresses his belief in the healing powers of psychiatric treatment and urges asylum reform so psychiatry could achieve its full potential (Beers 80). Likewise, the historical author, "[a]dept at graciously deferring to authority," was able to secure the support of multiple prominent US psychiatrists (Porter, *Social* 194; cf. also Grob 154), and later editions of Beers' memoir include letters in which they endorse the book. William James, for example, calls the memoir "full of instructiveness for doctors and attendants alike" and acknowledges, "you no doubt have put your finger on the weak spots of our treatment of the insane, and suggested the right line of remedy" (qtd. in Beers 111). Beers' praise for psychiatry likely ensured the support of prominent psychiatrists which added greatly to the Mental Hygiene Movement's success in instigating reforms in asylum conditions.

Beyond flattery, texts in my corpus encourage communication between the mad and those who treat them on the level of narrative structure. Chapters One and Two demonstrated that memoirs in my corpus appropriate culturally valued narratives of transformation and overcoming but also Gothic tales of threat and seduction to give shape and meaning to their lived experience. However, viewed through a medico-psychiatric lens, the (mostly) chronological structure of memoirs, the language they use, the types of information they include, and the attempt to weave illness-related events into a coherent narrative also resemble an elaborate case history. Even Ann Cvetkovich, who dismisses the medico-psychiatric understanding of depression as a neurochemical condition as "trivial" (15), appropriates this genre by "offering [her] own case history" (16), if only to demonstrate that her condition developed in response to stressful life transitions and academic pressures (17). Cvetkovich' example shows that the case history is a well-established format which aids the meaning-making process and the production of socially meaningful identities. Moreover, the appropriation of this specialized genre enables authors to engage mental healthcare professionals in their own idiom and to demonstrate their literacy in a discourse that is generally closed to persons outside the community of psychiatrists.

Memoirs in my corpus further emulate case histories by including information which psychiatrists elicit in diagnostic interviews such as the onset, duration, and severity of symptoms, a family history of mental disorders, a personal history of substance abuse, or other forms of transgressive behavior. Since narrating selves frequently apply psychiatric concepts and labels to the experiencing selves' behavior and state of mind, they perform both parts of diagnostic interviews. Specifically, they emulate and usurp psychiatrists' diagnostic powers and yield to the interpellation of self-specification that is so pervasive in the psychiatric dispositive (cf. Foucault, *Psychiatric* 157–161). This double role as patient-confessant and psychiatrist-confessor further illustrates that the appropriation of psychiatric concepts transcends binary oppositions of subversion and containment.

Moreover, in the address of psychiatrists, the inclusion of medico-administrative documents compounds the impression of a heavily annotated psychiatric case file, and the clinical judgment of other mental healthcare professionals further solidifies the objective truth of the experiencing selves' condition as well as the authors' claims to an identity as mentally disordered or mad. The stabilization of these identity claims is central to the textual selves' self-fashioning as textbook cases of their condition and it is based on this self-fashioning that authors claim the right to contribute to the psychiatric discourse.

Like several other memoirs in my corpus, Marya Hornbacher's *Wasted* includes reports by mental healthcare professionals as well as admission and discharge forms to stabilize her identity claims and to provide additional, supposedly objective perspectives on her eating disorders. By including excerpts of this privileged discourse as applied to her illness experience, Hornbacher endorses the psychiatric perspective as a legitimate and necessary addition to her life writing. Among other things, these records catalog the progressive deterioration of Hornbacher's mental and physical condition, classify her disorders according to the *DSM*, and code them into its numerical short-hands. The first report issues three diagnoses:

"I. AXIS I: A. Bulimia nervosa, 307.51 (w/anorectic features), B. Substance abuse, 305.00, C. Major Depression, 296.22" (*Wasted* 142) whereas the second one establishes that Hornbacher presents with

> I. AXIS I:
> A. 1. Anorexia nervosa, 307.10
> 2. Malnutrition secondary to severe starvation.
> B. 2. Bulimia nervosa, 307.51
> C. 3. Major Depression, recurrent, 296.33
> II. AXIS II:
> 1. Mixed personality features.
>
> Notes: BRADYCARDIA, HYPOTENSION, ORTHOSTASIS, CYANOSIS, HEART MURMUR. SEVERE DIGESTIVE ULCERATION [*Wasted* 178; cf. also 186, 277].

Unlike most of *Wasted*, where Hornbacher emphasizes her literacy in the psychiatric discourse by explaining technical terms to less knowledgeable readers, she fails to do so regarding the *DSM*'s organizations into axes and does not elaborate upon her medical diagnoses listed in the notes section. By including (presumably) unaltered internal communication written in the profession's shorthand, the memoir corroborates the objective truth of Hornbacher's narration and reveals psychiatrists as an intended audience.

In addition to explicit descriptions of extreme states of mind and their identification as symptoms of mental disorders, memoirs in my corpus also include passages whose language, tone, and structure can create the impression of an immediate representation of these symptoms which can further evoke the clinical interview for the memoirs' third group of addressees. As Bradley Lewis points out in his analysis of discursive practices in the psychiatric dispositive, the clinical psychiatric interview "works by prompting patients to give responses in which clinicians can find signs and symptoms" (*Moving* 55). When memoirs in my corpus include markedly disorganized passages or use exceedingly long or short sentences, they not only mark their texts as literature through these deviations from what is considered ordinary language (cf. Chapter Four). Instead, they also cater to selective reading or listening practices which psychiatrists use to identify "the objects ... of discourse so that she [the psychiatrist] can put them together into a conceptual grid or schema of psychiatric disorder" (B. Lewis, *Moving* 56).[6] Because the psychiatric dispositive fashions these listening or reading practices as objective and scientific methods (B. Lewis, *Moving* 49–51), literary passages that emulate symptoms can create the impression that they supply readers with the raw data based on which trained observers can arrive at the objective truth of the textual selves' condition. Despite this function in the production of objective truth, I discuss these poetic structures in Chapter Four, and turn now to the memoirs' emulation of the initial psychiatric interview, anamnesis.

Psychiatric anamnesis is generally very detailed as many psychological, psychosocial, and medical factors are relevant to the formulation of a diagnosis. Popular psychiatric textbooks such as Kaplan and Sadock's *Textbook of Clinical Psychiatry* instruct medical students to inquire into the nature, severity, and history of present complaints, as well as the patient's occupation, marital status, significant life events, other medical conditions, previous psychiatric diagnoses, treatment, medication, psychiatric conditions in the patient's family, the patient's consumption of alcohol or illicit drugs, sexual activity, and traumatic events such as abuse or loss of loved ones (Sadock and Sadock 1–15). Memoirs in my corpus provide answers to many if not all of these questions, thus aligning narrating selves with psychiatrists who conduct anamneses of the experiencing selves. Mental illness pathographies therefore cater to the psychiatric method of truth production and thereby present madness as knowable.

In this context, testimony by family and friends functions as heteroanamnesis, i.e., interviews with other informants that are conducted when the patient is deemed unreliable. Lori Schiller's account of schizophrenia provides extensive heteroanamnesis because her relatives, friends, and psychiatrist take turns narrating her story at times when Schiller considered her memory too impaired. The psychiatric case history that is reproduced in *The Quiet Room* even states, "Informants: Patient, unreliable. Parents, reliable" (Schiller and Bennett 74). Schiller's memoir therefore emulates psychiatric methods of truth production beyond information the narrating self can provide.

As the apotheosis of self-specifying life writing, Marya Hornbacher's memoir *Wasted* about her eating disorders provides information on all subjects listed in the textbook on clinical psychiatry above. While many forms of self-fashioning as a textbook case are also present in other mental illness pathographies, *Wasted* is unique in the extent to which they are made explicit. In the introduction, Hornbacher sketches the outlines of her history of eating disorders in a dispassionate manner that is at odds with the memoir's later literary and engaging passages:

> I became bulimic at the age of nine, anorexic at the age of fifteen. I … veered back and forth from one to the other until I was twenty, and now, at twenty-three, I am an interesting creature, an Eating Disorder Not Otherwise Specified. My weight has ranged … from 135 pounds to 52 … I am considered "moderately improved," "psychologically stabilized, behaviorally disordered," "prone to habitual relapse." I have been hospitalized six times, institutionalized once, had endless hours of therapy[7] [*Wasted* 2–3].

A little later, Hornbacher adds, "I get to be the stereotype: female, white, young, middle-class" (*Wasted* 7), thus adding the biographical information required in psychiatric interviews.

Hornbacher's summary of her illness experience strongly resembles the case reports reproduced in Susanna Kaysen's *Girl, Interrupted* (3, 11, 13, 69, 105, 145), David Smola's *A Waltz Through La La Land* (215–231), and Lori Schiller's *The Quiet Room* (51–52, 73–76) in the type of content, the use of professional jargon, and conciseness. The clinical assessment included in the appendix of his memoir describes David Smola as

> a twenty-two year old, single, white male who … [was admitted to Forestedge Hospital because of] his severe depression and potential for suicide. He claimed he had been feeling down since mid–August…. Prior to admission, outpatient therapy had been recommended but the patient refused…. Prognosis is good … given that this is the patient's first apparent major depressive episode [qtd. in Smola 215–217].

Like Kaysen's, Smola's, and Schiller's psychiatrists, Hornbacher includes her diagnosis, information about the onset of her mental illness, the severity of her condition as implied by her life-threateningly low weight, her current condition, her prognosis as well as the treatment she received. The major difference between the official case reports, which are exemplified by Smola's clinical assessment, and the passage from Hornbacher's introduction consists of Hornbacher's use of the first-person singular pronoun and the mild skepticism about her prognosis. Seizing the first-person singular in the emulation of a case report foreshadows Hornbacher's self-fashioning as a well-informed patient who seeks to enter a dialogue with mental healthcare professionals on (more) equal terms. Additionally, the inverted commas and the passive constructions ("I am considered 'moderately improved'…."), which Other psychiatric prognoses by reporting rather than embracing them, cast doubt on psychiatric prognoses rather than merely submitting to them. Hornbacher's embrace of psychiatric jargon and genres therefore show her belief in its methods of truth production but also alert psychiatrists among her readers to her desire to enter the discourse as a critical speaking subject.

Hornbacher further demonstrates this desire through the position of the passage quoted above and her reliance on technical jargon. By introducing herself in terms of psychiatric diagnostic categories, Hornbacher mirrors the clinical focus on the chief complaint, which is elicited first in psychiatric interviews (Sadock and Sadock 1–3).[8] Moreover, Hornbacher privileges the psychiatric idiom by adding explanations about the different types of eating disorders in a footnote rather than the main text which suggests that she considered the needs of the informed rather than the uninformed reader of this passage. In this manner, Hornbacher shows that she is so literate in the psychiatric discourse that its conventions inform her narrative structure and the dissemination of information.

Moreover, the passage shows that the narrating self accepted the identity the psychiatric dispositive bestowed upon her and foreshadows her attempts to use that identity to claim a voice. When Hornbacher states, "I am an interesting creature, an Eating Disorder Not Otherwise Specified," she embraces her current diagnostic label as an identity category through an essentializing *pars pro toto*. By reducing herself to her pathology in the jargon of a supposedly objective, scientific discipline, Hornbacher illustrates the tensions in her self-fashioning as "as an object of knowledge for a discourse with a scientific status" (Foucault, *Discipline* 24), as mad and normal (in the sense of rational enough to emulate the methods of said discourse), and as a speaking subject who can contribute legitimate knowledge. The latter is thrown into relief when Hornbacher fashions herself as a valuable case study. Even though the narrating self also claims to have transcended the state of being a collection of disorders or a personified "annotated Case" (4), the *pars pro toto* also foreshadows Hornbacher's claims about the typicality of her case. It is because of her lived experience as the "stereotype" (7) of eating disorders and her literacy in the psychiatric discourse, that she can provide an inside perspective and thus contribute to the truth production on her form of madness.

To support the claiming of voice based on their lived experience, authors in my corpus also explicitly refer to themselves as a "textbook case" of their disorder (Jamison, *Unquiet* 93; Hornbacher, *Madness* 74). In her memoir of living with bipolar disorder, Hornbacher states, "I have a glaring case of the disorder" (Hornbacher, *Madness* 7; cf. also Styron 47), and later, "[e]very symptom of mania I could have, I have, in force" (*Madness* 74; cf. also Styron 47). These and similar statements fashion authors as both objects of knowledge production as well as speaking subjects who are empowered by their literacy in the psychiatric discourse and wish to contribute their perspective. The self-fashioning and interaction with the psychiatric discourse, then, remains utterly ambivalent and characterized by tensions.

Despite their embrace of psychiatric truth, authors challenge the absolutism of the medico-psychiatric perspective. For example, Hornbacher's narrating self states, "[t]he history of my life—one version of it, anyway—is contained in [the] piles of paper and scrolls of microfiche" (*Wasted* 3) that make up her patient file. Her file describes her as "a 'hopeless case' … an invalid, a delusional girl destined, if she lived, for a life of paper gowns and hospital beds" (*Wasted* 3), and the narrating self claims that this representation of herself contributed to her decision to present her own view, not only on her lived experience but on eating disorders in general. Note how the narrating self does not dismiss the psychiatric interpretation of her life events but that she allows for additional perspectives on it when she states that her patient file only presents "one version" of her life. Moreover, the double meaning of "invalid" in Hornbacher's summary of her patient file speaks to the way psychiatry delegitimizes the opinion of those it deems unable to care for themselves. This passage at the beginning of *Wasted* therefore foreshadows Hornbacher's informed and critical engagement with the psychiatric discourse on eating disorders despite the psychiatric dispositive's delegitimization of patients.

Marya Hornbacher draws upon her lived experience and knowledge of psychiatric texts to propose specific corrections regarding the conceptualization of mental disorders and the implementation of psychiatric treatment. For example, Hornbacher criticizes the lack of differentiated analysis that pervades research on eating disorders and culture-wide assumptions (*Wasted* 122–123). She suggests abandoning both reductive neurochemical explanations that attribute eating disorders to errant neurotransmitters as well as Freudian interpretations of the anorexic body as a symbolic attempt to regress into a state of perpetual childhood but to account for the multiplicity of cultural, emotional, biological, and familial factors (cf. 122–123, 135; cf. also Kaysen 142–143). On the basis of her interactions with nurses on eating disorder wards and interviews with other eating disordered women, Hornbacher also proposes to screen nurses for issues with weight and eating of their own, as patients will not take advice from persons they perceive to be hypocritical (149). She furthermore explains that eating disordered persons may use caffeine to boost their metabolism or heart rate (146), rig the scales if left unmonitored, hide weights under their clothes, and drink copious amounts of water before being weighted (175). These revelations of her modes of deception simultaneously serve as a subtle reminder of the potential for resistance on part of the patient and fashion Hornbacher as an important ally who can provide practical advice on how to spot this kind of behavior (144). Hornbacher therefore addresses both the theoretical framework and treatment suggested by the psychiatric dispositive and offers concrete advice on how to improve both based on the knowledge she gained from her lived experience. In other words, she encourages the incorporation of her knowledge into psychiatric truth production and practice and does so from a position of confidence.

As this chapter showed, authors in my corpus draw upon the psychiatric discourse for a variety of reasons that complicate binary oppositions like subversion and containment or normal and mad. One of the central effects is that the psychiatric discourse adds even more meanings to the signifier madness. By producing madness to signify pathology and serious medical condition rather than a consequence of weak will, deviancy, erosion of intellect, eccentricity, or (artistic) genius, the psychiatric discourse destabilizes deeply ingrained stigma beliefs about madness as an individual responsibility or nonserious matter. At the same time, emphasizing the neurobiological or genetic basis of mental disorders supports the notion that the mentally disordered are radically Other, almost a different species.

Because it undermines some stigma beliefs and supports others, the appropriation of the psychiatric discourse illustrates that all responses to the stigma of madness become double-edged swords due to the contradictory nature of that stigma.

Moreover, the appropriation of the psychiatric discourse and other valued methods of truth production fulfills several stigma-political and personal functions. It legitimizes the claiming of a voice by marginalized subjects, authenticates their version of events, and enables them to become speaking subjects in a discourse that conceives of them as objects of a discipline with a scientific status. The psychiatric framework which interprets the disorienting experience of madness as pathology aids meaning-making and furthermore enables intellectualization and generalization as ways to manage shame, stigma, and intimacy. Another stigma-political effect of the appropriation of the psychiatric discourse is that authors can express their faith in psychiatric truth, thereby encouraging coalition politics with psychiatrists. Additionally, texts in my corpus fulfill multiple functions which Erving Goffman attributed to advocacy groups of stigmatized individuals when they introduce their Own to that discourse and empower them to spot malpractice, become informed consumers of mental healthcare services, and engage their therapists and psychiatrists on a more equal level. Lastly, methods and mediums associated with the production of objective truth such as the medical case history, the photograph, journalistic interviews, and academic methods of citation and reference corroborate the narrating selves' versions of events and create the impression of authenticity and truthfulness. This impression not only increases the memoir's perceived reliability but also satisfies voyeuristic drives and increases reading pleasures.

The appropriation of the psychiatric discourse as well as methods associated with the production of objective truth therefore contributes significantly to the conflicting self-fashioning in my corpus, yet, as several narrating selves in my corpus point out, the clinical language of psychiatry is woefully inadequate for communicating the affective center and emotional realities which lived experience entails (Styron 36; Jamison, *Unquiet* 179–183; Kaysen 75–77). To communicate these realities, authors turn to markedly poetic devices, which are the focal point of the next chapter.

Chapter Four

Producing
Subjective Truth

As the previous chapter demonstrated, authors in my corpus draw upon the psychiatric discourse which is produced through quantitative methods and interprets the lived experience of persons with mental disorders. Scientific practice requires that psychiatric truth claims are general and objective, which means that propositions about mental disorders hold true for all individuals who live with them and that experiments produce the same result if they are repeated (cf. B. Lewis, *Moving* 1–14). Accordingly, the language of medico-psychiatric truth claims avoids ambiguity, favoring instead the hedged language of statistical analyses and clear guidelines on which symptoms must be present to warrant a specific psychiatric diagnosis.

In this chapter, I turn to another form of truth which exists in a state of tension with what is presented as objective, psychiatric truth, namely artistic, subjective truth. Subjective truth refers to an individual's lived experience to which texts give expression by using literary devices and confessional tropes that are associated with the production of truth. It includes not only literary representations of the personal experience of symptoms but also artistic renditions of the experience of stigma or of a general sense of being devalued, cast out, abjected. Moreover, it describes the effect that madness has on the experiencing self's family, friends, and partners. In other words, mental illness memoirs present a subjective view of the social experience of madness, an aspect which the *DSM* barely addresses. In this sense, authors in my corpus claim a voice based on their status as writers and individuals with lived experience, thereby empowering themselves and influencing wider cultural representations of madness.

Texts in my corpus produce this subjective, artistic truth of madness in an explicit intertextual engagement with the psychiatric discourse. Memoirs combine and contrast the precise, clinical, markedly non-literary language of psychiatry with more literary, evocative modes of expression.

This practice enables and even privileges readings of literary devices as quasi-mimetic representations of symptoms, illness-related senses of self, and modes of being in the world. It furthermore strengthens the connection between madness and artistic expression and calls to mind the most positive stigma belief regarding madness, the trope of the mad artist. The artistic, subjective truth of madness therefore supplements the objective, psychiatric truth with more evocative descriptions of codified clinical conditions which complicates the notion of tensions in my corpus as binary oppositions and points to the interplay of both sides. Lastly, the intertextual engagement with the psychiatric discourse constitutes yet another attempt to enter into a dialogue with psychiatrists and to contribute to the discursive construction of madness.

When they produce the personal, artistic truth of madness, memoirs foreground and "defamiliarize" language in ways that undermine "automatic" responses and "habitualized" interpretations (cf. Shklovsky 11–12). Texts in my corpus include experimental narrative forms and decentered narrative subjectivities but also a high degree of aesthetic stylization and unusual figurative usages. These deviations from everyday speech and conversational storytelling are markedly constructed, "increase the difficulty and length of perception," and "make the works as obviously artistic as possible" (Shklovsky 11, 9). Literary theorist Viktor Shklovsky has claimed that these techniques lead to the defamiliarization of language which contributes to the impression of literariness and encourages a mode of reading that is characterized by both the assumption that a text conveys more than its denotative meaning and an increased willingness to accept ambiguity and explore uncertainties (cf. also Culler 27–29; Erlich 178, 183). These literary devices, therefore, discourage habitualized responses and enable new modes of thinking about the meaning(s) of madness, ways of being in the world, and the possibilities of its literary representation.[1]

The contexts in which these literary, defamiliarizing devices predominantly occur influences their effect and the range of possible interpretations. Experimental narrative forms, fragmented subjectivities, and a high degree of ambiguity are a hallmark of postmodern literature (Hutcheon 3–4). By employing forms of writing that are currently associated with high-brow literature, authors in my corpus establish their cultural capital and fashion themselves as writers. Moreover, the use of stylistic devices associated with postmodernism produces highly ambivalent, fragmented textual selves which not only contributes to the tension between normalcy and madness but also undermines the process of stigmatization which requires stable, unified selves. In these ways, these literary devices can have fortuitous stigma-political effects.

Additionally, narrative and chronological fragmentation, decentered narrative subjectivity, and uncertainty are established tropes of trauma writing and therefore encourage the mode of reception that is connected to the genre (Gibbs 20–21). The use of these tropes thus presents madness as utterly overwhelming, disruptive, even traumatic, and supports the production of madness as suffering (cf. Chapter Two). Moreover, the presence of tropes of trauma writing call attention to another property of literature, i.e., the ability "to impart the sensation of things as they are perceived and not as they are known" (Shklovsky 11). This focus on the transmission of experience is especially pronounced in the US trauma discourse and "the idea that audiences must suffer with, and even as, the victims emerge[d] as the dominant mode of reception" (Rothe 161). Through the representation of the extreme experience of madness by markedly literary tropes associated with trauma writing, texts in my corpus produce "forms of truth that are felt rather than proven by evidence" (Cvetkovich 77). In this manner, they not only encourage readers to empathize with textual selves and to cross the gap of Otherness, but they also produce a truth of madness that the clinical language of psychiatry cannot convey.

However, another literary device, the confessional mode, also complicates the creation of empathy through tropes of trauma writing. Mental illness pathographies include spectacular confessions that expose experiencing selves as persons who "break cultural conventions about what is acceptable appearance and behavior, while invoking other cultural categories—of what is ugly, feared, alien or inhuman" (Kleinman 163) and thereby encourage condemnation or even repulsion. In these cases, a confession no longer functions unequivocally as a ritual of purification that affirms norms but also provokes and scandalizes. Through the memoirs' use of tropes of trauma writing and scandalizing confessions, readers are caught in a tension between literary devices that draw them close and those that create the desire for distance. This chapter, then, further discusses the radical ambiguity and multifaceted tensions that characterize texts in my corpus.

In fact, the confessional mode creates yet another tension. Confession is a method of truth production, and mental illness pathographies emphasize the impression of truthfulness by adhering to established tropes of confessionalism. These tropes dictate that confessions are particularly truthful when they are made in colloquial, seemingly unpolished language that ignores the conventions of polite discourse (Rak 5). A focus on particularly visceral or shameful events further contributes to the truth effect of self-revelatory statements. In this manner, the confessional mode supports the impression of authenticity or truthfulness of memoirs but also creates a tension to the markedly artificial literary devices discussed above. Arguably, the combination of a deliberate increase in difficulty through defamiliarizing stylistic and narrative devices and the more colloquial language and base subject matter of confessionalism strike a balance between artistic appeal and accessibility that have made mental illness pathographies a commercial success.

Moreover, confessions in my corpus evoke the provocative artistic movements called "abject art" that protests discrimination by performing abject identities that simultaneously embrace and undermine stigma beliefs. Artists associated with abject art—usually members of the LGBTQIA+ community, people of color, and women—created works that exaggerate the stigma beliefs society held about them, e.g., homosexual male artists scandalized with depictions of perversion and disease. When authors in my corpus verbally emulate themes of abject art, they place experiencing selves in line with other marginalized subjects and establish madness as a politicized identity and a matter of performativity.

Even though there are some commonalities in the production of the subjective truth of specific disorders, such as the centrality of food imagery in memoirs about eating disorders, I refrain from organizing this chapter by pathology. There is too much internal variation within texts by authors who share a diagnosis to justify the imposition of a rigid, essentialist, author-centric typology. Instead, my analysis takes its starting points in the use of pronouns, narrative structures, imagery, and the use of the confessional mode. Because the narrative situation fundamentally affects the interpretation of prose texts, I turn first to deviations from the conventional first-person homodiegetic narrator of memoirs.

The Use of Pronouns and Narrative Situations

Even though genre conventions prescribe the use of the first-person singular in autobiographical texts, many authors in my corpus regularly depart from it. These deviations contribute to the literary representation of the authors' sense of self, interact with truth claims from the psychiatric discourse, and encourage readings of the choice of pronouns as a representation of the lived experience of symptoms of mental disorders. Thus, it illustrates how "discourse is appropriated and lived out at intimate levels" (Fee, "Broken" 2).

The choice of personal pronouns is particularly relevant to narratives about dissociative identity disorder (DID; previously known as multiple personality disorder). As Truddi Chase's therapist, Robert Philips, explains in his introduction to *their[2] memoir, the disorder's main characteristic is the presence of two or more distinct personalities (or alters) with unique behavior patterns and memories (ix). Its name derives from a mechanism of psychic self-defense, dissociation. Jane Phillips' experiencing self learned from *their therapist that dissociation may occur in threatening situations: After failed attempts at fight or flight, "the conscious mind simply abandons the body. It might 'watch' from some other vantage point, but later whatever happens will be sealed off somewhere out of reach of ordinary memory" and will only be known to the alters that develop to process it (29). According to the psychiatric discourse which authors appropriate, the lived experience of DID is thus one of fragmentation and multiplication of self which cannot be adequately conveyed with the traditional first-person singular pronoun.

The three authors in my corpus who narrate their experience of DID—Robert B. Oxnam, Jane Phillips, and Truddi Chase—provide three very different representations of their condition. Oxnam eventually accepts *their multiplicity as a fulfilling way of being in the world and decides against merging *their last three alters whereas Phillips sees *their multiplicity as a pathological reaction to and a reminder of the abuse *they suffered in childhood and eventually achieves singularity. Truddi Chase is still a multiple by the end of the memoir and occupies a position in-between. The authors' use of pronouns reflects the diversity of their lived experience and their stances toward their condition.

Robert B. Oxnam's memoir, *A Fractured Mind: My Life with Multiple Personality Disorder*, reflects *their positive attitude towards multiplicity and *their complex notion of selfhood on the level of narration. Even though all three accounts of DID in my corpus stress that the text is a collective effort which includes the perspective of many personalities, only Oxnam's memoir endows *their alters with enough individuality and agency to seize the narration. Whereas the majority of Chase's and Phillips' alters remain anonymous or even demand to be excluded from the narrative, Oxnam's eleven alters take turns narrating *their life in the first-person singular and, in the final chapters, in the first-person plural. Moreover, the memoir marks each switch from one alter's perspective to another's with a subchapter title consisting of the narrating alter's name and sometimes a quote. In this manner, the memoir stresses the individuality of the alters, the blockades and disconnections between them, and the lack of internal consistency that characterizes untreated DID (cf. Oxnam 3–4, 53; J. Smith 266).

Furthermore, Oxnam's memoir reflects the alters' distinct characteristics and their role within Oxnam's internal system on several textual levels, including the amount of space *their narrations take up within the memoir, the sentence structure and word choice of *their narration, the frequency of reader address, the amount of insight *they have into other alters' thoughts as well as the nicknames *they give Oxnam's psychiatrist. The text therefore uses distinctly literary means to represent the truth of Oxnam's lived experience. To illustrate this, I discuss the narrations of three of Oxnam's alters, Robert, Tommy, and Baby.

Robert is the "*dominant personality*" (Oxnam 11) and explains, "[s]ince I'm the most outspoken in the group, I get the job of 'narrator'" (3). "Narrator" in this case means that Robert's narration frames and connects the passages in which the ten alters present their account in the first person singular and that he functions as a guide through the story of Oxnam's life. While the other personalities can only draw upon *their limited perspective of events, Robert provides explanations of other alters' motivations, feelings, and thoughts by merit of his mergers with most of *them which further emphasizes his centrality to Oxnam's internal system. Moreover, Robert is a particularly overt narrator who frequently uses direct reader address and draws attention to the process and problems of narration, whereas other narrations often evoke an immediate report of experience without drawing upon metafictional techniques (see below). These differences in overtness of narration reflect both Robert's outspoken nature and his near-omniscience of intrapsychic processes.

Robert and another alter who merged with him seized control of Oxnam's body and mind whenever he attended classes, studied or wrote papers while other alters took over when Oxnam pursued his hobbies sailing and roller-skating or acted out by shoplifting or binging and purging. Depending on *their level of awareness about Oxnam's multiplicity, alters either watched *their fellow alters' actions or experienced periods of lost time, i.e., *they knew time had passed but did not know what Oxnam had done in those days or hours. To emphasize his leading role in Oxnam's academic pursuits, Robert uses the most intricate sentence structures, which frequently include multiple dependent and inserted clauses, as well as complex grammatical constructions, and an erudite choice of words such as "rancorous" (216), "cantankerous" (236), "doctrinaire" (248), and "meandering estuaries" (249). When referring to Oxnam's psychiatrist, Dr. Jeffrey Smith, he omits the "Dr." which reflects Robert's confidence, domineering style, and dislike of the power imbalance between therapist and patient. In Oxnam's memoir, then, the linguistic style of narration implicitly characterizes alters and establishes *their individuality.

The distinct abilities and personalities of alters become especially obvious when comparing Robert to Tommy, an angry teenager. Although Tommy is aware of other alters and narrates his encounters with them or Dr. Smith in the past tense, his contributions to the memoir never address the act of narration which reflects that his knowledge of internal processes is more limited than Robert's. Moreover, his style of narration differs greatly from Robert's performance of erudition and confidence: As Tommy represents Oxnam's pent-up rage, parts narrated from his perspective are consistently full of highly emotional words and insults. He refers to Dr. Smith as "the stupid shrink" (116), and his first contribution to the memoir begins with "'I don't like you. I hate you.' I was really mad. And I was on that stupid chair, in that stupid office.... Then that dumb shrink, he starts walking over to me, like he's going to do huggy-shrink junk" (49). The repetition of "stupid," the more limited range of vocabulary, short sentences, and *ad hoc* constructions like "huggy-shrink junk" suggest that Tommy's rage is so overwhelming that—unlike Robert—he is unable to verbalize his thoughts in a differentiated manner. These vast differences in the style of narration therefore not only produce the truth of a fragmented subjectivity but also emulate the noticeable switches in conversational style and personality that may characterize a direct encounter with a person with DID.

Additionally, the literary expression of Oxnam's sense of being in the world exacerbates the tension between a self-fashioning as normal and as mad. Tommy's self-representation suggests madness in the sense of a loss of wholeness and animalism: "When I'm mad, I'm like a mean dog. I tried to kill him [Dr. Smith] with my eyes. My mouth was angry and my teeth felt like I could bite him. I made those hissy noises like a snake" (49). Rather than assuming responsibility for his anger, Tommy projects it onto his personified mouth and teeth, which speaks to the sense of fragmentation and loss of agency that is a common occurrence among traumatized individuals (cf. Gibbs 12). Dissociated from his self and thus denied its status as a justified reaction to horrendous abuse, Tommy's anger grows until it exceeds the range of human emotions and becomes animalistic. It is the rage of a mean dog, a hissing snake, and throughout their interactions, Tommy "growled" (54), "hissed" (55), and "snarl[ed]" (116) at Dr. Smith. Whereas Robert's narrative performance suggests normalcy in the sense of self-control, rationality, and intelligence, Tommy's animalistic behavior and simple, aggressive language affirm the connection of madness to danger or a loss of humanity. Their narratives therefore depict them as distinct individuals and create an unresolved tension between normalcy and madness because these opposing personalities inhabit the same body.

Oxnam's memoir not only produces madness as aggressiveness and animalism but also establishes that it is the result of trauma. The narration of Baby—the alter who experienced sexual, emotional, and physical abuse at the hands of a family member who remains unnamed—contains several tropes of the literary depiction of trauma when he relives it during a therapy session:

> Who's coming? No, no. Not the door opening. Oh, no, no lights turned on. No lights at all. Light means happy. Dark means bad.... Then it's over. The door closes. I get into a little ball. My hands are over my eyes and mouth. Don't cry. Don't cry. It will happen

again if I cry. Bad boy! Don't cry. Now Dr. Smith comes over.... He won't hurt me. He doesn't have hurt in his eyes.... Then I feel something in my bottom. It's a finger. It hurts. I cry. Then something bigger than a finger. It hurts awful. I scream [141].

In this passage, as in the rest of his narration, Baby does not distinguish grammatically between the original experience of the trauma and the recall of it in the presence of Oxnam's psychiatrist. This is in line with theories from the field of Trauma Studies which suggest that an overwhelming event is not processed and integrated into memory but instead resurfaces in its *original, unmediated form* through flashbacks (Gibbs 4–5; cf. also Phillips 78).[3] In this context, "unmediated" means as it occurred in the individual's mind at the time, rather than put into context or imbued with meaning by retrospective analysis (Gibbs 14). The passage above conveys the immediacy of the experience and "the exactly literal quality of recollection in the flashbacks" (Gibbs 13) by narrating events through the filter of Baby's perception *as they unfold*. There are no expository remarks regarding the unnamed tormentor for the benefit of the reader, only a sudden panic at the abuser's presence which reduces Baby's already limited scope of expression to a mere "No, no" and "Oh, no." By representing the trauma of abuse through established literary techniques that represent the truth of experience as it was, Oxnam's memoir not only produces madness as the result of trauma but also creates the impression of authenticity.

The passage further represents the truth of Baby's experience through its interaction with psychiatric truth claims in the epilogue. Here, the historical author's psychiatrist Dr. Jeffrey Smith explains that the human mind frequently reacts to trauma with "a dis-association of feeling from fact" (J. Smith 264) and thus enables a retrospective interpretation of the passage quoted above as a literary representation of extreme emotional dissociation. Baby primarily reports on outside action and only implies feelings of fear or self-loathing ("Bad boy!"). Whereas Tommy is still articulate enough to identify his rage as such, Baby's narration can only acknowledge the facts of the abuse, not the feelings it caused. By presenting an interior monologue that lacks direct references to emotions and supplementing it with psychiatric truth claims, the memoir produces a literary representation of the subjective truth of abuse and dissociation.

While the youth and naiveté of the narrating voice and the narration in the present tense create the impression of an unmediated truth, i.e., one that is relived rather than recalled, they are also a staple of "dominant trauma aesthetics" (Gibbs 39; Rothe 120). The strict adherence to literary conventions of trauma writing reveals the constructedness of the passage, thereby creating yet another textual tension, this time between the impression of authenticity and artificiality. Like the objective, general truth of the psychiatric dispositive, subjective, artistic truth cannot provide immediate access to lived experience.

The narrative situation and stylistic devices, then, speak to multiple different aspects of Oxnam's lived experience: The shifts between markedly different narrating voices produce Oxnam's alters as distinct personalities with profound senses of individuality which expresses *their lived experience of DID. The fragmentation of the narrative into accounts by eleven personalities not only reflects the effects of Oxnam's abuse but also allows the text to adopt tropes of trauma writing that contribute to (and complicate) the production of subjective truth. Moreover, the narrative situation represents the mixture of division and unity in purpose that characterizes Oxnam's final decision to remain a multiple and to embrace the first-person plural pronoun in the last fifteen pages of the pathography.

Likewise, Jane Phillips' memoir, *The Magic Daughter: A Memoir of Living with Multiple Personality Disorder,* uses the choice of narrative situation to express *their stance towards multiplicity, which *they see as an unpleasant, pathological reaction to the physical and sexual abuse *they suffered at the hands of *their two older brothers. Even though Phillips' experiencing self sometimes acknowledges *their multiplicity by using the first-person plural pronoun in conversations with *their therapist, the narrating self fashions herself as a singular entity. Most of the time, she only *reports* on the thoughts and emotions of alters in the third-person singular or in the third-person plural in the case of the group of alters she calls "The Kids" but does not individualize any further. When describing *their internal system, Phillip's memoir relies on summaries and indirect speech rather than scenes and in the rare occasions when the text does include internal dialogues between alters, they never run longer than five lines (cf. 195). Through a narrative in the first-person singular without shifts and psycho-narration, Phillips' memoir places most of the focus on the singular narrating self and foreshadows the experiencing self's epiphany at the end: The experiencing self realizes that she created alters to deal with those emotions that her parents discouraged—namely anger, sadness –or the disappointment that her parents did not intervene and prevent the abuse (222). She understands that multiplicity and dissociation enabled her to be "the magic daughter" (60) that her parents wished for, i.e., a girl who was "bright and sweet, never sad or angry" (51), "who met most needs and fulfilled many wishes" (61). The experiencing self's return to singularity, then, not only relieves her of the horrors of uncontrollable switches between alters but also constitutes an emancipation from the unrealistic expectations of her parents and a healthy way to process her childhood abuse. Because the narrative situation reflects these changes, it strongly speaks to Phillips' understanding of madness as a pathological response to trauma.

In contrast to both Oxnam's and Phillip's memoirs, Truddi Chase's *When Rabbit Howls* is told by a heterodiegetic narrator in the third person with multiple focalizers to convey the intricate internal system of 92 alters and other aspects of *their lived experience. In the "authors' note,"— mark the plural—*they explain that *they narrate events in the third person because there is no alter with a complete memory of the abuse or *their life afterwards, so none can lay claim to it in the first person or serve as spokesperson (xxvi). Moreover, narration in the third person not only represents the process of dissociation but also avoids the intimacy and immediacy of the first-person perspective and thus mirrors Chase's need for distance. As the experiencing self's therapist observes during *their first session, there was "a gulf between them that would only be bridged with caution. He … [was] intent on giving her the measure of privacy most incest victims seemed to need" (3–4). In that passage, as in the rest of the first two chapters and about a third of the others, the memoir is narrated from the perspective of Robert A. Philips, Jr., Chase's therapist whom the experiencing self addresses as "Stanley."[4] *They inform him that *they chose "Stanley" because "it sounds like the name of an innocuous, lifeless entity … [and] will keep you [Dr. Philips] at a proper distance" (14). Similarly, the memoir begins without immediate access to the point of view of Chase's experiencing self (or rather selves) but provides the *imagined perspective* of an *observer*. It is thus twice removed from Chase's experiencing selves and reflects *their desire for distance and a careful management of intimacy. Moreover, the act of naming and the use of Stanley as a focalizer effectively turns him into a buffer between Chase's original set of alters and the reader. The creation of Stanley thus mirrors a core mechanism of DID, i.e., the creation of personalities that fulfill specific tasks. In this case, Chase created Stanley whose thoughts and emotions are accessible to the reader.

Like Oxnam's and Phillips' accounts of DID, Chase's memoir represents *their sense of self through the choice of pronouns. In direct speech, Chase's experiencing self frequently switches between the first-person singular and the first-person plural to refer to *themselves: "*I* spend a lot of time being scared that the mother would see the special badness that the stepfather hinted *we* were capable of " (90; emphasis added). In this case, the speaking alter considers herself as part of a group and fears that *their communal transgressions will be revealed. By attributing the worry exclusively to herself, the alter using "I" implies that not all personalities shared it or that *they did not (yet) possess enough awareness of *their multiplicity to use the first-person plural in reference to *themselves. The use of pronouns therefore represents the differing opinions and levels of awareness of multiplicity that characterize Chase's lived experience.

Even though Chase's experiencing self also enjoys aspects of *their multiplicity, *their experience of DID differs sharply from Oxnam's regarding the level of individualization and agency of alters. Only a little over twenty of the ninety-two (!) alters are named and individualized through linguistic idiosyncrasies like lisps, accents or markedly different registers. This cannot only be attributed to editorial demands for readability as the indistinguishability of alters is already established in the front matter and paratext which attribute authorship to "the Troops for Truddi Chase"—a collective name that evokes both large numbers and the uniformity of alters. Moreover, Stanley, the literary representation of Chase's therapist, frequently notices dramatic changes in Chase's speech but cannot attribute them to specific personalities as patterns of speech often vary from sentence to sentence, and there are too many alters to keep track easily. Whereas Oxnam's memoir presented a high degree of organization and a spirit of cooperation between the alters through the neat taking of turns in individual subchapters, Chase's narrative represents a rising cacophony of voices. When read side by side, these three accounts of DID address the limitations of generalizing psychiatric diagnostic categories that derive from a supposedly objective truth and illustrate the need for individualized forms of treatment, differentiated research, and the inclusion of the patient perspective.

While life writing by individuals with DID is a likely place for deviations from the first-person singular pronoun, several other memoirs in my corpus include pronoun switches that communicate extreme states of mind and that affect the management of intimacy. In Elizabeth Wurtzel's memoir about depression, a switch from the first- to the third-person singular occurs when the experiencing self is heavily medicated to calm her down after a miscarriage. For less than three lines, the text alters the narrative perspective to signify her chemically altered mental state: "No one would tell her what was wrong with her. She would just lie in her bed, staring at pink walls, taking pink pills that the nurse in white would give her. Between the green pills and the yellow ones. And all these blues" (189). In this quote, the switch from auto- to heterodiegetic narration with external focalization evokes the dissociative quality of the high. Just as the narrator is temporarily removed from the diegetic level, the experiencing self feels removed from the experience. The isolation of the passage into its own paragraph supports this impression, as does the narrowing of descriptions of her environment to one of its most basic features, colors.

The temporary deviation from the first person singular furthermore allows for a reassessment of the narrating self's inner turmoil. The passage has a timeless, strangely peaceful quality which is emphasized by the omission of verbs in the final two sentences and which presents a jarring contrast to the narrating and experiencing self's usual rapid-fire ruminations and declarations of suffering in the superlative mode. For example, before she went to the hospital, the experiencing self called her boyfriend and announced, "Stone, I'm dead. I know I said that on Saturday, and I'm sorry to wake you, but there's all this blood and I'm shaking and I'm in pain and I really think I might be dying and maybe I should see a doctor" (187–188). Tellingly, her boyfriend's reply to her breathless assessment is only "Again?" (188). The passage in the third person therefore constitutes a brief respite for the reader as much as for the experiencing self and speaks to the meaning of madness as suffering that applies when Wurtzel relates to herself and the world in the first person.

Marya Hornbacher's *Wasted: A Memoir of Anorexia and Bulimia* includes many deviations from the first-person singular pronoun to the second- and third-person singular as well as the first-person plural pronoun. In some cases, these deviations constitute literary representations of extreme states of mind, as the narrating self suggests: When the experiencing self is close to death by starvation and finds that she can no longer write, the narrating self muses that it is because she had "lost the sense of first person, the sense of being in the world that writing requires" (*Wasted* 261). However, unlike Wurtzel, who deviates from the first-person singular only briefly, and unlike authors diagnosed with DID and whose choice of pronouns and narrative situations emphatically speaks to their sense of being in the world, Hornbacher's use of pronouns often constitutes an explicit, extended retreat of the textual selves from the narrative that fulfils multiple related functions.

In some cases, intertextual references to the psychiatric discourse enable interpretations of pronoun switches as literary representations of the subjective experience of symptoms such as an intense sense of disconnection. For example, the narrating self explains that from earliest childhood, she often assumed a disembodied perspective outside of herself. She states that "copious research" calls this phenomenon "objectification consciousness" and found that women with eating disorders have the habit of "perceiving themselves through other eyes, as if there were some Great Observer looking over their shoulder" (*Wasted* 14). *Wasted* frequently emulates this habit in passages like the following:

> The girl gets up each day and creates herself out of cloth and paint. She writes at night about men who looked, and boys who touched, and weight…. She remembers … waiting for the man who will corner her in her room, with his knife, and slice her apart….
> She wants her mother and father to save her. She says this, and Dad asks in earnest: From what?
> *From myself.*
> My night fears ended as suddenly as they began [86–87].

Here, Hornbacher further emphasizes the sense of disconnection that the third-person singular creates by establishing the artificiality and construct-edness of "[t]he girl … herself" rather than that of her social identity or façade. It furthermore *reports* that the girl writes about men, boys, and her weight rather than including excerpts from her writing and is thus twice removed from the lived experience of being looked at, touched or weighted down by one's body. Finally, rather than allowing the one and a half pages in the third-person singular to float untethered and isolated from the rest of her narrative in a way that would suggest a more general statement about female teenage angst and questions of identity, Hornbacher specifically identifies as the girl when she claims the girl's night terrors as her own, thus representing her shifting, detached sense of self. By establishing a connec-tion between a sense of being removed from oneself and eating disorders, the memoir privileges interpretations of pronoun switches as representa-tions of Hornbacher's lived experience of madness. However, Hornbacher's self-fashioning as an authority on eating disorders and her copious refer-ences to psychiatric concepts and research also elevate these passages from being merely about her personal, subjective experience and instead con-tribute to the production of a larger truth about eating disorders that she happened to "liv[e] out at intimate levels" (Fee, "Broken" 2). In this manner, pronoun switches contribute to the production of a subjective truth that is validated by psychiatric truth *and simultaneously* shift the focus from her specific life story to the literary illustration of more general concepts.

While Hornbacher's use of the second-person singular pronoun can also represent detachment from lived experience and her (past) self, its effects are far more varied. Because the shift to "you" frequently occurs when Hornbacher describes the indignities of life on eating disorder wards (cf. *Wasted* 144–152) or expounds on her eating disorders in a particularly graphic fashion, it also manages her shame. For example, she switches to the second-person singular for three pages to narrate in a spectacularly vis-ceral fashion how the experiencing self bought ipecac syrup to induce vom-iting and overdosed on it. The narrating self claims, "you don't even get the stall door shut. You vomit in insane, ripping heaves, blood spattering on the seat. You throw up a carrot stick, a pretzel, quarts of water, blood…. Your hands will not do as they're told, you have to use both hands to get toilet paper, wipe off the seat, the walls, the floor" (*Wasted* 171). In this passage, the second-person singular elevates the shameful revelation of a complete loss of control over her body in a public bathroom to the abstraction of general statements or instructional discourse. Hornbacher thus uses the second-person singular to create distance between herself and the events she narrates.

However, unlike a narration in the third-person singular which could be used for general claims as well—"if *one* overdoses on ipecac …"—the second-person singular eventually leads to "the projection of story experientiality," i.e., the "the quasi-mimetic evocation of real-life experience" (Fludernik 226; 12).[5] As Monika Fludernik's explains in her analysis of narratives in the second-person singular, the "[y]ou here at first seems to involve *me*, the reader, projecting an everyday situation with which one can identify" (Fludernik 227), in this case, Hornbacher's desire to become thin. Even though the "you" eventually loses its deictic relation to (non-eating-disordered) implied readers by merit of its increasingly specific descriptions of the process of purging, this passage and others like it still implicate readers. Despite a growing sense of disgust for the narrated events, the continued use of the second-person singular pronoun and the immediacy suggested by the present tense force readers to keep imagining themselves purging in the same uncontrollable fashion as Hornbacher did, thereby transmitting shame or fear and blurring the boundaries between the non-eating-disordered, normal implied reader and the mad experiencing self (cf. Fludernik 226–232). The switch to "you" and the affective identification it entails constitute a very aggressive way of communicating the lived experience of eating disorders but also manages intimacy. The transmission of story experientiality draws implied readers close at the precise moment Hornbacher's graphic descriptions of gut-wrenching sickness create a desire for distance. The passage therefore not only mirrors Hornbacher's own sense of being perversely drawn to and simultaneously repulsed by her bulimia (cf. Chapter Three) but also symbolically replays the ravenous taking in and expelling of food in the management of intimacy and distance to the reader. As such, Hornbacher's use of the second-person singular pronoun not only reproduces the subjective truth of eating disorders for readers but also constitutes an aggressive reaction to stigma that Erving Goffman calls "hostile bravado" (*Stigma* 17): Hornbacher aggressively lingers on those aspects of her stigmatized condition which implied readers will find repulsive and thus exerts control over the reactions her confessions of deviance will receive.

Moreover, the use of "you" manages shame and complicates power relations between author and readers because it turns the voyeuristic potential of the scene on its head. The passage quoted above not only presents the experiencing self as an object engaging in clandestine, pathologized behavior and satisfies voyeuristic desires but also forces readers to imagine *themselves* in the position of said object. Hornbacher's textual selves thus also evade the voyeuristic look that humiliates and shames its object (cf. Laine 33), reverses it, and fixes it on the reader. Hornbacher's memoir thus includes titillating descriptions of deviant behavior while also managing the shame connected to offering her experiencing self to the voyeuristic gaze. Furthermore, her account produces a tension between the

representation of madness as a spectacle and as something to be hidden, a
cause for shame.

Just like her narration in the second-person singular, Hornbacher's use
of the first-person plural pronoun incriminates the female implied reader
but also elevates her claims to a socio-cultural critique of gender roles and
female beauty standards. As such, the use of "we" makes truth claims about
how women in contemporary Western society relate to food and speaks to
the social aspects of her lived experience. For example, the narrating self
mocks the fact that a lack of appetite is a core aspect of the performance of
femininity:

> To hear women tell it, we're never hungry.... Food makes us queasy, food makes us
> itchy, food is too messy.... And yet, this maxim is hardly new. A lady will eat like a bird.
> A lady will look like a bird, fragile boned and powerful when in flight, lifting weightless
> into the air. We feign disinterest and laugh, and creep into the kitchen some nights, ...
> shoveling cold casseroles, ice cream, jelly, cheese, into our mouths, swallowing without
> chewing.... Ashamed of this, we turn skeletons into goddesses [117–119].

In this passage, the "we" suggests a socio-cultural environment *perpetuated
by all women* in which starving denotes the acceptance of disempowering
gender norms such as feminine fragility but also romanticizes the tran-
scendence of the traditionally feminine realm of the material ("powerful
when in flight"). In combination with Hornbacher's socio-cultural critique,
the use of the first-person plural pronoun not only generalizes her experience and reproduces mechanisms of female bonding over shared concerns
of eating and weight (cf. *Wasted* 283–284) but also restores agency since
it presents beauty ideals as self-imposed rather than merely enforced by
patriarchal structures. In this manner, Hornbacher's use of "we" can allevi-
ate the sense of aloneness, empowers women, and makes claims about the
subjective, cultural, and psychosocial truth of having an eating disorder.
Moreover, it represents (her type of) madness as a response to unhealthy
socio-cultural pressures and creates a tension to the medicalizing framework of the psychiatric discourse which predominantly roots it in neurobi-
ology and genetic predispositions, i.e., the individual and more specifically
herself. Overall, pronoun switches contribute to Hornbacher's careful management of shame and intimacy to both the implied reader and the experiencing self.

As this section showed, the switches in pronouns and narrative perspective in combination with intertextual references to the psychiatric discourse contribute to the representation of the artistic, subjective truth of
madness. However, variations in the use of pronouns within a diagnostic category also illustrate the diversity of lived experience and therefore
problematize the general truth claims which the psychiatric discourse
formulates. Memoirs in my corpus thus express their highly conflicted

relationship to the truth claims of the psychiatric discourse on the level of narration. Additionally, the use of pronouns produces further meanings of madness like trauma or a loss of the sense of self and ultimately contributes to the creation of madness as a floating signifier.

Markedly literary techniques such as deviations from the traditional first-person singular pronoun produce other textual tensions as well. Especially the second-person pronoun contributes to the tension between the creation of intimacy or affective identification and the desire for distance or even repulsion. Likewise, narrative situations other than autodiegetic narrations of singular and unified textual selves add to the transmission of story experientiality or the impression of authenticity. However, the marked constructedness of texts that rely on literary techniques creates the impression of artificiality, thus introducing another tension.

Defamiliarized Narratives

Impressions of artificiality and constructedness are further increased by elements of narratives that have a "defamiliariz[ing]" effect (Shklovsky 11–12) due to their deviation from the fluid literary conventions for the "quasi-mimetic evocation of real-life experience" (Fludernik 12). Examples of these defamiliarizing textual elements are a high degree of narrative fragmentation, representations of mental processes that destabilize common sense notions of how the human mind works, and scenarios that contradict known laws of the physical world.[6] Of course, some deviations from conversational storytelling and the realist mode, such as omniscient narrators, have long been habitualized, as have impossible scenarios in non-realist genres such as science fiction or fantasy. In fact, the tropes of trauma writing have even conventionalized the fragmentation of narrative chronology or experiencing selves. What interests me here, then, is how texts in my corpus use defamiliarizing narrative techniques to convey their lived experience in a genre whose conventions dictate the realist mode.

As Russian literary critic Viktor Shklovsky suggested, defamiliarizing uses of language and narrative "increase the difficulty and length of perception … [thereby] remov[ing] objects from the automatism of perception" (11, 13), and enabling new ways of seeing them. Literary language and unusual narrative structures, then, allow for new ways of understanding the subjective, artistic truth of madness and the mad.

However, these new ways of understanding madness are predicated upon the reader's willingness to employ the literary mode of reading, whose central features are an increased willingness to explore ambiguity as well as the assumptions that a text conveys more than its denotative meaning and that "complications of language ultimately have a communicative purpose" (Culler 27). Readers are more disposed to engage with "obscurities and apparent irrelevancies, without assuming that this makes no sense" (Culler 27) when texts receive the institutional label "literature." Once a text has undergone a process of selection—they have been published, reprinted, received prizes—and found to be well-constructed, it "gives us reason to expect that the results of our reading efforts will be 'worth it'" (Culler 27). The assumption that complications have a point and that individuals and institutions vouch for it by bestowing the label "literature" is called the "hyper-protected cooperative principle" (cf. Culler 25–27). While texts in my corpus have indeed undergone a process of selection and even reached best-seller status, the fact that their authors are discredited subjects and that deep-seated stigma beliefs associate madness with incoherence (Wood 1–3) endangers the hyper-protected cooperative principle.

Nevertheless, texts in my corpus allow readers to find significance in defamiliarized uses of narrative conventions through their intertextual references to the psychiatric discourse. The psychiatric discourse creates a frame of reference that enables readers to recuperate, e.g., fragmented narrative subjectivities as representations of trauma because psychiatric truth claims establish dissociation and splitting as reactions to horrific abuse. Because texts in my corpus tend to use defamiliarizing techniques only when they narrate periods of acute madness and employ much more conventional forms to describe times of remission, readers can assume that authors are able to express themselves in a coherent, straightforward prose and use defamiliarizing techniques for literary effects. I therefore hold that, despite the authors' status as discredited subject, the hyper-protected cooperative principle remains intact, and readers readily assume that defamiliarized uses of narrative serve a purpose.

Truddi Chase's memoir of dissociative identity disorder draws upon the artistic and self-referential but increasingly conventionalized tropes of trauma narratives. To readers familiar with the aesthetics of trauma narratives, the narrative representation of *their traumatic experience is relatively conventional: Like several other trauma narratives, Chase's memoir uses chronological fragmentation, repetitions with incremental new revelations, circularity, and fragmentation of narrative personae to convey "horrific actions that seem to defy the normal methods of ordinary narratives" (Richardson, "What" 38; cf. also Gibbs 14–35). However, Chase's memoir goes beyond even these narrative devices and challenges basic notions of personhood in the representation Chase's original singular self and mirror images to convey the utterly disturbing subjective truth of her lived experience.

These challenges to the nature of personhood do not derive from contradicting statements that are made by individual alters and the written version of Chase's therapist as the story is told by an extradiegetic, heterodiegetic omniscient narrator. This choice alone is unusual in life writing as "[n]arratorial omniscience in the authorial mode is certainly unavailable to real narrators in natural interactions; yet it is the kind of privilege, that … affords the reader the comforting illusion of reliability, objectivity and absolute knowledge" (Fludernik 168). In this case, however, the supposed reliability and omniscience of the narrator only exacerbate the contradictions and the resulting mystification which transmits one of the central aspects of Chase's lived experience to the reader, i.e., confusion and a deep sense of incongruity.

Chase's original singular self—the so-called "first-born child"—presents the first instance in a chain of paradoxes that characterize the representation of narrative subjectivity in the memoir. During the first experience of sexual abuse, "the first-born child died at two years old, she split into two cores: one potential child, the other potential adult" (Chase 340). Alternately, the narrator and alters who, the narrator claims, know "the truth of her own reality" (80), state that these cores "slept" (340), that they "died" and that this death was permanent (235), or that they are once more "coming alive; not as the dictionary defined 'alive,' but as it was defined within the mechanisms of the Troop Formation [Chase's internal system of alters]" (119). Like Schrödinger's cat, the fragmented cores of the first-born child are therefore simultaneously dead and alive and thus defy conventional notions of existence and personhood which reflects Chase's highly complex sense of self on the level of narrative subjectivity.

The complexity of narrative subjectivity is further increased because *after* the split cores of the first-born child "died," an ever-growing number of "mirror-images" was created to absorb the sustained abuse and, after the "deaths" of some of them, even mirror-images of mirror-images (340, 277). Even considering the unstable nature of death in Chase's internal system, the notion of a mirror-image whose object of reflection no longer exists creates another unthinkable phenomenon. Yet another passage that transcends conventional cognitive structures describes a part of the setting of Chase's internal world, "the Tunnel": "The child core and her mirror-image hung inside … a space that was not a space because they were contained by nothing. The first-born child and her mirror-image shared that same space and shared nothing because there was nothing left" (276). Paradoxes such as these reproduce the experiencing selves' difficulties of coming to terms with their internal reality for the reader and therefore transmit a central aspect of Chase's lived experience through defamiliarization, that is, literary techniques. Beyond this "quasi-mimetic evocation of real-life experience" (Fludernik 12), these cryptic passages also suggest that there remain aspects of madness that cannot be broken down and remain beyond conventional modes of thought.

In Lori Schiller's memoir of schizophrenia, Schiller's narrating self generally distinguishes carefully between her detached perspective and the experiencing self's immediate experience of symptoms. However, in the second chapter of the memoir, the narrating self embraces two contradictory realities and reproduces an aspect of the lived experience of madness for the reader, i.e., the challenge of telling reality from horrific psychotic beliefs that the schizophrenic individual faces.

The defamiliarizing and shocking effect of mirroring symptoms on the level of narration depends on the first chapter's more distanced representation of the experiencing self's first bout of psychosis. The narrating self explains that one summer, during her late teens, "my head was filled with wild, strange thoughts" and voices that were always "pounding into my head. They began to curse and revile me: 'You whore bitch who isn't worth a piece of crap!' they yelled at me" (Schiller and Bennett 6). In these quotes, the narrating self retains a strict conceptual distance to both the experiencing self and the symptoms of madness by using the past tense and by concretizing symptoms into entities—"the Voices" (Schiller and Bennett 6), the capitalization of which suggests a proper name—who use direct speech to communicate with the experiencing self. Even though the narrating self admits, "[s]ince that time, I have never been completely free of those voices" (7), the distance to the past self and symptoms fashion the narrating self as a somewhat normal person who describes the intense madness of a past self. The memoir further strengthens the impression of normalcy when the second chapter moves away from the first manifestation of symptoms and begins the narration of her childhood—a time when she "felt well, a happy healthy girl … with a normal head and heart" (7), thus returning to the genre-typical chronological account of her lived experience.

However, the second chapter immediately defies expectations of a nostalgic account of a happy childhood when Schiller narrates an incident that is not only horrifying in its content but—through its narrative construction—reproduces for the reader a fundamental distrust in the reality of events as textual selves perceive them. At the very beginning of the second chapter, the narrating self confesses that there is one childhood memory that "plagues" her (9), namely that of the family dog, a black mongrel, who was kept on a very short chain.

> One day as I was in the kitchen with him, I suddenly grew very angry.
> In a burst of rage, I grabbed a nearby golf club and began beating the dog furiously. At first he barked hysterically. But because of the chain, he could not escape. He began to foam at the mouth. As I beat him, one by one his legs collapsed. He kept struggling to rise, but I wouldn't let him. I kept hitting him, and hitting him, and hitting him.

He fell to the ground. Then he stopped barking. His body writhed in horrible spasms, blood dribbling from his ears and mouth. After a while he stopped moving. Dead.

To this day, I do not know why I did it …

But there is one big problem with this memory: It isn't true. It never happened.

My mom and dad say we never had such a dog. They say that the incident I remember so clearly never took place. My brothers, Mark and Steven, agree [9–10].

Because the narrating self, who previously fashioned herself as reliable, first affirms and then undermines the reality of the event, the passage quoted above reproduces aspects of Schiller's lived experience for the reader, albeit in a mediated, less extreme form.

Among these aspects is a shock, relief, and confusion at the realization that the events never took place in the reality occupied by Schiller's family and that the narrating self is not reliable after all. The text creates this shock by producing the truth of the dog's death in several ways. Before the narrating self reveals that the event only ever took place in her mind, the narrating self's self-fashioning as reliable and the evocation of the confessional mode through the admission that the "memory" "plagued" her, lead the reader to assume that Schiller produces the truth of an atrocity she committed through confession. Furthermore, the detailed description of the dog's gruesome death, which is free from obvious embellishment or interpretation, "call[s] to mind the abundance of objects surrounding us in everyday life and thereby support[s] the effect of well-observed, faithful representation" (Fludernik 160). The passage further contributes to the impression of truthfulness when it plays on "cultural verisimilitude" (Todorov 19). Cultural verisimilitude refers to the relation between the text and what readers believe to be probable courses of events based on "a scattered discourse that in part belongs to each of the individuals of a society but of which none may claim ownership; in other words, … *public opinion*" (Todorov 19) or, in this case, stigma beliefs. Due to widespread stigma beliefs that individuals with schizophrenia are violent, unpredictable, and dangerous, the description of the incident appears to be true. By drawing upon these literary techniques of truth production, Schiller therefore conveys the lived experience of having hallucinations so vivid that they seem "more real than the outside reality" (Schiller and Bennett 103) and furthermore reproduces her pervasive sense of confusion to the reader. Moreover, the passage complicates neat distinctions between a mad experiencing self and a carefully managed narrating self which contributes to the central tension in self-fashioning that runs through my corpus.

The passages analyzed above use defamiliarizing narrative structures and paradoxical representations of narrative subjectivity to establish that one meaning of madness is confusion and that it cannot be grasped with conventional modes of thought. Moreover, these confrontations with transgressive narrative situations emulate a mechanism common to trauma writing, i.e., they "leave the reader in a situation similar to that which the witnesses [here: mad persons] themselves are facing, though the stakes are radically different" (Iversen 98). That is, they use markedly literary techniques to evoke complex, unpleasant emotions like incomprehension, horror, confusion or irritation and thereby transmit "suffering that approximates that of the victims" (Gibbs 20).

Defamiliarizing Uses of Language

Another markedly literary technique that communicates the symbolic, artistic truth of madness in ways that the clinical language of psychiatry cannot, is the use of self-referential, defamiliarized language. For example, cryptic passages mirror the confusion of individuals with lived experience of psychosis and speak to the problems of communication whereas sentence length reflects sluggish or overexcited minds. As with unconventional narrative structures, intertextual references to the psychiatric discourse privilege readings of defamiliarized language as representations of the lived experience of madness.

Kristina Morgan's *Mind Without a Home* enables a reading of defamiliarized language and narrative structures as representations of her lived experience of schizophrenia right from the beginning when she presents a description of her condition that is adapted from the *DSM V*, and marked as such in a footnote, as the memoir's epigraph. The epigraph reads, "Schizophrenia may be characterized by delusions, hallucinations, disorganized speech (e.g., frequent derailment or incoherence), grossly disorganized or catatonic behavior, and other negative symptoms (e.g., diminished emotional expression and reduced drive)…" (viii). Epigraphs are usually reserved for quotations from canonical literary texts that invite comparisons or supply a context and mode of interpretation. In Morgan's case, the epigraph establishes the centrality of the psychiatric discourse for the interpretation of Morgan's memoir.

The epigraph's reference to incoherence as a characteristic of schizophrenia enables a reading where the degree to which Morgan's language is defamiliarized mirrors the severity of the experiencing self's symptoms. Morgan's writing style is fairly conventional at the beginning of her memoir when she describes a childhood that was free from symptoms. For example, she portrays her younger sister and her friends coherently and concisely as quintessential teenage girls who start to discover their femininity: "Rose wears ankle bracelets and small heart necklaces. She hangs with friends who giggle over boys in teen magazines. When anyone in her group is threatened, they are ferocious, like small radios turned up high" (15). The simile, while somewhat unusual, still conveys succinctly that the girls express their aggression through words rather than actions and that they are surprisingly loud considering their size. Passages written in this relatively conventional style not only keep the memoir accessible, establish biographical data, and relate family anecdotes, but they also show that Morgan *can* write about her lived experience normally or coherently.

However, imagery and language become increasingly cryptic in sections that describe the onset of Morgan's condition and even more so when her experiencing self is confined to mental hospitals. The memoir further emphasizes the experiencing self's confusion and disorientation in its structure as it is organized into short, disjointed, journal-like entries that range in length from a third of a page to five pages. While surrounding entries provide a small degree of context by alluding to the experiencing self's stay at a mental hospital, the following excerpt stands by itself under the title "Recognition":

> The earth broke in front of me. I could not grab the sun; holy shit!—I'm glad it will be over soon. Life is not a canister filled with gummy bears. End this conflict with skinny therapists who dismiss me because I say red is more than red. Don't they see death lingers in the crevice of earth at whose lip I stand? The sun throws me no handle but slips behind the line of roofs marched up against the mountain. I am left to wish for ears that have been taught exactly how to hear. The earth did break in front of me. I could not grab the sun [216].

The information from the epigraph enables narrativizations of this and similar passages as literary representations of the experiencing self's altered state of mind while also transmitting (a weaker, mediated version of) the disorientation that is part of Morgan's lived experience.

This passage does not merely provide an example of the disorganized speech of an individual with schizophrenia—textbooks for clinical psychiatry do that as well (cf. Black and Andreasen 38–42; B. Lewis, *Moving* 55–56)—but it also speaks to a part of the lived truth of her condition that goes beyond the experience of codified symptoms. In fact, the passage addresses the social experience of having a mental disorder, which, for Morgan, includes the incomprehension of others and the rejection of her speech as meaningless. Although the passage quoted above does not provide details, it conveys that the experiencing self just lived through a cataclysmic event ("The earth broke in front of me") and could not find a point of orientation ("I could not grab the sun"). The content of previous chapters suggests that the narrating self refers to the death of her grandmother to whom the experiencing self was very close. Therapists dismiss her because of the alternate meanings she perceives ("red is more than red") and are oblivious that Morgan feels herself to be on the brink of death or suicide ("death lingers in the crevice of earth at whose lip I stand"). The sun, which represents a central organizing force that structures life and provides orientation, does not come to her aid ("throws me no handle") but leaves her field of sight as it recedes behind the well-ordered lives and social limitations which the line of roofs and the mountain symbolize. Morgan thus desperately yearns for a person who understands her. The last two sentences have multiple communicative purposes. The repetition of the first two sentences at the end of the entry constitutes a plea to be heard this time, alludes to her inability to express herself in another manner but also insists on the validity of her subjective truth when she alters the first sentence to "The earth *did* break..." (emphasis added). Morgan thus uses defamiliarized language to reproduce the experience of impeded communication and to convey the desperation she felt when she lived through extreme states of mind and could not make herself understood.

A couple of pages later, the narrating self even pleads with the implied reader directly to try and understand by first relating another instance of being dismissed as incoherent and then switching to the imperative mode. One time, a therapist asked her during group therapy how she felt, and the experiencing self's reply was "[t]he trees are bent, shed leaves. I need brooms to sweep them up" (229). When the therapist moves away and starts talking to someone else, the narrating self wonders, "Can't she hear my ABCs, hear that I'm dying over a missing broom?... Stay listening to me long enough to learn that a broom ties me to leaves, ties me to Grandmother, ties me to the grief of Grandma, to my heart.... Please help me be less silent. Don't forget about me because I speak on slant" (229). Through her reference to "my ABCs," the narrating self implies that her communication is organized, albeit in an idiosyncratic manner. The expression furthermore suggests that the experiencing self tries to communicate sentiments that are as basic to human nature as the alphabet is to writing. Her switch to the imperative mode not only addresses the therapist but also implores the reader to be patient with her attempts at communication and not to discard her utterances simply because she expresses herself in unusual ways ("speak on slant"). In these entries, Morgan calls attention to the social experience of mental illness in a culture that associates meaninglessness with her condition and forestalls any attempts at communication. Moreover, both entries represent mental healthcare professionals who exclusively interpret Morgan's speech as symptomatic and thus formulates an implicit but strong critique of the way the mad are pathologized and dismissed by therapists.

Morgan's memoir increases the defamiliarizing effect of passages such as those quoted above by emulating the disorganized language of the psychotic experiencing self on the level of narrative transmission. Unlike Lori Schiller, who was also diagnosed with schizophrenia and restricted associative leaps or neologism to the direct speech or interior monologues of her experiencing self (cf. Schiller and Bennett 149–152, 183–184), Morgan does not domesticate her representation of schizophrenia by mediating between the experiencing self's madness and the reader through a (mostly) normal narrating self. Instead, Morgan's narrating self switches back and forth between the highly idiosyncratic language that suggests an immediate, quasi-mimetic representation of the experiencing self's state of mind and a more conventional language that accompanies a detached, retrospective perspective. For example, the entry that follows "Recognition" reads,

> I run through the shadows of hills, cast off at a loss. My heart's pump, loudly triumphant, silencing nothing—not a trombone for humanity, but a pipeline for the personal. It beats hard. I prolong introductions. Splice. One artery to another. Spliced. Following flowing, ferocious. The poet Howe, I salute open water.
> I had a bad night. They jacked me up on Haldol.[7] We have a nation that pushes medication for everything [216–217].

In this passage, only a new paragraph marks the abrupt transition from allusive imagery and fragmented sentences to a retrospective evaluation of the experiencing self's state of mind and a more general critique of the reliance on psychotropic drugs in the US mental healthcare system. In this manner, the memoir illustrates another truth of the lived experience of schizophrenia, namely the quick and fluid transitions between states of normalcy and madness. Additionally, Morgan's incorporation of defamiliarized language that emulates symptoms on the level of narration forces readers to engage with this mode of expression which imitates interactions with a floridly psychotic person who drifts in and out of conventional language. These passages from Morgan's memoir therefore make a point about the importance and problems of communicating with the mad by using defamiliarized language.

Although Marya Hornbacher's use of language does not show the same degree of defamiliarization as Kristina Morgan's, her changing style still creates the aesthetic illusion of being a direct representation of the experiencing self's state of mind. In her memoir *Madness: A Bipolar Mind*, Hornbacher uses a combination of psychiatric truth claims and literary techniques such as marked differences in sentence structure and sentence length to evoke the two extreme states that characterize her condition, i.e., depression and mania. As the narrating self points out at the beginning of the text, typical symptoms of clinical depression include despair, lethargy, and a preoccupation with dark thoughts (*Madness* 6). In passages that narrate how the experiencing self lived through depressive episodes, sentences tend to be very short and paratactic. For example, Hornbacher describes her behavior during her first depressive phase in the following manner: "I sigh. I despair of ever getting up again. I cannot move. I will not move. Everything is horrible. I want to go to sleep forever" (19). During another depressive phase, the text reads "I am in my mother's guest room. I am lying in bed. I am utterly still. The light is blinding. I pull the pillow over my face" (141). The shortness of the sentences evokes the lethargy of a depressed person who needs to rest frequently whereas the paratactic structure suggests that the experiencing self reduces everything—movement, interaction with the outside world, and variety in self-expression—to the bare minimum. Furthermore, the first-person pronoun occupies the prominent first position in most of the sentences which mirrors how the experiencing self's awareness of the world is reduced to an egocentric focus on one's own suffering that can characterize extreme depression. Sentence structure and sentence length therefore contribute to a literary representation of the sluggish, depressed mind as well as the monotony of suffering that formed part of Hornbacher's lived experience.

Similarly, during the experiencing self's manic phases, sentences are significantly longer and more complex to reflect her rapid speech and agitation. For example, one sentence runs fifteen lines before it comes to a full stop, which emulates the experiencing self's loquacity (*Madness* 39–40). Another passage narrates the experiencing self's agitation and elation in the following manner: "I stand up in my chair, sit down in my chair, hop out of my chair, do a little Snoopy dance, my hospital gowns flapping about me like wings—I've grown inordinately fond of these gowns and am wearing several at once, 'for dramatic effect'—and I sing the Snoopy song, stand on my chair again, imitating Snoopy as vulture, plop down" (73). The verb phrases, which share a subject but repeat the object "chair" three times, emphasize the action rather than the acting subject. This relative absence of the subject evokes an uncontrolled, mindless activity and a restlessness which finds an outlet in the intense interaction with the experiencing self's environment, in this case, the chair. The progressive forms "flapping" and "imitating" add to the impression of agitation by implying simultaneity. The marked differences in style therefore evoke the diametrically opposed states of Hornbacher's condition and lend literary expression to both psychiatric truth claims and her lived experience.

The passage that describes the experiencing self's physical agitation does not merely represent the lived experience of symptoms in a literary manner but also reflects attempts at shame management and contributes to the double self-fashioning as normal and mad. Throughout *Madness*, the narration creates the impression of immediacy through the present tense and the reflection of the experiencing self's condition on the level of language which obscures the distance between the narrating and the experiencing self. However, the passage also undermines the impression of immediacy through the ironic and distanced way the narrating self assumes the experiencing self's point of view. For example, the narrating self no longer shares the experiencing self's fondness of hospital gowns but rather describes it as "inordinate" (73), that is, excessive, and only provides the experiencing self's reason for putting on several at once in quotation marks. Moreover, the phrase "I've grown inordinately fond of these gowns and am wearing several at once, 'for dramatic effect'" (73) is isolated from the rest of the passage through dashes which interrupts the flow of narration and evokes a narrating self who seeks to demonstrate her ironic distance and light-hearted mocking of the mad experiencing self. In this manner, the narrating self manages her shame about the experiencing self's insouciant behavior and presents herself as normal in the sense of able to identify and (mockingly) reject transgressions of social norms. Nevertheless, the present tense and the emulation of the experiencing self's state of mind on the level of language still connect the two textual selves and thereby reinforce the self-fashioning as normal *and* mad.

As this section showed, authors in my corpus use defamiliarized language and intertextual references to the psychiatric discourse to communicate the subjective experience of mental disorders. However, memoirs do not merely depict madness as it is defined in the *DSM* in a literary manner but also claim a voice in the discursive construction of madness when they represent the social experience of having a mental illness. Their production of subjective truth therefore goes beyond a mere literary illustration of psychiatric truth claims and shows that madness also means being dismissed as incoherent, being ashamed of one's behavior during bouts of madness, and having a double sense of self. In other words, they establish that being subject to stigma is a crucial aspect of the lived experience of madness and thereby promote an understanding of their condition that does not restrict itself to the neuropsychological perspective but also takes the patient's point of view into consideration.

While the speaking position of the psychiatric patient does not have much discursive weight, authors in my corpus still need to authenticate their inside perspective of madness before they can hope to claim a voice in its discursive construction. Beyond providing reproductions of parts of their patient file, eliciting witness testimony from their psychiatrists or families that confirm their patient status (cf. Chapter Three), authors also produce the truth of their identity and of their narrative of madness by employing one of the West's most trusted methods of truth production, namely confession.

Confessing Madness: Truth and Sexuality

All authors in my corpus rely heavily on the confessional mode, and with good reason. As Leigh Gilmore points out, "For many readers, the bedrock of autobiographical narrative is confessional in the sense that the writer and reader can be taken in a particular relation to each other, bound by a demand upon the writer to render a transparent truth" ("American" 661), in this case, the truth of an individual deemed mad. This truth is produced according to the "logic" of contemporary US confessionalism, which "is one of infinite regression. The farther one delves into the juicy details of visceral life … the more truth about that individual shall be known" (Olson 132). The production of truth in life writing is therefore intimately tied up with voyeuristic—and exhibitionistic—pleasures.[8]

Although authors in my corpus confess all kinds of transgressions such as mendacity, theft, and addiction to alcohol or illegal substances, this section focuses on confessions relating to the sexual. Confessions of deviant sexual fantasies and the loss of male sexual potency or what is deemed feminine purity contribute to the conceptualization of madness as (moral) degeneration. Moreover, these confessions illustrate that madness entails further blemishes, particularly when mad individuals try to numb the suffering connected to mental disorders with transgressive behavior. Spectacular confessions of sexual behavior—or the lack thereof—therefore don't merely entertain or titillate but actively contribute to the production of meaning in my corpus.

Mark Vonnegut's memoir of schizophrenia includes particularly spectacular confessions of his deviant sexual thoughts which fashion the experiencing self as a morally and intellectually degenerate madman: During one of his psychotic episodes, the experiencing self stayed with a friend and her family, and the narrating self explains, "Mary made me tea now and then or a sandwich or gave me paper and crayons to play with. She was terse with me but not unloving, just a harried mother with a big problem son. Trying to keep me out from underfoot. Trying to reason with me on an adult level wasn't very rewarding" (Vonnegut 182). The narrating self immediately extends this impression and imagines himself as a part of that friend's family, referring to her husband as "Daddy" and their toddler as his sister. He states, "If Daddy knew that Marky wanted to fuck Mommy, Daddy probably wouldn't like it very much. If Daddy knew that Marky wanted to fuck his sister, Daddy would most likely not approve. If Daddy knew that Marky wanted to fuck the little doggy, he might think his son a little weird. He maybe might think that Marky should have an operation" (182). Note how Vonnegut abandons the nuanced perspective of a narrating self who looks back upon his past incapacitation and his friend's efforts to assume the language and mindset of his experiencing self. The simple, childish language ("Mommy," "Daddy," "the little doggy") and parallel sentence structure in combination with the coarse term "fuck" creates the impression of a regressed, yet highly sexualized man and thereby evokes the trope of the mad sexual deviant as well as stigma beliefs that conflate madness with mental incapacitation. Since this state of mind is mirrored on the level of narrative transmission, the passage is particularly scandalizing as it blurs the boundaries between a past, mad experiencing self and a present, normal narrating self.

While the passage quoted above certainly includes spectacular revelations about the experiencing self, the passage also violates central tropes of confessional writing that were established by Jean-Jacques Rousseau. Dave Tell summarizes Rousseau's tenets succinctly by stating that only "the unhinged and exclamatory, in direct opposition to words 'organized as discourse' can bespeak the uninhibited effusion of the heart" (134). Consequently, Rousseau was deeply suspicious of "scripted or articulate speech [as it] indicates the manipulation of the inner self or its strategic deployment" (Tell 135). Vonnegut's passage, by contrast, is carefully calibrated for effect: The abrupt deviation from the narrating self's usual academic and poetic register to a coarse language and moral naiveté, the self-reference in the third-person singular, and the diminutive form of his name all constitute literary, i.e., markedly constructed, attempts at representing the experiencing self's extreme state of mind. Due to this violation of conventions of confessional writing, it cannot unambiguously produce the truth of the experiencing self's deviant thoughts or redeem the speaking subject through the ritual of purification that is confession.

Instead, the primary function of this passage is to manage Vonnegut's shame. After admitting that the experiencing self—a college-educated man in his mid-twenties—was treated like a child by a well-intentioned friend who felt that he did not respond to reason, the narrating self begins an aggressive, over-the-top performance of mental incapacitation, regression, and sexual deviance. By acting out the harshest stigma beliefs about the intellectual degeneration and sexual threat of the mad in an exaggerated and artificial manner, the narrating self points to the constructedness of stigma beliefs. Moreover, the passage demonstrates that Vonnegut's condition entailed the humiliation of having his friends talk down to him and therefore shows that his lived experience of madness is intimately connected to the affect of shame—an aspect that the *DSM* does not address at all. Vonnegut's confessional performance of regression therefore produces a more complete view of his lived experience and thus supplements the psychiatric discourse.

Other confessions regarding sexual behavior contradict popular beliefs about the sexual magnetism of mad artists and fictional mad-women and furthermore create a tension to the romanticizing and eroticizing descriptions of madness in my corpus (see Chapter Two). Robert B. Oxnam, William Styron, and David Smola all confess that they lost all interest in intercourse. When discussing the physical and emotional effects of his condition, William Styron explains that his "libido also made an early exit [after the onset of the depressive episode], as it does in most major illnesses—it is the superfluous need of a body in beleaguered emergency" (47). When his psychiatrist puts him on new antidepressants and informs him that they can have the side effect of impotence, the narrating self comments scathingly, "I wondered if he seriously thought that this juiceless and ravaged semi-invalid with the shuffle and the ancient wheeze … woke up each morning … eager for carnal fun" (60). As he had been similarly affected by his mental disorder, David Smola's experiencing self even heralds the first erection after the onset of his depressive episode as the sign of his return to normalcy (207). Confessions of a loss of sexual potency therefore further establish the truth of madness as a loss of vitality and undermine popular stereotypes.

Tropes of the sexually attractive madwoman are deeply embedded in Western literature and art. Katarzyna Szmigiero states that some of the most famous examples of the trope of the erotically appealing madwoman are Shakespeare's Ophelia in *Hamlet*, Scott F. Fitzgerald's Nicole in *Tender Is the Night*, and Erich Maria Remarque's Francis in *The Black Obelisk*. Ophelia's madness, Szmigiero claims, "was manifested in her disarrayed, frequently incomplete clothing and loose hair," as well as in the singing of bawdy songs which "signified that insanity robbed her of her feminine modesty" and promised sexual abandon (58). The eroticization of the mad Ophelia is particularly striking in paintings of her by Eugène Delacroix, Arthur Hughes, and Alexandre Cabanel who depict her seductively sprawled in or next to a river, the scene of her suicide. They painted her with her breasts exposed, caressing her chest (Delacroix), down on her back (Hughes), and richly adorned with symbols of sexuality like flowers or her long, lush hair (Cabanel). All three painters show Ophelia facing the viewer with an expression that pleads for rescue or beckons the viewer to come closer. Whereas Delacroix' painting is kept in dark, earthy tones, Hughes and Cabanel's Ophelias are rendered in the vivid colors and lush detail preferred in the romantic pre–Raphaelite and *l'art pompous* traditions known for their aestheticized, even kitschy depictions of female beauty and intense emotion. This short description shows how well-established the trope of the madwoman, whose "deranged mind adds to her charms … [rendering her] seductive and vulnerable at the same time," really is (Szmigiero 58).

While several female experiencing selves are highly promiscuous and refer to the psychiatric discourse to interpret this behavior as an attempt to cope with the suffering their madness causes (cf. Hornbacher, *Wasted* 73; Hornbacher, *Madness* 140–147; Wurtzel 120–122), their representations of their promiscuity tend to focus on the mundane and mechanic aspects of indiscriminate sexual encounters and are anything but erotic. Elizabeth Wurtzel explains that she started having vaginal intercourse for the sole reason that "[her] mouth was getting tired and chapped from giving so many blowjobs" (160). As her pragmatic reasoning suggests, "there was never any pleasure, no element of partying" in her promiscuity (121). Likewise, Marya Hornbacher's memoir *Wasted* suggests self-destructive impulses rather than pleasure as the driving force behind the experiencing self's promiscuity. Starting at the age of twelve, she had sex with strangers, usually "skanky sons of bitches I picked up like crusty green pennies from the gutters of neighboring towns" (*Wasted* 85). These boys were "butt-ugly," had "obscene pubic mustaches," and tended to "stick their tongue down your throat" after "routine flirtation" (70). The narrating self's low regard for the experiencing self's sexual partners ("pennies"), their repulsive physique, and the intrusion of her body reveal the experiencing self's actions as joyless attempts to numb herself through casual sexual contacts. Like male experiencing selves who lost their ability to comply with the sexual norm of virility, promiscuous behavior in women is a deviation from gendered sexual norms. Authors in my corpus thereby show that madness entails other blemishes, either by directly affecting the afflicted person's bodily functions or by causing them to numb the pain in ways that are socially sanctioned.

This section showed that confessions of the sexual do not merely entertain and titillate but actively contribute to the production of the subjective truth of madness which, in many cases, means suffering, incapacitation, and shame and frequently causes individuals to develop traits that stigmatize them further. Moreover, these confessions create a tension to romanticizing and erotic depictions of madness in my corpus as well as dominant cultural tropes.

Madness as Abject Corporality

Authors in my corpus further elaborate on these truths of madness when they show that mad persons evoke disgust, rejection, and morbid fascination through provocative textual performances of what French-Bulgarian literary theorist and psychoanalyst Julia Kristeva called "the abject" (1).[9] Regardless of the desensitization by the culture of extreme confessionalism in contemporary US media, there are some revelations so intimate and transgressive that audiences will recoil. While a large part of the desire for distance derives from disgust for the deviant, fragmented, and unclean, there is also the need to escape the morbid fascination which these self-representations evoke despite their threat to contaminate the subject, to transgress its boundaries. Mental illness pathographies create this morbid fascination and desire for social distance when they aggressively depict experiencing selves as polluted, polluting, and transgressive in ways that destabilize boundaries between inside and outside, self and Other and thereby simultaneously affirm and undermine stigma beliefs through grotesquely exaggerated performances of stigmatized identities.

According to Kristeva, the earliest form of abjection takes place when the infant develops its subjectivity by learning to distinguish between inside and outside, self and Other (1). It begins with the preverbal child's rejection of the maternal body and continues when the child further establishes its corporal boundaries through the expulsion of certain food items. This expulsion is coupled with an intense, gut-wrenching revulsion and the horror of becoming once more submerged and undifferentiated in the maternal body. The process of abjection is therefore one of purification that constitutes the subject and is repeated when filth, waste, pus, bodily fluids, the dead body, the "immoral, sinister, scheming, and shady ... a terror that dissembles, a hatred that smiles" are excluded from the social order (Kristeva 4; cf. Arya).

The abject, however, is not merely the dirty and pathogenic, an object facing the I which can be pushed away or properly assimilated but "something rejected from which one does not part ... [which] disturbs identity, system, order. What does not respect borders, positions, rules" (Kristeva 4). It inflicts upon the self an intolerable, taboo element that "beseeches, worries, and fascinates desire" (Kristeva 1) to lose one's boundaries once again, and it can therefore be intensely pleasurable as erotic imagery of binging and purging illustrates (cf. Chapter Two). Simultaneously, it produces a "massive and sudden emergence of uncanniness, which, familiar as it might have been in an opaque and forgotten life [i.e., in the maternal body], now harries me as radically separate, loathsome" (Kristeva 2). The concept of the abject, then, accounts for the cultural fascination with and repulsion by the transgression of boundaries and laws that are symbolized by particularly ruthless serial killers and certain types of horror movies that play on disgust, sadism or the fragility of the human body. In this section, I show that passages in my corpus have quite similar effects and produce madness as abjection.

By linking their Otherness to abjection, authors in my corpus evoke the artistic outgrowths of identity-political movements of the 1980s and 1990s that drew upon Kristeva's concept as "the keynote" of their works (Menninghaus 366). These artists held that "all cultural rules ... had, first, to be read from the perspective of what they serve to rule out.... And, secondly, what was officially considered abject had to be embraced, more or less provocatively, as a positive alterity, thus challenging the legitimacy of the cultural discrimination in each case" (Menninghaus 366). Feminists,

African Americans, and homosexual men, particularly those concerned with the discrimination against gay victims of AIDS, "used their bodies as platforms for their politics" (Arya 34). To represent Othered subjectivities and symbolize their societal state of abjection, artists depicted and incorporated bodily fluids and waste matter or used obscenity and images of fragmented, composite or wounded bodies. In this manner, abject art and texts in my corpus displace tensions between the affirmation and deconstruction of marginalized identities into the psychoanalytic realm and play them out on the stage of the body (Cf. Harrison 140; A. Zimmermann 31–55).[10]

Abject art and memoirs in my corpus not only comment on the artist's or author's personal sense of abjection but make larger identity-political claims because the expressive resources of the body and symbolic systems can be read in parallel. In the words of anthropologist Mary Douglas, certain forms of impurity and transgression "are used as analogies for expressing a general view of the social order" (3) and "as symbols of the relation between parts of society, as mirroring designs of hierarchy or symmetry which apply in the larger social system" (4). As such, the abjection depicted in memoirs of madness not only "represents the ultimate coding of our [here: the authors'] crises, of our [here: their] most intimate and most serious apocalypses" (Kristeva 208; my addition) but also forces the reader to confront their assumptions and fears regarding the mad. Moreover, the representation of experiencing selves as abject can be both revolting in its depiction of that which is a feared Other and produces a spectacle that satisfies voyeuristic desires. In their emulation of techniques used to negotiate the socio-cultural status of highly politicized identities, memoirs in my corpus furthermore produce madness as a socially constructed category akin to race, gender, and sexual orientation.

When memoirs link madness to abjection, they not only insist on the constructedness of social identities but also reveal other aspects of their authors' lived experience. Memoirs, that describe the experiencing self in states of abjection or describe both the grotesque destruction of bodies and the revulsion of those that witness it, show that the lived experience of madness is characterized by the realization that one is indeed abject or by the stigma and social exclusion that follows ascriptions of abjectness. In many cases, texts in my corpus manage the author's shame through especially provocative descriptions of experiencing selves that are covered in excrement or splatter blood, bile, and other bodily fluids over their immediate surroundings to symbolically communicate the literal and metaphorical pollution of mad persons and thereby evoke an aggressive reaction to stigma that Erving Goffman calls "hostile bravado" (*Stigma* 17). Mental illness pathographies therefore enable stigma-political mechanisms in their negotiation of abjection.

To reveal the vastly different personal truths that representations of the abjection in and of madness can produce, I turn to two seemingly similar scenes of emaciation, defilement, and debasement. Once when he was floridly psychotic, Mark Vonnegut's experiencing self was "[d]own from one fifty-five to about one twenty pounds, deaf, dumb and blind, convulsing in [his] own puke, shit and piss" in a padded cell (118; cf. also 189). In a seemingly similar scene, Cherry Boone-O'Neill's experiencing self overdosed on laxatives and lost bowel control in her sleep. The morning after the overdose, the experiencing self's husband woke to find that she looked like "death warmed over" (110) and that her face had turned overnight into "a mummy's…. It might as well [have been] just a skull with a thin layer of skin stretched across it" (108). Horrified, he then realizes that the mattress of their bed was "soggy … [with] liquefied excrement" (108–109), "recoiled at the sight of the dirtied linens[,] and quickly made his way to the shower" (109). Weakened by extreme dehydration, sustained self-induced vomiting, and starvation, the experiencing self could only lie there, "in [her] own defecation, writhing with what was obviously excruciating pain" (109). Throughout the incident, the narrating self recalls, "I could not reply intelligently, I could only groan" (109).

While both memoirs fashion experiencing selves as abject, the incidents in Mark Vonnegut's memoir primarily establish that times of madness constitute his "most intimate and most serious apocalypses" (Kristeva 208) and hint at the need for mental healthcare reforms. The passage reveals the experiencing self's state of abjection as he lost the ability to communicate ("deaf, dumb and blind"), move deliberately ("convulsing"), and no longer kept himself clean of bodily discharge. However, in these scenes, the experiencing self was already excluded from society by merit of the double liminality[11] of his *acute* psychotic *break* and the confinement to a padded cell, a status that is visually and symbolically marked by the staff's decision to take away his regular clothes and only provide a papery hospital gown (Vonnegut 118). Unlike the closed ward where a mad individual can be kept indefinitely, the padded cell is reserved for those patients in acute but transitory states of crisis that put themselves or others at risk. While Vonnegut's descriptions may evoke disgust, pity or fear and thus affirm the stigma beliefs that individuals with schizophrenia are helpless yet also uncontrollable and dangerous (cf. Angermeyer and Dietrich 170), it also firmly establishes the temporary nature of his abjection and invites the question why the staff did not clean his cell more frequently. In this manner, Vonnegut's memoir implicitly protests the inhumane conditions in institutions of marginalization that contain abject individuals and produces madness as a temporary crisis and suffering.

However, Vonnegut also undermines these protests and productions of madness as a variant of human difference that is marginalized when he criticizes attempts to use the experience of abjection for political capital. Assuming the perspective of an experiencing self that still embraces anti-psychiatric beliefs about the marginalization of transgressive Others, the narrating self states,

> The humiliations and restrictions I had suffered made blacks, women, and homosexuals look like fat-cats basking in the good graces of the powers that be.... Admittedly my oppression and suffering hadn't been long-term, but if blacks could identify with and be outraged by what the slaves went through, I could certainly identify with all inmates of mental institutions, past, present, and future.... I was no longer a male wasp heterosexual of upper-middle-class origins with good intentions.... I had credentials [146].

This highly problematic comparison to the African American experience of slavery certainly invites discussions about the conditions in mental hospitals and illustrates his sense of victimization. However, the passage, in its blatant exaggeration and provocation, also functions as a scathing indictment of those who relativize the suffering of others to claim a voice and a critique of attempts to present madness as a way of being in the world that is marginalized in the same manner as some racial, gender or sexual identities. In this manner, Vonnegut not only undermines the formation of identity-political movements around madness but also creates a tension to other statements in his memoir that present madness as a core part of who he is.

By contrast, Cherry Boone-O'Neill's scene of abjection presents the experiencing self as defiled and defiling and constitutes a sincere plea to take the destructive effects of eating disorders seriously. Boone-O'Neill symbolizes the damaging results of her madness through the defilement of the experiencing self and her husband by her feces. Her husband, who experienced intense anger, worry, and incomprehension at Cherry's inability to stop fasting, purging, and then lying about it, is literally and symbolically polluted by the physical manifestations of her madness, i.e., feces that evade her control and transgress the boundaries of her body. He "recoils" in a horror that illustrates societal reactions to acts of abjection and madness. Additionally, Boone-O'Neill disturbs the glamorous yet wholesome image she projected as a member of The Pat Boone Family and illustrates how far eating disorders can remove even a woman of strict evangelical upbringing from her prescribed purity and role as a devout wife. In this way, she implicitly calls for improvements in the treatment of eating disorders as they have severe physical and psychological effects that endanger strict adherence to Christian values.

The scene also demonstrates the damage caused by the experiencing self's madness through tropes of the uncanny. Boone-O'Neill's experiencing self is not merely emaciated like Vonnegut's but is represented as undead when her husband compares her face to "a mummy's," a skull covered in skin or "death warmed over." In other words, she evokes a corpse, which Kristeva called "the utmost of abjection … death infecting life" (3–4), as well as incarnations of the uncanny that transgress the boundaries of life and death. In these comparisons, the experiencing self is a mummified body—or rather a fragment thereof—that retains some life or regains it. She is uncanny like a corpse that once again shows aspects of life like body heat while lacking a complete miraculous resurrection ("*death warmed over*"). These images are all the more horrifying as they occur in the bed of newlyweds, traditionally a space for the creation of life, not a grotesque mirage of its end. In this way, Cherry Boone-O'Neill reveals the transgressive and uncanny elements of madness that are felt both by the mad person and their loved ones as an additional feature of the lived experience of madness. Moreover, she presents the spectacle of her abject mad self in a manner that simultaneously repulses and fascinates through its voyeuristic pleasures and thereby illustrates the conflicted reactions that madness evokes.

Marya Hornbacher's memoir *Wasted* also includes passages that depict abject bodily fluids that transgress boundaries. In her case, these representations illustrate how the abject practices of madness contributed to the experiencing self's attempts to establish corporeal boundaries as well as symbolic ones in a family structure that was shaped by an intrusive and overprotective father and a distanced, overly critical mother. Hornbacher recalls two occasions when the pipes in her family home broke due to her frequent purging, "spilled my undigested dinners, in their spaghetti entirety, for any and all to see" (176), and flooded both bathroom and basement with vomit (223). Just as the child in Kristeva's famous example, who was repulsed by the creamy skin on the milk, which her parents urged her to drink, and spit it out, the experiencing self rids herself of spaghetti, the quintessential North American family meal. As the phrase "in their spaghetti *entirety*" (emphasis added) suggests, the experiencing self expulses the dinner with all its symbolic meanings in the complex communications of love, need, and belonging that are negotiated via food in her family. These negotiations take place both between the parents—"My father, voracious, tried to gobble up my mother. My mother, haughty and stiff-backed, left my father untouched on her plate" (23)—and between each parent and Marya: Both competed for the experiencing self's love and had special foods only they were allowed to give her, each dish representing "a statement of nurturance, a statement about the other parents lack thereof" (26). Like the child in Kristeva's text, the experiencing self communicates "'I' want none of that element, sign of their [the parents'] desire…. But since the food is not an 'other' for 'me,' who am only in their desire, I expel *myself*,

I spit *myself* out, I abject *myself* within the same motion through which 'I' claim to establish *myself*" (Kristeva 3). Hornbacher makes this contradictory process explicit when she states that an eating disorder is "an attempt to find an identity, but ultimately it strips you[12] of any sense of yourself" (*Wasted* 6), and that "my emotional survival" depended "upon my mastery, if not total erasure, of my physical self" (134). As these claims suggest, the experiencing self expanded her abjection of food to the abjection of her body and self. With her entire identity based upon abjection, she herself becomes utterly abject, prone to be marginalized and looked upon with disgust or morbid fascination. Madness is therefore the process of abjection taken to extremes and supplies the basis of the experiencing self's identity.

In her memoir of bipolar disorder, Marya Hornbacher also produces the meaning of her madness as abjection through imagery that mirrors abject art's focus on fragmented or repulsive bodies which are tied to marginalized subjectivities, the loss of a unified sense of self, and alienation (A. Zimmermann 31, 78–81). During a suicide attempt, Hornbacher cuts her arm, "glimpse[s] the bone, and then blood sprays all over the walls" (*Madness* 2). On the way to the hospital, the experiencing self looks down but "there is an enormous gaping red thing where my arm used to be. It is bloody, it looks like a raw steak, it looks like the word *flesh*, the word itself" (*Madness* 4). Delirious, drunk, and in shock, the experiencing self then realizes that she herself is a steak and that the paramedics "are carving me up to serve me. They will serve me on a silver-plated platter" (*Madness* 4). In these passages, Hornbacher transposes the alienating, violent experience of madness onto the stage of her body when she reveals that the experiencing self has lost all sense of kinship to her mutilated arm: Not only has the arm become "an *enormous* gaping red *thing*" (emphasis added), i.e., an object unconnected to her that no longer matches her bodily proportions, but it has also lost its actuality as a body part and only exists as an abstract signifier ("it looks like the word *flesh*, the word itself"). As noted at other points in this study, Hornbacher repeatedly negotiates her sense of alienation and mental or physical fragmentation through her deviations from the first-person singular, the externalization of her madness as well as the Othering of her body and mind, but in this passage, she also conveys the horror and violence that characterize her subjective experience of madness as abjection and alienation from self.

Descriptions of the mutilated body and the steak simile furthermore foreshadow the memoir's spectacular confessional representations of the experiencing self at her most abject as well as the text's careful composition. Notably, her arm looks like "raw steak," i.e., specific, valuable parts of flesh cut in a distinct manner, and later the experiencing self herself feels like a steak that is carved up and served "on a silver-plated platter." This metaphor conveys that *Madness: A Bipolar Life* does not contain her undifferentiated lived experience but only includes carefully selected aspects which, nevertheless, produce the impression of a raw and violent representation of madness. The historical author prepared and served a selection of her memories and sense of self "on a silver-plated platter" for the reader's consumption, thus alluding to the confessional memoir's status as a commodity. Moreover, the metaphor reinforces the tension between the artificiality of editorial decisions imposed on her life narrative and the impression of authenticity, truthfulness, and immediacy that is produced through the suggestion that her self can be consumed by the reader—if only its most sought-after parts.

Hornbacher further prefigures the spectacular and intimate nature of her memoir through recourse to another aspect of the abject body that frequently featured in abject art, namely the permeability of bodily boundaries and the depiction of that which is usually hidden (cf. Zimmermann 60–67). When Hornbacher violates the bodily boundary of her skin with a knife and even "glimpse[s] the bone," her blood transgresses that boundary so forcefully that it defiles her immediate surroundings. This not only symbolizes that abject subjects like the mad threaten to infect the social order but the graphic descriptions of transgressed bodily boundaries presage the spectacular confessions of the memoir and thereby appeal to voyeuristic pleasures. Hornbacher therefore extends the range of meaning expressed by her abject body from statements about the meaning of madness to statements about confession, i.e., the mode which produces and communicates these meanings.

Elizabeth Wurtzel's narration of a miscarriage constitutes a similarly spectacular and self-conscious scene that evokes abject art. However, unlike Hornbacher, Wurtzel uses the body to signify the doubly abject state of being female and mad. After describing how her doctor dismissed her complaints about abdominal pain and reassured her that it was the result of her taxing therapeutic process, there is an ellipsis in the narration to a few days later when the experiencing self "woke up in blood. There was blood on the sheets, blood between the sheets, blood on my nightgown … [and I] felt the plasmatic bits of blood that encrusted my inner thighs, saw the thick clots of burgundy" (Wurtzel 186–187). When she got up to call her boyfriend, she looked back and "saw a trail of blood, left in dots and splatters on the floor and smears on the wall like a Jackson Pollock painting" (Wurtzel 187). As her reference to Jackson Pollock suggests, Wurtzel inscribes herself into the tradition of provocative art but, as the blood came from her vagina, also more specifically into the tradition of abject art concerned with the female body.

As feminist literary critic Elizabeth Grosz points out, "in the West …

the female body has been constructed not only as a lack or absence but … as a leaking, uncontrollable, seeping liquid … a disorder that threatens all order" (203). Consequently, artists associated with abject art like Cindy Sherman, Judy Chicago, and Shigeto Kubota aggressively flaunted imagery of menstruation, the epitome of this conceptualization of female corporality. Chicago depicted menstruation in close-up photographs of bloody tampons being pulled from a vagina, and Kubota, a performance artist, filled her vagina with paint and let it seep onto a canvas. Both artists simultaneously affirmed and undermined cultural constructs of femininity as abjection by focusing on the uncontrollable, seeping female form in an aggressive and excessively graphic manner. In line with this motif, Wurtzel describes uncontrollable bleeding that saturated her sheets and nightgown and even left smears and splatters on the wall. When taken as an analogy of her madness, her profusely bleeding abject body signifies how her depression tainted her life and affected her environment in a belligerent, explosive fashion. Moreover, the enormous amount of blood speaks to the intensity of the experiencing self's psychic pain and her desire to convey this pain to her family and friends to get help. At other points in the memoir, Wurtzel confesses that the only small delight her depression left her was "knowing that others worry" (49) and letting them know that, to help her, "they need to do more and more and more, they need to try to get through to me until they haven't slept or eaten or breathed fresh air for days, they need to try until they've died for me" (51). Wurtzel thus flaunts both her desire to cause disorder in the lives of others with her dramatic cries for attention as well as her own psychic pain through her representation of her unruly body which mirrors the aggressive representation of abject femininity in the abject art movement. Wurtzel therefore produces madness as a disturbance of order, not just for those diagnosed with it but also for their loved ones.

Through its focus on a spectacularly bleeding uterus, the passage furthermore evokes the historical diagnosis of hysteria and points to Wurtzel's double delegitimization as a woman and a mad person. Hysteria, derived from the Greek word for the uterus, *hystera*, is a medically outdated diagnosis that linked a variety of symptoms such as irritability, selective muteness, fainting, anxiety, paralysis, and being sexually transgressive to a wandering, over- or understimulated uterus. The diagnosis enjoyed intense scientific and psychoanalytic interest during the Victorian Age and was frequently used to disempower women based on their alleged constitutional weakness (Scull, *Hysteria* 66, 195). By the 1980s, feminists such as Hélène Cixous started to view hysteria as a bodily response to patriarchal oppression, a "bombard[ment]" of the male analyst with "carnal and passionate body words" (886). Although Wurtzel's experiencing self also expressed her anguish by transposing it onto the stage of the body, the passage presents an ironic reversal of the Victorian *modus operandi*: The experiencing self's doctor refused to consider a possible medical origin of the abdominal pain and assumed that her symptoms were a psychosomatic expression of her mental disorder and the strains of therapy. In this manner, and by describing herself and other women as "hysterical" 21 times in the memoir, Wurtzel links a specifically female medical complication, a miscarriage, to the experiencing self's dismissal by her doctor who treated her like a discredited person because she had the stigma of madness. The experiencing self's discredited state is therefore a mirror image of the delegitimization women faced in the Victorian Age which further fashions madness as a politicizable identity like gender. Moreover, Wurtzel's memoir shows how stigma beliefs affect medical practice even at the end of the twentieth century. Stigma thus remains a central aspect of the lived experience of madness, and authors in my corpus allude to it on several textual levels.

While I do not propose that all aspects of the textual response to stigma in my corpus are a conscious stigma-political strategy, mental illness memoirs constitute an important contribution to the contemporary conversation on how to define madness and how to treat those who experience it. As the last two chapters showed, this contribution to the definition of madness (also) derives from the interplay of methods connected to the production of subjective and objective truth. In my corpus, subjective and objective modes of truth production do not exist in opposition but supplement and qualify each other. On the one hand, the interaction of intertextual references to the supposedly objective truth of psychiatry and a subjective truth which is expressed through literary techniques enables readings of defamiliarizing language, associative leaps, switches in pronouns or the fragmentation of narrative subjectivity as quasi-mimetic representations of specific symptoms of mental disorders. On the other hand, the objective truth of psychiatry can provide an interpretive framework that reduces the unsettling effect of a language or narrative that resists easy narrativization. Just as the psychiatric discourse imposes order on madness through its rigid nosologies and produces the impression that madness is knowable, intertextual references to psychiatric truth claims provide an interpretive framework for readers, thereby reducing irritation and enabling the reader's continued consumption of the memoirs.

However, the interaction of objective and subjective truth in memoirs of my corpus not only enables new modes of understanding or proves fortuitous in attempts by the mad to claim a voice in the discursive construction of their condition. The combination of intertextual references to the psychiatric discourse and literary techniques for the representation of lived experience also encourages essentializing readings that reduce artistic expression to outgrowths of the historical author's diagnosed psychiatric condition. The inclusion of witness testimony has similarly ambiguous effects. On the one hand, witness testimony authenticates the identity and truth claims made in memoirs in my corpus and thereby facilitates the authors' claiming of a voice as a person with lived experience of madness. On the other hand, witness testimony by normal witnesses perpetuates the discredit of individuals deemed mad by making allowances for stigma beliefs that associate madness with permanent unreliability, thereby legitimizing them. Like the unresolved tension between contradictory meanings of madness, the tension between the empowering and disempowering effects of the interaction of objective and subjective truth ultimately points to the double bind in which stigmatized individuals find themselves: Whenever they respond to one stigma belief in their discursive construction of madness, they also affirm another one. When they empower themselves by drawing upon a combination of methods of truth production, they also disempower themselves through that very combination.

Lastly, the combination of objective and subjective modes of truth production exacerbates the other central tension in my corpus. In their appropriation of the objective, scientific discourse of psychiatry or established academic means of truth production, narrating selves present themselves as normal in the sense of rational, whereas literary techniques evoke the trope of the mad artist and emphasize the narrating self's madness. Through these complex textual effects, tensions, ambiguities, as well as the combination of spectacular confession and ambitious literary techniques, memoirs in my corpus do important cultural work and are a popular commodity.

Conclusion

There is a cacophony of discourses on madness and large numbers of discursive agents who support vastly different understandings. The very term madness evokes, among other things: Romanticized suffering and artistic genius; states of abject horror and pervasive unease; a loss of self; "a social category among other categories like race, class, gender, sexuality, age, or ability that define our identities and experiences" (Liegghio 10); a persistent blemish; a condition that can be overcome; a loss of control and of the faculty of reason; spiritual growth and prophetic knowledge; the result of an imbalance of neurotransmitters, overexcited nerves, imbalanced bodily humors—in short: pathology; the result of sin, or the lack of willpower; an impairment in the legal sense; a propensity for violence and unpredictable behavior; a state of childlike innocence and utter helplessness; quirkiness and hilarious eccentricity; a coping strategy in the face of trauma, environmental stressors, or an insane society; a source of shame; a source of pride; a label to discredit transgressive individuals; the mark of a weak constitution; animal strength and cunning; a variant of human difference; extremes of mood and thought; a divine blessing; a discursive construct.

The only point the psychiatric dispositive, advocacy groups, academics, the media, high and popular culture, and authors of mental illness memoirs can agree on is that madness is heavily stigmatized. Like the meanings of madness itself, the stigma beliefs attached to those diagnosed with it are multifaceted and contradictory. For example, there is the stigma belief that the mad are utterly incapacitated by their condition but also that they could "pull themselves together" or "snap out of it" if they wanted to (Corrigan and Watson 477). Any mad person who calls for (professional) help in the management of their condition risks supporting the former stigma belief, any mad person who shares a narrative of overcoming and self-reliance the latter. Those among the mad who wish to narrate their lived experience, therefore, find themselves in a double bind, i.e., they cannot reject one stigma belief without supporting another one.

This double bind is not specific to stigma beliefs about madness but a general mechanism. Stigma beliefs immunize themselves through contradictions: African Americans are dangerous beasts *and* childlike, innocent creatures. Jewish people are capitalists *and* communists. Women are inherently sinful *and* angelic. Stigma-political campaigns that seek to combat any one of these beliefs and attempt to construct arguments free from internal contradictions are easily caught up in this double bind, as the mixed results of recent campaigns that present madness as a "brain disorder" suggest (cf. Corrigan and Watson).

The complexity, ambiguity, and radical openness of meaning afforded by literary texts such as memoirs paradoxically circumvents that double bind by presenting narrating and experiencing selves in a contradictory manner. When memoirs present textual selves as *both* normal *and* mad, they problematize the binary oppositions that the process of stigmatization needs and creates. Memoirs exacerbate this contradiction when authors appropriate the objective truth of psychiatry that is associated with normalcy in the sense of rationality, yet also claim the authority of lived experience and convey their personal, subjective truth of madness through markedly artistic means that evoke the mad genius. Thus, texts in my corpus contain two central tensions between opposing types of self-fashioning (as normal and mad) and types of truth (objective and subjective), which are never resolved and have fortuitous stigma-political effects.

Memoirs not only complicate binary oppositions between normals and mad people but also destabilize the very meaning of madness—and, by extension, normalcy—by presenting textual selves in accordance with a plethora of culturally valued discourses, narratives, tropes, and popular stigma beliefs about the mad. For example, textual selves are *both* enabled *and* incapacitated, *both* harmlessly eccentric *and* monstrous, and their madness is *both* an expression of their repressed, true selves *and* a demonic Other intruding into their minds, *both* (the result of) sin *and* (supposedly morally neutral) pathology. Authors may switch from one trope to the other and back, depending on their narrative and rhetorical needs. Consequently, textual selves in my corpus embody the inconsistencies of stigmatizing beliefs about the mad through the very act of affirming all those beliefs while simultaneously undermining notions of unified essential selves—which are the basis of stigma beliefs—in a very postmodern manner.

Because memoirs affirm so many contradictory claims about madness and normalcy, the tension in self-fashioning cannot be understood as a strain between two clearly defined, stable attributes. Instead, it should be viewed as a continual oscillation between claims to two labels with shifting, context-dependent, vast webs of meaning that are created by many different discursive agents. In short, normal and mad signify highly variable things to different people. In reference to Stuart Hall, I therefore claim that memoirs in my corpus reveal madness (and by extension normalcy) to be a "floating signifier," much like "race" and "gender" (Hall 5). In Hall's words, floating signifiers "gain their meaning, not because of what they contain in their essence, but in the shifting relations of difference, which they establish with other concepts and ideas in a signifying field" through the constant loss, appropriation, and contraction of new ones and "the endless process of being constantly re-signified, made to mean something different in different cultures, in different historical formations, at different moments of time" (8). The active destabilization of the meaning of madness through the attribution of contradictory contents to this label then undermines the process of stigmatization which marks and discredits individuals for supposedly stable traits and blemishes.

While authors are highly invested in the stigma-political work their memoirs can perform, this does not mean that the creation of tensions in self-fashioning and truth production is a conscious stigma-political maneuver embraced by all authors in my corpus. Instead, similarities in my corpus exist because authors respond to a similar set of stigma beliefs and make sense of their experience by drawing upon a culture-wide set of narratives and tropes of life writing. Any features beyond that—escaping the double bind of stigma beliefs and (further) destabilizing the meaning of madness by affirming *all* stigma beliefs—are a function of literature. In other words, these stigma-political advantages are the result of a mode of reading encouraged by literary texts that is accepted by producers and recipients alike. Literariness allows for unresolved tensions, ambiguity, and openness of meaning, and therefore literary texts like memoirs can perform cultural work that more pragmatic texts like manifestos could not.

However, this does not mean that literary accounts of the lived experience of madness are more effective or able to replace traditional stigma-political campaigns. While traditional stigma-political campaigns may be seen as moralizing or prescriptive because of their straightforward condemnation of discrimination, their explicit rejection of stigma theories or definite calls for softer social labels, they generally manage to get their point across. Literature, with its radical openness of meaning, can only undermine the binary oppositions or destabilize the meaning of terms when readers are willing to employ the literary mode of reading and to question their own attitude towards the mad: Unless readers assume that contradictions have a communicative purpose, they may interpret them as the author's inability to tell a coherent story and find their stigma beliefs about the conflation of mental illness and mental incapacitation confirmed. Similarly, they could see representations of experiencing selves as monstrous Others as a validation of stigma beliefs by the very people they describe. While literature may be able to do stigma-political work that manifestos cannot, the opposite is also true.

Notwithstanding these restraints, a major aspect of the commercial and, I argue, stigma-political success of memoirs in my corpus is their ability to combine the impression of authenticity and literariness. Even though mental illness pathographies create the impression and expectation of authenticity through the confessional mode or authenticating documents and are often read as true accounts of lived experience, they are still literature. Literariness is not tied to fictionality, and the memoirs' poetic language and complex negotiation of themes central to the human condition can foster a readiness to employ a literary mode of reading.[1] Furthermore, readers do not enjoy pathographies for their factual iterations of the course of a particular illness but because they *construct* narratives that *interpret* lived experience. This constructedness and capacity for meaning-making further ties pathographies to literature and its openness of meaning while the impression of authenticity is central to stigma-political goals such as the creation of sympathy.

Another stigma-political function in mental illness pathographies—and a central feature of postmodern literature—is "a more general questioning of any totalizing or homogenizing system" (Hutcheon 11–12). In this case, mental illness pathographies problematize the order which the psychiatric dispositive attempts to impose on the phenomenon of madness through the ever more complicated bureaucratization of mental disorders in the *DSM*.

As is common in postmodern critical and artistic practice, memoirs of madness position themselves firmly within the system they seek to challenge. Authors empower themselves and circumvent the processes of rarefication and specialization by learning to decipher the technical language of the psychiatric "fellowship of discourse" (Foucault, *Discourse* 225). They establish their literacy in the psychiatric discourse by explaining technical terms and theories to less knowledgeable readers, referencing specialist literature, and (also) interpreting their lived experience through the hegemonic interpretation of madness as mental disorder. Expressions of gratefulness for the treatment they received and narratives of conversion to the truth of the psychiatric dispositive further cement authors' embrace of the psychiatric discourse. These rhetorical moves not only affirm mental disorders and pathology as meanings of madness but can also be read as attempts to engage psychiatrists and psychologist in their own technical language and encourage coalition politics.

At the same time, authors also point to inconsistencies between psychiatric truth claims and their lived experience to reveal that psychiatric truth is not universal but must be seen as "fictions or as ideological structures. This does not necessarily destroy their 'truth' value, but it does define the conditions of that 'truth'" (Hutcheon 13). Additionally, authors use markedly literary means to represent their lived experience and to recreate (weaker, mediated versions of) their emotional responses to specific symptoms. In this manner, authors communicate personal truths of madness which the clinical language of the psychiatric discourse cannot convey and provide a more immediate, tangible experience of the (subjective) truth of the experiencing self's condition. In this way, authors not only challenge the psychiatric dispositive's claims to a general truth but also establish the need to draw upon patient experience to achieve a more complex understanding of madness through the affective responses of those that live with it.

Memoirs in my corpus thus merge two supposedly contradictory kinds of knowledge that are produced about madness: objective and subjective truth. This merger provides authors with the rhetorical, stigma-political, and identity-political advantages outlined above and reveals that the distinction between objective and subjective truth is arbitrary and unsupported by current practice. Even though psychiatry increasingly advances its understanding of the impact of genetics and biochemical processes in the development, outbreak, and treatment of mental disorders, its objective studies still rely on patients' reports on symptoms since suicidal ideation or obsessive thoughts cannot be detected in the same manner as tumors or inflammations can be. Truth production in the psychiatric dispositive thus (also) relies on conclusions drawn from patients' subjective experience.

Conversely, the production and communication of a subjective truth of madness in my corpus is never separate from psychiatric discourses on mental illnesses. Authors need to reference their diagnostic labels because an official psychiatric diagnosis legitimates the authors' claims to an inside perspective of the diagnosed condition and any subjective truth they produce about it. Secondly, any criticism authors voice about inconsistencies between their lived experience and their diagnostic category needs be made in recourse to the technical terms and framework of the psychiatric dispositive to be intelligible. Even Suzanna Kaysen, who is the most radical author in my corpus in her rejection of the psychiatric dispositive and its truth about madness, uses a close reading of the *DSM* to demonstrate the underlying misogyny of the diagnostic label she received, borderline personality disorder. Lastly, the confrontation with the psychiatric truth of their condition and the treatment they received shaped the authors' lived experience of madness and thus the subjective truths they produced. Because these two modes of truth production are so intimately tied up with each other, authors in my corpus may embrace both, just as they embrace multiple, supposedly mutually exclusive meanings of madness.

Interestingly, the front matter of the fifth and most recent edition of the *DSM*—the official diagnostic manual by the American Psychiatric Association—creates so many unresolved tensions and conflicting meanings of madness that the text verges on literature as well. The introduction states that the "DSM is a medical classification of disorders and as such serves as a historically determined cognitive schema imposed on clinical and scientific information" (American Psychiatric Association, Introduction 10), i.e., that it is a rather rigid categorical classification of separate disorders with (more or less) "well-defined boundaries around symptom clusters" (6). However, recent scientific findings and clinical practice have shown that "boundaries between disorders are more porous than originally perceived" so that "many, if not most," disorders are placed on a spectrum of related symptoms (6). Despite these issues, the preface insists that the *DSM* "can aid in the *accurate diagnosis* .... of mental disorders ... [and] an *objective* assessment of symptom presentations" (Kupfer and Regier xli; emphasis added). The front matter thus acknowledges that the *DSM*'s truth production is culturally and historically rooted in a specific tradition of thought that is increasingly challenged by more recent (and presumably better) means of truth production, yet it also insists that it helps to produce a general truth that can be recognized accurately and objectively by clinicians.

Likewise, the *DSM*'s medical framework and tentative gestures towards genetic and physiological risk factors (Kupfer and Regier xlii) conceive of madness as a medical disorder. However, it also undermines this medical meaning of madness with the claim that "[m]ental disorders are defined in relation to cultural, social, and familial norms and values. Culture provides interpretive frameworks that shape the experience and expression of the symptoms, signs, and behaviors that are criteria for diagnosis" (Introduction 14). Furthermore, "[t]he boundaries between normality and pathology vary across cultures for specific types of behaviors" as does "tolerance for symptoms and behaviors" (14). In other words, madness is also understood as transgressive behavior and the subjective, culturally determined experience of distress. The experience of distress and the resultant need for treatment or care do not serve as reliable markers of mental disorders either: "Mental disorders are *usually* associated with significant distress or disability in social, occupational, or other important activities" (American Psychiatric Association, Introduction 20; emphasis added). Yet, "the diagnosis of a mental disorder is not equivalent to a need for treatment" (20) and by extension distress or serious impairment. Likewise, "individuals whose symptoms do not meet full criteria for a mental disorder" may require treatment or care (20). In this manner, mental disorder is not defined consistently in recourse to distress or impairment either. The *DSM* thus creates a tension by insisting on medical, intrapersonal, and cultural factors that determine the experience and official diagnosis of madness: the practice of medicine traditionally depends on the objective presence of pathogens, genes, or tumors whereas judgment based on internalized cultural norms or need for assistance on the part of patients, family members, and clinicians is a much more subjective matter.

This incongruity is further emphasized when the *DSM* also rejects deviancy as a meaning of madness. The *DSM* states that "[s]ocially deviant behavior (e.g., political, religious, or sexual) and conflicts that are primarily between the individual and society are *not* mental disorders unless the deviance or conflict results from a dysfunction in the individual" (20; emphasis added). The *DSM* goes on to define this dysfunction as "a clinically significant disturbance in an individual's cognition, emotion regulation, or behavior that reflects a dysfunction in the psychological, biological, or developmental processes underlying mental functioning" (20). The latter suggests that explicit criteria must be met to justify the diagnosis of a mental disorder and to ensure that transgressive individuals are not unduly pathologized. However, this is immediately qualified by the statement that there are "individuals whose symptoms do not meet full criteria for a mental disorder but who demonstrate *a clear need* for treatment" (20; emphasis added). In the passages quoted, the *DSM* first emphatically rejects the pathologization of socially deviant behavior by evoking an objective, medical framework ("clinically significant," "dysfunction," "biological, or developmental processes") only to allow for exceptions on the basis of a subjectively determined "clear need" for psychiatric treatment that will effectively pathologize the individual just as much as an official diagnosis. In conclusion, the *DSM* creates multiple tensions between various meanings of madness including biological, medical, bodily disorder, distress, (culturally determined) deviancy, and impairment to function thus echoing the ambiguities and tensions negotiated in my corpus of pathographies.

Scholars on life writing by individuals with disabilities, illnesses or disorders have long emphasized the significance of narrative "in shaping both the experience of illness and discourse about illness, indeed shaping professional understanding, medical knowledge itself" (Clark, Introduction 3).[2] While I do not suggest an exclusive, causal relationship between the destabilization of the meaning of madness in autobiographical texts and the tensions present in the most recent edition of the *DSM*, I propose that literature exposes the unresolved conflicts that exist in the cultural imagination of madness. Through literature and other cultural products, these conflicting meanings become part of the backdrop that is internalized by individuals, including discursive agents such as mental healthcare professionals or researchers in fields pertaining to madness. Conversely, the truth produced by these agents becomes a part of the sediments of knowledge on madness and is negotiated in art and literary texts such as mental illness memoirs. I thus conclude that this process of cross-fertilization is moving towards a greater ambiguity regarding the meaning of madness as suggested by the memoirs in my corpus and the examples drawn from the *DSM*.

That the meaning of madness becomes so ambiguous that it even constitutes a floating signifier like race and gender allows for comparisons between mad people and individuals who are subjected to racism or sexism as well as comparisons of the interpretive frameworks that surround these attributes. It is widely accepted, Tobin Siebers states, that while some bodies are "black" or "female," these attributes "do not define individual bodies," but "denote large social categories having an interpretation, history, and politics well beyond the particularities of one human body" (17). Adherents of the theory of social construction claim the same about the mind and/or brain and the meaning, history, and politics that certain states of mind acquire. However, at the point of writing, key differences between the categories of race, gender, and state of mind remain: Attempts to reduce individuals to the characteristics "black" or "female" are largely rejected as racist or sexist, and these reductive frameworks as well as the "characteristics, experiences, emotions, and rationales that determine their [racist and sexist] usage … have become objects of knowledge and political interpretation for many people" (Siebert 17). Sanism—as some activists call the discrimination against people labeled mad—is not (yet?) subjected to the same theoretical scrutiny and political interpretation as racism and sexism. Unlike outright racism or sexism, sanism is still fairly widespread in US popular culture. Much stigma-political work remains to be done and the politics and mechanisms of sanism are far from fully explored.

Moreover, this study raised new questions in related fields. For example, how do these forms of self-fashioning, the negotiation of the ambiguous meaning of madness, and the stigma attached to the condition play out in other forms of life writing such as (video) blogs, personal essays, letters, or journals? What about the rapidly growing genre of autobiographical graphic novels on the subject of mental illness? Which additional meanings of madness are produced (and undermined) in this medium and its "connections and disconnections between the verbal and the visual" and the way it "produces specific engagements with disjunctions, complexity, and the ineffable" (Quesenberry and Squier, 63)? Do autobiographical films or performance art also produce multiple meanings, and if yes, how?

Asked in a different direction, are similar readings possible in life writing by individuals with conditions of the mind that are not generally considered madness by laypersons but still included in the *DSM V*, such as ADHD, Tourette's disorder, narcolepsy, kleptomania, substance abuse disorders, or neurocognitive disorders such as Alzheimer's disease and multiple sclerosis? Are there differences in stigma-management or in the emphasis of specific meanings that can be linked to the severity of stigma?

Lastly, are there changes as the number of people diagnosed with a mental disorder at some point in their life rises to 25 percent? That is, to which extent does the widespread nature of mental illness, which a study of the World Health Organization (*Mental*) places in the group of the most serious health problems worldwide, alongside cancer and heart disease, affect stigma politics, identity politics, and the production of the meaning of madness as deviance and pathology ("Mental" 3–4)? And how does what Campbell and Manning call "the emergence of a victimhood culture" (692), i.e., the emphasis of one's stigmatized characteristics as a conflict strategy in the face of oppression, influence modes of disclosure, shame management, and stigma politics?

Regardless of these open questions, this study not only contributes to the understanding of mechanisms of self-fashioning in life-writing by stigmatized individuals, but it also illuminates the potential which literature and its openness of meaning have in stigma-political, identity-political, and cultural work: It is the potential to demonstrate a stigmatized person's basic humanity, to give (mediated) access to another perspective, a glimpse into another way of being in the world.

Chapter Notes

Preface

1. The only exception is Clifford Beers' 1908 memoir of what is now called bipolar disorder. I included this text because of the influence Beers exerted on the conceptualization of madness and the treatment of the insane as the spokesperson for the Mental Hygiene Movement. See Capps; Pols.

2. According to Jane Tompkins, literature does "cultural work within a specific historical situation," i.e., it "provid[es] society with a means of thinking about itself, defin[es] certain aspects of a social reality which the authors and their readers shar[e], dramatiz[es] its conflicts, and recommend[s] solutions" (200).

3. I acknowledge that the authors discussed in this study are not representative of the entire population of persons with mental illnesses. Unlike many who share their conditions, authors in this study have access to treatment which allows them to be stable and productive enough to narrate their experience of madness in memoirs. Moreover, many of them hold down high-status jobs, are famous or have worked as writers before, which provides them with connections to the publishing industry. This is not the case for the vast majority of people with mental illnesses.

4. According to the National Institute of Mental Health (NIMH)—the US federal agency for research on mental disorders—the conditions discussed in my corpus are among the most common in contemporary US society: Up to .64 percent of adults experience schizophrenia or closely related psychotic disorders at some point in their lives ("Schizophrenia"). The lifetime prevalence is 1.4 percent for borderline personality disorder ("Personality"), 2.7 percent for anorexia and bulimia ("Eating"), 4.4 percent for bipolar disorder ("Bipolar"), and 6.7 percent for major depressive episodes ("Major"). The NIMH does not provide statistics on dissociative identity disorder, a condition the existence of which is still contentiously debated, but the largest advocacy group in the US, the National Alliance on Mental Illness (NAMI), states that an estimated 2 percent of adults experience it ("Dissociative"). As these numbers suggest, a significant portion of the population is diagnosed with a mental disorder at some point of their life, and according to a 2014 WHO report, these numbers continue to rise ("Mental").

5. For the representation of persons with mental disorders in film and television, see Byrne; Cross, *Mediating*; Rohr; J. Zimmerman. In journalism, see McGinty et al. In literature, see Crawford et al. For a general overview, see Rubin.

6. I included Susanna Kaysen's *Girl, Interrupted* due to its immense commercial success and its cultural impact: In 2000, it was turned into a movie of the same name, featuring well-known actresses Winona Ryder as Kaysen as well as Whoopi Goldberg and Angelina Jolie in supporting roles.

7. The only exception is Kristina Morgan, who describes relationships with men and women in her memoir, and Truddi Chase who grew up in poverty but became a successful real estate agent.

8. For analyses that tackle these issues of intersectionality, see Donaldson.

9. Because memoirs in my corpus frequently blur the lines between narrating and experiencing selves, I introduce the term "textual selves" to refer to the totality

of textual self-representation, i.e., both the experiencing and the narrating self.

10. For a discussion of the pronounced surge of interest in personal memoirs, see Rak, *Boom*; Smith and Watson; Zwerdling.

11. I use "discourse" in the Foucauldian sense that was aptly summarized by Weedon: "Discourses ... are ways of constituting knowledge, together with social practices, forms of subjectivity and power relations which inhere in such knowledges and the relations between them. Discourses are more than ways of thinking and producing meaning. They constitute the 'nature' of the body, unconscious and conscious mind and emotional life of subjects which they seek to govern. Neither the body nor thoughts and feelings have meaning outside their discursive articulation, but the ways in which discourse constitutes the minds and bodies of individuals is always part of a wider network of power relations, often with institutional bases" (108). Cf. also Foucault, "Discourse"; S. Mills.

12. I use "dispositive" in the Foucauldian sense, meaning the system of relations established between institutions, discourses, administrative mechanisms, architectural forms, knowledge structures, and philosophical or moral propositions. The dispositive thus includes "the said as much as the unsaid" and "is always inscribed in the play of power" and knowledge production (Foucault, "Confession" 194–196). I use the term "psychiatric dispositive" rather broadly to include the so-called psy-sciences (psychiatry, psychology, psychoanalysis), as well as all older forms of knowledge and truth production about madness and its treatment.

13. At the same time, novelistic techniques such as verisimilitude, the inclusion of scenes rather than summaries, and a focus on episodes that symbolize the truth an individual ascribed to their experience draw attention to the constructed nature of this truth, thereby creating yet another tension in my corpus.

14. Distinctions between memoir, autobiography, and life writing remain the subject of scholarly debate. While some use autobiography and life writing to denote "all modes and genres of telling one's own life" (Schwalm par. 1), others differentiate based on prestige or scope. I use "life writing" as an "umbrella term ... to refer

to all nonfictional representations of identity" whereas "autobiography" refers to a comprehensive account of a person's life (Couser, *Memoir* 23–24). Historically, "memoir" used to refer to (supposedly subliterary) accounts of single, incisive incidents, usually written by marginal populations. However, recently it has become a more prestigious term (Rak "Are") that "often signals autobiographical works characterized by a density of language and self-reflexivity about the writing process" (Smith and Watson 4).

15. Unless otherwise indicated, quotes retain the original emphasis.

16. For a distinction between testimony and confession, see Radstone.

17. For analyses of self-making through narrative, see Eakin *Fictions*; *Living*.

18. Other terms for the genre exist but are unfitting for my purposes. Pryal suggests "mood memoir" for texts about affective disorders, but the term is too narrow to cover the scope of conditions addressed in my corpus. Couser named memoirs of illness and disability "autopathography" (*Recovering*) or "autosomatography" (*Signifying* 2), but he abandoned the former due to the negative connotations of the root patho- which implies suffering or illness that may not be present in the lived experience of individuals with disabilities (*Memoir* 44). The Greek word for body, *soma*, is unfitting for memoirs about conditions of the mind.

19. This also finds expression in the reluctance of many mad or disabled activists to unite their efforts for fear of incurring additional stigma (cf. Brewer).

20. For other analyses that understand self-fashioning in memoirs in terms of containment and subversion see E. Young; Burr and Butt 204.

21. Magi et al. criticize the trend in research that "makes madness into something general and symbolic" (140).

Introduction

1. The terminological shift from "mental illness" to "mental disorder" in the psychiatric dispositive is based on the evolving understanding of conditions of the mind: According to the American Psychiatric Association, the type of pathology denoted

by "disorder" is closer to madness than the type denoted by "illness" (cf. Aftab). In this project, the terms "mental illness" and "mental disorder" are used interchangeably. In this manner, my language reflects both the word choice in my corpus—authors tend to write "mental illness"—as well as the terms currently endorsed by psychiatric authorities, allowing my project to keep its analytical distance from both groups. For a problematization of both terms and a historical overview of the scientific debate surrounding them, cf. Aftab.

2. For the ongoing debate of whether madness should be incorporated into the disability framework, cf. Spandler et al. For a delineation of the terms "consumer," "survivor," and "ex-patient," see Jones and Kelly; Diamond. For a detailed discussion of the neurodiversity movement, cf. Chapter Two.

3. For a critical assessment of the efficacy of this strategy, see White and Pike; Corrigan and Watson.

4. I share Christian Perring's doubts that the supposedly neutral language of psychiatry or softer social labels promoted by advocacy groups like "brain disorder" or "neurodiverse" can reduce stigma. Perring states that over time even medical terminology becomes derogatory, as was the case for "moron": It was originally introduced in 1910 as a scientific label for people with a mental age between eight and ten and is now exclusively used as an insult (Perring 12). I suspect that "neurodiverse" will undergo a similar development.

5. For the development of this movement, see Lewis "Mad"; Menzies et al.; Starkman.

6. For many scholars in the field of Mad Studies, the capitalization of "Mad" marks it as a politicized term that refers to an oppressed identity, whereas the non-capitalized version still has sanist implications (Cresswell and Spandler). I retain the capitalization of "Mad" in quotes but won't capitalize the term myself. While I do not wish to offend, I hold that it is important to uphold the ambiguity as well as the negative and positive connotations of the non-capitalized form. Only by not restricting myself conceptually to the politicized usage of the term, can I fully explore how authors in my corpus negotiate the meanings of madness.

7. For more on "symbolic violence," see Bourdieu, *Language*. For a discussion of "structural violence," see Rylko-Bauer and Farmer. I elaborate on epistemic violence in Chapter Three.

8. The social model of disability distinguishes between "impairment" and "disability" to reveal the exclusionary, dehumanizing, discrediting tactics with which society reduces the opportunities of persons with physical or mental impairments for participation, visibility, and access to resources. These reductions of opportunity then constitute disability. For more, see Spandler et al.

9. For more comprehensive accounts, see de Young; Gilman; Morall, *Madness*; Scull, *Madness*.

10. The Americans with Disabilities Act of 1990 affords similar legal protections for individuals with mental illnesses or impairments as the Civil Rights Act of 1964 did for other marginalized groups. However, as is the case for other marginalized groups, discriminatory actions in terms of housing and jobs still occur (Angermeyer and Dietrich 163). Summarizing multiple studies from the 2000s, Cross stated that one in eight people in the US would not want to live next door to a person with a mental illness, and one third of respondents did not think the mentally ill have the same right to a job as anyone else (*Mediating*, 20–21).

11. During the nineteenth century, distinct national schools of thought resulted in a diversity of terms. Those who treated the mad in Anglophone countries called themselves "mad doctors," and, when that term acquired derogatory overtones, "asylum superintendent," "medical psychologist" or (in reference to the French school of *aliénisme*) "alienist." The terms "psychiatry" and "psychiatrist" originated in nineteenth-century Germany and were rejected by English-speaking specialists until the early twentieth century (Scull, *Madness* 12).

12. Even with the advent of the talking cure and a more general reliance on confession as a method of truth production in medicine and psychiatry, truth was not to be found in the patient's speech but only in the doctor's interpretation thereof (Foucault, *Sexuality* 66).

13. Antonio Gramsci called notions held by the general public "common sense" and proposed that they are sediments of

knowledge that accumulated in the social stratum over centuries (419–425).

14. For more inclusive genealogies of confession, see Bauer; Grobe; Lofton; Tambling.

15. This desire for meaning-making is also present in the private confessional writing by North American Puritans. In these texts, believers reflected upon significant spiritual events in their lives and relentlessly questioned their righteousness to discern their state of salvation (Bauer 4–5, 26; cf. Chapter One).

16. For more on postmodern literature, see Ashley et al.; Geyh; Hutcheon; McHale, *Cambridge*.

17. Pierre Bourdieu defines "cultural capital" as an individual's social assets such as education or intellect which are expressed through ownership of art, academic credentials as well as behavior and opinions. Cultural capital provides an advantage in achieving a higher social status and is therefore valuable for discredited subjects who want to overcome their marginalization ("Forms" 47–50).

18. Alternately, the discredit that results from being labeled "mad" could also support readings of these textual tensions as evidence for the historical authors' intellectual incapacitation or mental disorder. This possibility is discussed in Chapter Four.

Chapter One

1. "Normification" is a response to stigma and consists of "the effort on the part of a stigmatized individual to present himself as an ordinary person, although not necessarily making a secret of his failing" (Goffman, *Stigma* 31). I introduce the term "normalization" to refer to attempts to present one's blemish as the norm, i.e., an attribute shared by most people.

2. Other responses are normification, hostile bravado, and presenting one's condition as a blessing in disguise (cf. Goffman, *Stigma* 7–31). I elaborate on these responses when they become relevant to my analysis.

3. I define shame as "a self-directed adverse judgement" (Taylor 151) of the entire self which results from the subject's sustained investment in an object combined with the realization that a mutually

enjoyable relationship with said object is not possible (cf. B. Williams 94; Tomkins 133–145). This can include the rejection as a lover, employee or valued participant in a discussion as well as one's failure to adhere to one's own, private standards of will-power, interpersonal conduct or the prototypically American value of self-reliance. Following Ullaliina Lehtinen, I furthermore hold that shame in "inferiorized" (4) subjects like mad persons can be both a pervasive experience and occur episodically as the result of actions a culture deems shameful (4–15). For more on shame, see M. Lewis; Heller.

4. In this memoir, "narrator" is a more appropriate term than "narrating self," since the entity who tells the story is omniscient and gives insight into the thoughts of nearly all persons who interact with Smola's experiencing self, thus suggesting a more disinterested evaluation of the story's characters. Simultaneously, this heterodiegetic narrator with zero focalization calls into question the truthfulness of the memoir, since the narrative situation is markedly novelistic and at odds with human forms of knowledge.

5. For more on the intersection of literary texts and sociological analysis, cf. Franke, Müller, and Sarkowsky.

6. While this passage is incongruent with previous descriptions of intrusive voices and delusions, it is noteworthy that the quote does not attribute the insistence on normalcy to a past, experiencing self who has not yet come terms with her madness. Instead, this passage creates a tension between the self-fashioning as normal and as mad by not ascribing one to a past and one to a present self.

7. I chose "*they" as a non-binary, gender-neutral pronoun that accounts for fluid states of singularity and multiplicity to refer to Phillips, Oxnam, and Chase in *their entirety as *they have male and female alters.

8. See Scheid and Brown for an overview on the debate whether mental illness and mental health constitute a spectrum or a dichotomy.

9. Convinced that he was persecuted by the police, he interpreted every interaction and every object in his vicinity as either an instance of torture to make him confess, as marks of infamy or as a ruse to incriminate

him. He furthermore believed that his family had been replaced by doubles and that eating his food in a certain order could be used against him as a confession of guilt.

10. Other authors in my corpus perform their normalcy *qua* rationality through appropriations of the markedly scientific—read: rational—discourse of psychiatry (see Chapter Three).

11. The phrase "anti-psychiatry movement" is a misnomer insofar as there never was a unified social movement or school of thought. Cf. Morrall, *Ideas* 80–114; Itten and Young.

12. The notion that madness is a deeply spiritual, transformational experience is one of the central theses of *The Divided Self* by R. D. Laing, a key figure of anti-psychiatry.

13. This is a reference to one of the treatments for hysteria (from the Greek *hystera*, meaning "uterus"). The condition is now frequently understood as a reaction to restrictive gender roles in Victorian times and as a method to delegitimize women's claims to more independence and political participation (cf. Arnaud; Meek "Medical" and "Wandering"; Scull, *Madness* 268–289 and *Hysteria*). As such, the reference foreshadows Kaysen's charges of sexism against the psychiatric dispositive.

14. Anti-psychotic medication that brought about the psychopharmacological revolution (cf. Scull, *Madness* 378–383). It was introduced shortly before Kaysen's stay at the prestigious McLean Hospital.

15. For a critique of Szasz's conceptualization of disease, see Kendell.

16. For more on the rest cure, see Kelly; Scull, *Hysteria* 98–102.

17. Cf. Patrick Corrigan's analysis of the impact of social desirability on the expression of stigma beliefs in "Public."

18. I retain the term "self-made man" despite its conceptual exclusion of women in narratives of transformation. I hold that attempts to account for both sexes through phrases like "self-made (wo)man" constitute an anachronism in a discussion of the history of this myth. After all, the ideal of self-making was "constitutive of American masculinities" (Carden 22). Novels about the personal transformation of women tended to be grouped under the label "sentimental novels." Though there are similarities in structure and tropes (cf.

Williamson 1–22; Cawelti 101–164), the respective genres have acquired distinct connotations. In this project, "self-made man narrative" refers to texts that stress the protagonist's individual development whereas sentimental novels focus on the evocation of sympathy, even though such simple distinctions are hard to maintain. For more on the conceptual exclusion of women in narratives of self-making, see Carden.

19. For a discussion of self-improvement literature, see McAdams 119–145; McGee 11–18; Yagoda 7–29.

20. For the origins of conversion narratives, see Caldwell; Hindmarsh; Shea. For their theological background, see Bauer. See G. Smith and McAdams 24–34 for the language of conversion narratives. For different types of literary conversion, see Hawkins, *Archetypes*. For the impact of Puritan conversion narratives on literature until the twentieth century, see A. Young.

21. Further strong examples from my corpus are William Styron's and Mark Vonnegut's memoirs. Styron's text describes a journey from darkness into light and bears similarities to the conversion narrative of Jonathan Edwards. Vonnegut's narrative chronicles how he turned from a hippie with anti-psychiatry views (18–19) into a "convert" to the biochemical model of mental illness (194).

22. Though Elizabeth White was English, not American, I reference her narrative since it was so widely received in America that it appears in "the most complete bibliography of American autobiographies" (Caldwell 2–3). Distinctions to American conversion narratives written at the same time consist mostly of the absence of references to Puritan ministers as well as her use of terms like "parish" (Caldwell 6–7) and are therefore irrelevant to my analysis.

23. The term "restoration" carries religious connotations such as the restoration of Israel and of believers in captivity—another key motif in Boone-O'Neill's narrative—as well as the restoration to health (e.g., *New English Translation*, Psalm 14:7). This choice of words immediately suggests that the experiencing self's recovery occurred through divine grace and provides a first hint to the genre Boone-O'Neill emulates.

24. Whereas the narrating selves of

Puritan conversion narratives do not devi-ate from the knowledge of their sinful nature to avoid sowing doubt about their salvation (cf. White 3), Boone-O'Neill's memoir blurs the line between the perspec-tives of her normal and mad self, thereby illustrating the tensions that permeate my corpus and complicating a seemingly straightforward narrative of the return to normalcy.

25. It is a matter of debate whether senti-mental texts increased the political engage-ment of its middle class, mostly female readers or whether "the sentimental novel gave readers permission to retreat from actual social engagement by replacing [it] … with private, sentimental scenes of read-ing" (Boudreau 15). For the present anal-ysis, I assume that "sentimental and even sensationalist literature served a regula-tory purpose" (Boudreau 15) as it attempts to shape and guide its readers' communal, "affective, passionate, embodied responses … in order to produce political effects" (Burgett 3). For more on Franklin's *Autobi-ography*, see D. Anderson; Bell. For Doug-lass' life writing, see Buschendorf; Drake; Levine, "Identity," *Lives*. For Alger's novels, see Birkenstein-Graff.

26. The title creates a tension with pas-sages where Beers describes the return of reason as a "miracle," "salvation," and rebirth (41–42). This speaks to the multiple, contradictory types of self-fashioning—as either the passive recipient of salvation or as the central driving force of recovery –in my corpus. Additionally, it proves that authors may rely on one mode more heavily than others but that striking contradictions and ambiguities remain which ultimately complicate any conceptualization of mad-ness and its treatment.

27. For an overview of the tropes, the history, and the socio-political impact of sentimental literature, see Hendler; Lang; Strick.

28. The insertion of an adjective that comments on his grandiose state of mind during his time of elation is an example of the ironic distance and wry humor that characterizes much of Beers' narration. These wry comments on his altered state speak to the tension that exists in Beers' memoir between the self-fashioning as nor-mal and humorous acknowledgments of his madness.

29. I analyze authors' comparisons to various marginalized groups in Chapter Two.

30. Kathryn Hume makes a related argu-ment about what she calls "aggressive fic-tions," a type of contemporary prose that irritates by undermining values, reveling in the grotesque, or challenging ontological assumptions. Whereas Hume believes that aggressive fictions break with established literary patterns and expectations com-pletely, I suggest that discredited subjects who are engaged in stigma-politics cannot afford to alienate readers to the extent that texts in Hume's corpus do. Hence my claim that textual elements spill over patterns rather than break them.

31. For alternate readings, see Breton.

Chapter Two

1. For a disambiguation, see Bloom.
2. For an overview of this debate, see Ellis.
3. For theoretical background on identity-political movements that focus on race, (dis)ability, gender, and sexuality, see Alcoff et al.; Heyes; Roth.
4. For more on these groups, see Reaume; LeFrançois et al.; Spandler et al.
5. For the founding documents of the neurodiversity movements, see Sinclair; Singer. For more on the neurodiversity movement, see Armstrong "Myth"; Herrera and Perry.
6. While some cooperation does exist between disability or autism activists and those in Mad Pride, forming stable coa-litions has been difficult: Some disabil-ity activists do not want to incur stigma by associating with the mad, whereas many in Mad Pride do not see their conditions as a form of disability but rather as a valued trait (B. Lewis, "Mad" 117).
7. A similar mechanism is at work in Marya Hornbacher's *Wasted* which links the experiencing self's eating disor-ders to Christian ascetic practices and to the so-called "starving saints" (86, 153) and ultimately reframes her madness as a quasi-religious quest for purity and self-control. For more on the relation of Christian asceticism and eating disorders, see Bordo.
8. I chose *they as a non-binary,

gender-neutral pronoun that accounts for fluid states of singularity and multiplicity to refer to Phillips, Oxnam, and Chase in *their entirety as *they have male and female alters.

9. As always, authors in my corpus create tensions by affirming the opposite to any meaning of madness they produce. Textual representations of the experiencing selves' incapacitation are discussed below.

10. For more on the US tradition of minstrelsy, see Johnson; Lott.

11. Since most passages that create humor are rather long and lose their impact when summarized, I restrict myself to a single example. For passages that use humor in similar ways, cf. Jamison, *Unquiet* 76–77; Beers 53–55; Styron 73–74; Kaysen 52–53; Vonnegut 176.

12. Exact delineations of these two modes are difficult as they share several features such as physical jokes, exaggerations, and stereotyped characters. However, the farce is described as a "'slice of life' dramatically or comically distorted but still very close to reality" insofar as it is concerned with "the accidents of humdrum existence" (Cannings 558; cf. also J. M. Davis). Slapstick tends to focus more on "broad humor, horseplay, absurd situations, or violent actions" (Marshall 700). Cf. also Fry.

13. The reference to the tragic figure Sisyphus also points towards the frustrating and cyclical nature of Hornbacher's condition: Despite her best efforts, her mood keeps rising in mania like Sisyphus' rock on the mountain, only to plummet into depression, as the rock rolls back to the foot (cf. 274–279). In this manner, the passage embeds meaning of what it means to be mad in a humorous and innocuous way.

14. The illusion of unselfconsciousness is destroyed when Hornbacher's experiencing self puts her hope in modern psychiatry to answer the question, "why the *fuck* I am like this" (233). This also allows for a more sympathetic evaluation of her struggles.

15. Michael Oliver suggests that individualizing and medicalizing approaches conceive of disability as a "personal tragedy" and are "pathological and problem-oriented" (129).

16. For more on how the Holocaust was represented, reinterpreted, and incorporated into US culture to such an extent that it was turned into an American, rather than Jewish, symbol, see Flanzbaum, "Americanization" and "Imaginary"; Gross 200–24; Novick.

17. Just as Wurtzel assumes that only Jewish people possess the in-group knowledge to understand references to the Holocaust, several authors in my corpus express the belief that madness is "nearly incomprehensible to those who have not experienced it in its extreme mode" (Styron 5; cf. also Hornbacher, *Wasted* 279). They thus claim for their lived experience what has been a consensus in the reception of Holocaust survivor testimony: that it is both unimaginable to those who have not lived it and to a certain extent inexpressible to those who have (Gibbs 19).

18. Another aspect of the Holocaust metaphor that is evoked in my corpus is the strength of the human spirit in the face of cruelty (Flanzbaum, "Americanization" 91–94). *When Rabbit Howls* provides an example of that when Chase's therapist encourages the experiencing self by saying "[s]omehow you managed to survive against pressures, tortures, as great as any concentration camp ever devised" (299–300), thus allowing *them to form a more positive identity based on *their strength while also affirming the extent of *their abuse.

19. "The United Nations' Convention on the Rights of Persons with Disabilities" (2006) explicitly includes persons with mental health difficulties and considers detention on grounds of mental disorders to be a breach of human rights. For a discussion of what this reform means for the conceptualization of madness or mental illness, see Spandler et al.

20. According to Ruth Helyer, the postmodern Gothic increasingly "move[s] away from clichés such as ghosts" and focuses on "the exploration of our own psyche" (728) and is thus well-suited for appropriations by authors in my corpus. I consider horror fiction to be a genre that began as a subset of Gothic romance but developed independently by the early twentieth century (Reyes, "Introduction" 13). For further information on these genres, see Smith and Hughes; Cherry et al.; Anolik; Andrew Smith.

21. I use the term uncanny (or *unheimlich*) in the Freudian sense: "a class of the terrifying which leads back to something

long known to us, once very familiar" but "estranged only by the process of repression" ("Uncanny" 217–218, 230). Therefore, "[a]n uncanny experience occurs either when repressed infantile complexes [such as the belief that inanimate objects are alive] have been revived by some impression, or when primitive beliefs we have surmounted seem once more to be confirmed" ("Uncanny" 230).

22. Although Beers, Vonnegut, and Oxnam address pleasurable aspects of their condition such as euphoria, high self-esteem or a general erotic charge, none of them shapes it into a dangerous lover narrative. This suggests that the representation of madness differs along gender lines when it comes to the appropriation of gendered genres.

23. Unlike some characters in this this list, the personifications of various disorders are never redeemed, and seduction is the experiencing selves' downfall. This leaves them to await salvation or to overcome the dire circumstances themselves. Authors therefore combine appropriations from different narrative templates to tell a coherent story.

24. The theory of degeneration was a highly influential concept that mixed ideas from social and biological sciences. It assumed that the opposite of evolution—a development towards less complex, more primitive organisms—could occur in races and individuals if a hereditary taint was acquired through immoral behavior (cf. Scull, *Madness* 224–267). Robert Louis Stevenson also alludes to this theory when a character assumes that Mr. Hyde has so much influence on Jekyll because the latter was wild in his youth and now "the ghost of some old sin, the cancer of some concealed disgrace" forces him to comply with Hyde's demands (Stevenson 23).

25. For a discussion of the grotesque in contemporary literature, see Hume 77–114.

26. For an extended discussion of the concept of abjection, see Chapter Four.

27. In this respect, likening her appearance to a zombie when she describes her skin as "the gray color of rotten meat" (*Wasted* 266) already hints at her indifference about her self-destruction as well as the single-minded focus on the consumption of the attention—or brains—of others.

28. It is this aggressiveness that Hornbacher's narrating self most urgently wants to hide when she presents her eating disorder as a purely defensive mechanism. Before describing the experiencing self's body, Hornbacher explains that the roommate reminded her why she was an anoretic: "fear. Of my needs, for food, for sleep, for touch, for simple conversation, for human contact, for love. I was an anoretic because I was afraid of being human. Implicit in human contact is the exposure of the self, the interaction of selves. The self I'd had, once upon a time, was too much. Now there was no self at all. I was a blank" (*Wasted* 266). In this passage, she fashions herself as a tragic figure, whose monstrosity derived from an incapacity to allow the most basic human needs to be fulfilled and who consequently missed out on all kinds of connection, such as an erotic one to the roommate she was attracted to. When she insists that "there was no self at all. I was a blank," she rejects all agency and responsibility for her mad behavior.

29. Cold-wet-packing was abandoned by most hospitals after the advent of Thorazine, a powerful anti-psychotic drug, in the 1950s, but some hospitals continued the practice until the late 1980s (Noll 285).

30. This subgenre depicts the asylum as a dreary, labyrinthine place with sadistic orderlies and doctors who take liberties with patients, neglect them, and perform experiments or cruel and humiliating procedures on them (cf. Earle 260–263).

31. For an analysis of instable selves in the postmodern moment, see Gergen, *The Saturated*; "The Self"; Surry.

Chapter Three

1. For a similar self-fashioning as more knowledgeable than individual mental healthcare professionals, see Phillips. The experiencing self tells *their therapist, "Maybe you should reread Putnam [an authority in the field of dissociative identity disorder] (186), thus contradicting him based on his discourse's truth claims.

2. Despite the medicalization as mental disorders, their high prevalence, and the fact that madness "can be as serious a medical affair as diabetes" (Styron 7), the stigma of madness is (one of) the reason(s) why these conditions only receive a

small percentage of the research funding allocated to diabetes (Hornbacher, *Madness* 283). William Styron also points out that individuals with diabetes can find hope in the knowledge that "immediate measures [can be] taken to rearrange the body's adaptation to glucose ... [whereas] depression in its major stages possesses no quickly available remedy" (Styron 8). With these comparisons, authors urge the medical community to follow through on the medicalization of madness and to allocate as much funding and research to mental disorders as befits the number of those that experience them. In other words, they (also) embrace the medico-psychiatric truth of madness but demand the benefits of the patient role in return.

3. Though she avoids direct references, Hornbacher evokes the sociological concept of symbolic power (see Bourdieu, *Language*), i.e., the tacit, everyday ways of dominating subjects, disciplining them, and confirming their place in the social hierarchy by means of institutions and education which has been fruitfully applied to analyses of psychiatry (see Lee; Crossley).

4. Jean-Martin Charcot was a nineteenth-century French neurologist who exhibited some of his patients—mostly women in acute hysteric fits—for the edification and entertainment of his colleagues and friends (Scull, *Hysteria*).

5. "Disciplinary power" is a Foucauldian concept that refers to a combination of technologies such as surveillance, record-keeping, insertion of individuals into strict timetables, and the elicitation of confessions that produces "docile bodies" that function well in factories, military regiments, and schools (cf. *Discipline* 152–156).

6. Lewis uses "objects" in the Foucauldian sense, that is, as "the signs, or basic semiotic elements, of a discourse" which are organized into larger conceptual models (*Moving* 41). In the case of psychiatry, certain behaviors, opinions, and moods are identified as symptoms—the objects of psychiatry—which are then organized into disorders, the concepts that structure them.

7. Note how the term "creature"—whose etymology suggests creation and construction—calls attention to the social constructedness of diagnostic categories but

also points to the sociocultural and familial circumstances which helped engender Hornbacher's eating disorders. The emphasis on constructedness creates another tension to the "neurochemical causal theory of mental disorders" (B. Lewis, *Moving* 48) that is endorsed by contemporary psychiatry and produces further meanings of madness.

8. A more spectacular variation of this focus on the chief complaint is present in memoirs that depart from the chronological order of events and begin with a flash-forward to particularly severe manifestations of symptoms such as suicide attempts (Hornbacher, *Madness*; K. Morgan; Phillips), excessive binge eating (Apostolides) or the first experience of mania or florid psychosis (Jamison, *Unquiet*; Schiller and Bennett).

Chapter Four

1. For more on the definition of literariness and Russian Formalism, the school that studied it, see Erlich; Gorman.

2. I use "*they" as a non-binary, gender-neutral pronoun that accounts for fluid states of singularity and multiplicity to refer to Phillips, Oxnam, and Chase in *their entirety as *they have male and female personalities or alters. Individual alters who identify as male or female retain traditional third-person singular pronouns.

3. For the most well-known theorists who embrace this notion, see Caruth; Tal. For criticism, see Gibbs.

4. I henceforth use "Stanley" to refer to the *character modeled after* Robert A. Philips, the historical author's therapist who wrote an introduction and an epilogue to the memoir.

5. Other narratologists understand the "you" in second-person narratives as "an 'I' in disguise" (Bal 29) or as a stand-in for the third-person pronoun in so far as it constitutes a character's narration of another character (McHale, *Postmodernist* 223). This openness of meaning further establishes the use of you as a markedly literary technique and contributes to the blurring of boundaries between self and Other that is prominent in my corpus.

6. Monika Fludernik coined the term "unnatural narrative" to analyze these types

of narration. According to her, narratives that exceed the "*cognitive frames*" of conversational storytelling are "unnatural" (12). I avoid this term because I find her definition of natural narratives as straightforward imitations of conversational storytelling too narrow and the resulting binary distinction between natural and unnatural narratives unproductive for my analysis. While I occasionally draw upon insights from the field of Unnatural Narratology, I embed them in the framework of Russian Formalism and the concept of defamiliarization. For more on Unnatural Narratology, see B. Richardson *Narrative*; *Voices*; Alber.

7. Haldol is a powerful anti-psychotic drug. While the narrating self criticizes the use of this medication, the switch to more conventional language can also reflect the effects of that drug which renders the passage more ambiguous.

8. For a critical discussion of confessionalism in contemporary US life writing, see Gilmore, "American." For the centrality of confessionalism in US entertainment, see Lofton; Grobe.

9. For more on the concept of abjection, see Arya; McAfee.

10. For more detailed analyses of abject art cf. Arya; Menninghaus; Zimmermann.

11. Liminality means "slip[ping] through the network of classifications that normally locate states and positions in cultural space … [It means being] betwixt and between the positions assigned and arrayed by law, custom, convention, and ceremonial" (Turner 95).

12. Note how the absence of a first-person singular pronoun emphasizes the loss of a sense of self.

Conclusion

1. For a debate of the cultural standing of memoirs and its contested status as literature, see Couser, "Rhetoric"; Yagoda.

2. Notable scholars in this field are G. Thomas Couser, Arthur Frank, Arthur Kleinman, Anne Hunsaker Hawkins, Kathryn Montgomery, Ann Jurecic, and Hilde Lindeman Nelson.

Works Cited

Primary Sources

Apostolides, Marianne. *Inner Hunger: A Young Woman's Struggle Through Anorexia and Bulimia.* W.W. Norton, 1998.

Beers, Clifford Whittingham. *A Mind That Found Itself: An Autobiography.* Doubleday, 1956.

Boone-O'Neill, Cherry. *Starving for Attention.* Continuum, 1982.

Chase, Truddi. *When Rabbit Howls.* Jove, 1987.

Cvetkovich, Ann. *Depression: A Public Feeling.* Duke UP, 2012.

Hornbacher, Marya. *Madness: A Bipolar Life.* HarperCollins, 2009.

_____. *Wasted: A Memoir of Anorexia and Bulimia.* HarperCollins, 1998.

Jamison, Kay Redfield. *An Unquiet Mind: A Memoir of Moods and Madness.* 1995. Picador, 2011.

Kaysen, Susanna. *Girl Interrupted.* Virago, 1993.

Morgan, Kristina. *Mind Without a Home: A Memoir Schizophrenia.* Hazelden, 2013.

Oxnam, Robert B. *A Fractured Mind: My Life with Multiple Personality Disorder.* Hyperion, 2005.

Phillips, Jane. *The Magic Daughter: A Memoir of Living with Multiple Personality Disorder.* Viking, 1995.

Schiller, Lori, and Amanda Bennett. *The Quiet Room: A Journey Out of the Torment of Madness.* 1994. Grand Central, 2011.

Smola, R. David. *A Waltz Through La La Land: A Depression Suvivor's Memoir.* Kirk House, 2010.

Styron, William. *Darkness Visible: A Memoir of Madness.* 1991. Vintage, 2004.

Vonnegut, Mark. *The Eden Express.* Praeger, 1975.

Wurtzel, Elizabeth. *Prozac Nation: Young and Depressed in America.* 1994. Riverhead Books, 1995.

Secondary Sources

Aftab, Awais. "Mental Illness vs Brain Disorders: From Szasz to DSM-5." *Psychiatric Times,* vol. 31, no. 2, 28 Feb. 2014. www.psychiatrictimes.com/dsm-5/mental-illness-vs-brain-disorders-szasz-dsm-5. Accessed 5 Jan. 2019.

Alber, Jan. *Unnatural Narrative: Impossible Worlds in Fiction and Drama.* U of Nebraska P, 2016. *Ebscohost.* http://search.ebscohost.com/login.aspx?direct=true&scope=site&db = nlebk&AN=1155225. Accessed 13 Jan. 2019.

Alcoff, Linda Martín, et al., eds. *Identity Politics Reconsidered.* Palgrave Macmillan, 2006.

Aldana Reyes, Xavier. "Introduction: What, Why and When Is Horror Fiction?" *Horror: A Literary History,* edited by Xavier Aldana Reyes. British Library, 2016, pp. 7–17.

_____. "Obsessed with Pain: Body Politics and Contemporary Gothic." *Twenty-First-Century Gothic,* edited by Brigid Cherry et al. Cambridge Scholars, 2010, pp. 53–67.

American Psychiatric Association. Introduction. *Diagnostic and Statistical Manual of Mental Disorders.* 5th ed. American Psychiatric, 2013, pp. 5–24.

_____. "Use of the Manual." *Diagnostic and Statistical Manual of Mental Disorders.* 4th ed. American Psychiatric, 1994, pp. 1–12.

Anderson, Douglas. *The Unfinished Life of*

Benjamin Franklin. Johns Hopkins UP, 2012.

Anderson, Leon. *Deviance. Social Constructions and Blurred Boundaries.* U of California P, 2017.

Andreasen, Nancy, and Donald Black. *Introductory Textbook to Psychiatry,* 2nd ed. American Psychiatric Association P, 1995.

Angermeyer, M.C., and S. Dietrich. "Public Beliefs About and Attitudes Towards People with Mental Illness: A Review of Population Studies." *Acta Psychiatrica Scandinavica,* vol. 113, no. 3, Apr 2006, pp. 163–179. *Researchgate,* doi: 10.1111/j.1600-0447.2005.00699.x.

Anolik, Ruth Bienstock. "Introduction: Diagnosing Demons: Creating and Disabling the Discourse of Difference in the Gothic Text." *Demons of the Body and Mind: Essays on Disability in Gothic Literature,* edited by Ruth Bienstock Anolik. McFarland, 2007, pp. 1–19.

Armstrong, Thomas. "The Myth of the Normal Brain: Embracing Neurodiversity." *AMA Journal of Ethics,* vol. 17, no. 4, 2015, pp. 348–352. https://journalofethics.ama-assn.org/article/myth-normal-brain-embracing-neurodiversity/2015-04. Accessed 10 Jan. 2019.

Arya, Rina. *Abjection and Representation: An Exploration of Abjection in the Visual Arts, Film and Literature.* Palgrave Macmillan, 2014.

Ashley, Kathleen, et al., eds. *Autobiography & Postmodernism.* U of Massachusetts P, 1994.

Bal, Mieke. *Narratology: Introduction to the Theory of Narrative.* Translated by Christine Van Boheemen. 3rd ed. U of Toronto P, 2009. *Ebscohost.* http://search.ebscohost.com /login.aspx?direct=true&scope=site&db=nlebk&db=nlabk&AN=468878. Accessed 10 Jan. 2019.

Bär, Gerald. *Das Motiv des Doppelgängers als Spaltungsphantasie in der Literatur und im deutschen Stummfilm.* Rodopi, 2005.

Barthes, Roland. *A Lover's Discourse: Fragments.* Translated by Richard Howard. Hill and Wang, 2001.

Bauer, Susan Wise. *The Art of the Public Grovel: Sexual Sin and Public Confession in America.* Princeton UP, 2008.

Beilke, Debra. "The Language of Madness: Representing Bipolar Disorder in Kay Redfield Jamison's *An Unquiet Mind* and Kate Millet's *The Loony-Bin Trip.*" *Depression and Narrative: Telling the Dark,* edited by Hillary Clark. SUNY P, 2008, pp. 29–39.

Bell, Robert H. *The Rise of Autobiography in the Eighteenth Century: Ten Experiments in Literary Genre—Augustine, Bunyan, Rousseau, Locke, Hume, Franklin, Gibbon, Fielding, Sterne, Boswell.* Edwin Mellen P, 2012.

Berger, Arthur Asa. "Humor: An Introduction." *American Behavioral Scientist,* vol. 30, no. 1, 1987, pp. 6–15. *Academic Search Premier,* doi: 10.1177/000276487030003002.

The Bible. English Standard Version. www.biblestudytools.com/esv/. Accessed 10 Jan. 2019.

"Bipolar Disorder." *NIH: National Institute of Mental Health,* Nov. 2017. www.nimh.nih.gov/health/statistics/bipolar-disorder.shtml. Accessed Oct. 4, 2018.

Birkenstein-Graff, Cathy. *Rereading the American Rags-to-Riches Story: Conflict and Contradictions in the Works of Horatio Alger, Booker T. Washington, and Willa Cather.* 2003. Loyola U, Dissertation.

Black, Donald W., and Nancy C. Andreasen. "Interviewing and Assessment." *Introductory Textbook of Psychiatry.* 6th ed. American Psychiatric, 2014, pp. 17–56.

Bloom, Clive. "Horror Fiction: In Search of a Definition." *A Companion to the Gothic,* edited by David Punter. Blackwell P, 2001, pp. 155–166.

Bordo, Susan. "Anorexia Nervosa: Psychopathology as the Crystallization of Culture." *Food and Culture: A Reader,* edited by Carole Counihan and Penny Van Esterik. Routledge, 1997, pp. 226–250.

Boudreau, Kristin. *Sympathy in American Literature: American Sentiments from Jefferson to James.* UP of Florida, 2002.

Bourdieu, Pierre. "The Forms of Capital." *Handbook of Theory of Research for the Sociology of Education,* edited by J. F. Richardson, translated by Richard Nice. Greenwood P, 1986, pp. 241–258.

_____. *Language & Symbolic Power.* Harvard UP, 1991.

Brain, Tracy. "Dangerous Confessions: The Problem of Reading Sylvia Plath Biographically." *Modern Confessional Writing: New Critical Essays,* edited by Jo

Gill. Routledge, 2006, pp. 11–32. *Ebscohost,* http://search.ebscohost.com/login. aspx? direct=true&scope=site &db=nlebk&AN=155672. Accessed 10 Jan. 2019.

Breton, Rob. "Diverting the Drunkard's Path: Chartist Temperance Narratives." *Victorian Literature and Culture,* vol. 41, 2013, pp. 139–152.

Brewer, Elizabeth. "Coming Out Mad, Coming Out Disabled." *Literatures of Madness: Disability Studies and Mental Health,* edited by Elizabeth J. Donaldson. Palgrave Macmillan, 2018, pp. 11–30.

Brontë, Charlotte. *Jane Eyre.* Classics Arawá, 2016.

Browne, Jessica L., et al. "'I Call it the Blame and Shame Disease': A Qualitative Study about Perceptions of Social Stigma Surrounding Type 2 Diabetes." *BMJ Open,* vol. 3, no. 11, 2013, doi:10.1136/bmjopen-2013-003384. Accessed 10 Jan. 2019.

Burgett, Bruce. *Sentimental Bodies: Sex, Gender, and Citizenship in the Early Republic.* Princeton UP, 1998.

Burns, Tom R. "Towards a Theory of Structural Discrimination: Cultural, Institutional and Interactional Mechanisms of the 'European Dilemma.'" *Identity, Belonging and Migration,* edited by Gerard Delanty, et al. Liverpool UP, 2011, pp. 152–172.

Burr, Vivien, and Trevor Butt. "Psychological Distress and Postmodern Thought." *Pathology and the Postmodern,* edited by Dwight Fe., Sage, 2000, pp. 186–206.

Burrus, Virginia. *Saving Shame: Martyrs, Saints, and Other Abject Subjects.* U of Pennsylvania P, 2008.

Burstow, Bonnie. "A Rose by Any Other Name: Naming and the Battle against Psychiatry." *Mad Matters: A Critical Reader in Canadian Mad Studies,* edited by Brenda A. LeFrançois et al. Canadian Scholars' P, 2013, pp. 79–90.

Buschendorf, Christa. "'Properly Speaking, There Are in the World No Such Men as Self-Made Men': Frederick Douglass' Exceptional Position in the Field of Slavery." *Intellectual Authority and Literary Culture in the US, 1790-1900,* edited by Günter Leypoldt. Winter, 2013, pp. 159–184.

Byrne, Peter. *Screening Madness: A Century of Negative Movie Stereotypes of Mental Illness.* Time to Change, 2009.

Cabanel, Alexandre. *Ophelia.* 1883, Private Collection.

Caldwell, Patricia. *The Puritan Conversion Narrative: The Beginnings of American Expression.* CUP, 1983.

Campbell, Bradley, and Jason Manning. "Microaggression and Moral Cultures." *Comparative Sociology,* vol. 13, no. 6, 2014, pp. 692–726. *Academia,* www.academia. edu/10541921/ Microaggression_and_ Moral_Cultures. Accessed 14 Jan. 2019.

Cannings, Barbara "Towards a Definition of Farce as a Literary 'Genre.'" *The Modern Language Review,* vol. 56, no. 4, Oct. 1961, pp. 558–560.

Cannon, Eoin F. *The Saloon and the Mission: Addiction, Conversion and the Politics of Redemption in American Culture.* U of Massachusetts P, 2013.

Capps, Donald. "Mental Illness, Religion, and the Rational Mind: The Case of Clifford W. Beers." *Mental Health, Religion & Culture,* vol. 12, no. 2, March 2009, pp. 157–174.

Carden, Mary Paniccia. *Sons and Daughters of Self-Made Men: Improvising Gender, Place, Nation in American Literature.* Bucknell UP, 2010.

Caruth, Cathy. *Unclaimed Experience: Trauma, Narrative, and History.* Hopkins UP, 1996.

Castle, Terry. *The Female Thermometer: Eighteenth Century Culture and the Invention of the Uncanny.* OUP, 1995.

Cawelti, John G. *Apostles of the Self-Made Man.* U of Chicago P, 1965.

Chandler, Daniel. *Semiotics: The Basics.* Routledge, 2017.

Cherry, Brigid, et al. "Introduction: Twenty-First-Century Gothic." *Twenty-First-Century Gothic,* edited by Brigid Cherry, et al. Cambridge Scholars P, 2010, pp. 1–5.

Chory-Assad, Rebecca M., and Ron Tamborini. "Television Doctors: An Analysis of Physicians in Fictional and Non-Fictional Television Programs." *Journal of Broadcasting and Electronic Media,* vol. 45, no. 3, 2001, pp. 491–521.

Cixous, Hélène. "The Laugh of the Medusa." Translated by Keith Cohen and Paula Cohen. *Signs,* vol. 1, no. 4, 1976, pp. 875–893.

Clark, Hillary, ed. *Depression and Narrative: Telling the Dark.* SUNY P, 2008.

_____. "Repenting Prodigal: Confession,

Conversion, and Shame in William Cowper's *Adelphi*." *Depression and Narrative: Telling the Dark,* edited by Hilary Clark, SUNY P, 2008, pp. 55–65.

Corrigan, Patrick W. "Lessons Learned from Unintended Consequences about Erasing the Stigma of Mental Illness." *World Psychiatry,* vol. 15, no. 1, 2016, pp. 67–73.

Corrigan, Patrick W., and Amy C. Watson. "Stop the Stigma: Call Mental Illness a Brain Disease." *Schizophrenia Bulletin,* vol. 30, no. 3, 2004, pp. 477–79.

Corrigan, Patrick W., et al. "Challenging Two Mental Illness Stigmas: Personal Responsibility and Dangerousness." *Schizophrenia Bulletin,* vol. 28, no. 2, 2002, pp. 293–309.

_____. "Does Humor Influence the Stigma of Mental Illness?" *Journal of Nervous and Mental Disease,* vol. 202, no. 5, 2014, pp. 397–401.

_____. "The Public Stigma of Mental Illness Means a Difference Between You and Me." *Psychiatry Research,* vol. 226, 2015, pp. 186–91.

Couser, Thomas G. "Body Language: Illness, Disability, and Life Writing." *Life Writing,* vol. 13, no. 1, 2016, pp. 3–10.

_____. "Introduction: Human Conditions: Illness, Disability, and Life Writing." *Recovering Bodies: Illness, Disability, and Life Writing.* U of Wisconsin P, 1997, pp. 3–17.

_____. "Introduction: Some Body Memoir." *Signifying Bodies: Disability in Contemporary Life Writing.* U of Michigan P, 2009, pp. 1–16.

_____. "Medical Discourse and Subjectivity." *Recovering Bodies: Illness, Disability, and Life Writing.* U of Wisconsin P, 1997, pp. 18–35.

_____. *Memoir: An Introduction.* OUP, 2012.

_____. "Rhetoric and Self-Representation in Disability Memoir." *Signifying Bodies: Disability in Contemporary Life Writing.* U of Michigan P, 2009, pp. 31–48.

Crawford, Paul, et al. *Madness in Post-1945 British and American Fiction.* Palgrave Macmillan, 2010.

Cresswell, Mark, and Helen Spandler. "Solidarities and Tensions in Mental Health Politics: Mad Studies and Psychopolitics." *Critical and Radical Social Work,* vol. 4, no. 3, 2016, pp. 357–373. doi: 10.133 2/204986016X14739257401605. Accessed 10 Jan. 2019.

Cross, Simon. "Laughing at Lunacy: Othering and Comic Ambiguity in Popular Humor about Mental Distress." *Social Semiotics,* vol. 23, no. 1, 2013, pp. 1–17.

_____. *Mediating Madness: Mental Distress and Cultural Representation.* Palgrave Macmillan, 2010.

Crossley, N. "Not Being Mentally Ill: Social Movements, System Survivors and the Oppositional Habitus." *Anthropology & Medicine,* vol. 11, no. 2, 2004, pp. 161–180.

Crowley, John William. "Slaves to the Bottle: Gough's *Autobiography* and Douglass' *Narrative*." *The Serpent in the Cup: Temperance in American Literature,* edited by David S. Reynolds and Debra J. Rosenthal. U of Massachusetts P, 2011, pp. 115–35.

_____, ed. *The Drunkard's Progress: Narratives of Addiction, Despair, and Recovery.* Johns Hopkins UP, 1999.

Culler, Jonathan D. *Literary Theory: A Very Short Introduction.* OUP, 1997. *Ebscohost,* http://search.ebscohost.com/login.aspx?direct=true&scope=site&db=nlebk&db=nlabk&AN=100295. Accessed 10 Jan. 2019.

Davis, Jessica Milner. "Farce." *Encyclopedia of Humor Studies,* edited by Salvatore Attardo. SAGE, 2014, pp. 233–237.

Davis, Lennard J. "Introduction: Normality, Power and Culture." *The Disability Study Reader,* 4th ed., edited by Lennard J. Davis. Routledge, 2013, pp. 1–14.

Davis, Mark. *Asylum: Inside the Pauper Lunatic Asylum.* Amberley, 2014.

Davison, Carol Margaret. "The Victorian Gothic and Gender." *The Victorian Gothic: An Edinburgh Companion,* edited by Andrew Smith and William Hughes. Edinburgh UP, 2012, pp. 124–42.

Delacroix, Eugène. *The Death of Ophelia.* 1838. Die Pinakoteken, Munich.

De Young, Mary. *Madness: An American History of Mental Illness and Its Treatment.* McFarland, 2000.

Diamond, Shaindl. "What Makes Us a Community? Reflections on Building Solidarity in Anti-Sanist Praxis." *Mad Matters: A Critical Reader in Canadian Mad Studies,* edited by Brenda A. LeFrançois et al. Canadian Scholars' P, 2013, pp. 64–78.

"Discredit." *Merriam-Webster.com.* www.

merriam-webster.com/dictionary/ discredit. Accessed 19 July 2016.

"Discrimination." *Merriam-Webster.com.* https://www.merriam-webster.com/ dictionary/ discrimination. Accessed 19 July 2016.

"Dissociative Disorders." *NAMI: National Alliance on Mental Illness,* www.nami. org/Learn-More/Mental-Health-Conditions/Dissociative-Disorders. Accessed Oct. 4, 2018.

Dolar, Mladen. *A Voice and Nothing More.* MIT P, 2006.

Doller, Jane. Foreword. "Chapter 25" *The Quiet Room: A Journey out of the Torment of Madness,* by Schiller and Bennett, 1994. Grand Central, 2011, pp. 229–238.

_____. *The Quiet Room: A Journey out of the Torment of Madness,* by Schiller and Bennett, 1994. Grand Central, 2011, pp. xi-xiii.

Donaldson, Elizabeth J., ed. *Literatures of Madness: Disability Studies and Mental Health.* Literary Disability Studies, Palgrave Macmillan, 2018.

Donovan, Courtney. "Graphic Pathographies." *Journal of Medical Humanities,* vol. 35, no. 3, 2014, pp. 273–299.

Douglas, Mary. *Purity and Danger: An Analysis of Concepts of Pollution and Taboo.* 1966. Routledge, 1984.

Douglass, Frederick. "Self-Made Men." *Frederick Douglass Heritage,* www. frederick-douglass-heritage.org/self-made-men/. Accessed 24 Nov. 2018.

_____. "The Trials and Triumphs of Self-Made Men." *The Portable Frederick Douglass,* edited by John Stauffer and Henry Louis Gates, Jr. Penguin Classics, 2016, pp. 292–302.

Drake, Kimberly. "Rewriting the American Self: Race, Gender, and Identity in the Autobiographies of Frederick Douglass and Harriet Jacobs." *The Slave Narrative,* edited by Kimberly Drake. Grey House, 2014, pp. 43–64.

Eakin, Paul John. *Fictions in Autobiography: Studies in the Art of Self-Invention.* Princeton UP, 2014.

_____. *Living Autobiographically: How We Create Identity in Narrative.* Cornell UP, 2008.

Earle, Harriet E. H. "'A Convenient Place for Inconvenient People': Madness, Sex and the Asylum in *American Horror Story.*" *Journal of Popular Culture,* vol. 50, no. 2, 2017, pp. 259–75. doi: 10.1111/ jpcu.12508. Accessed 10 Jan. 2019.

"Eating Disorders." *NIMH: National Institute of Mental Health,* Nov. 2017. www. nimh.nih.gov/health/statistics/eating-disorders.shtml. Accessed Oct. 4, 2018.

Ellis, Kate Ferguson. "Can You Forgive Her? The Gothic Heroine and Her Critics." *A Companion to the Gothic,* edited by David Punter. Blackwell Publishers, 2001, pp. 257–267.

Erlich, Viktor. *Russian Formalism: History—Doctrine.* 4th ed. De Gruyter Mouton, 2010. *Slavistic Printings and Reprintings,* vol. 4. *Ebscohost,* http:// search.ebscohost. com/login.aspx?-direct=true&scope=site&db=nleb-k&AN=559073. Accessed 10 Jan. 2019.

Federman, Cary, et al. "Deconstructing the Psychopath: A Critical Discursive Analysis." *Cultural Critique,* vol. 72, 2009, pp. 36–65.

Fee, Dwight. "The Broken Dialogue: Mental Illness as Discourse and Experience." *Pathology and the Postmodern: Mental Illness as Discourse and Experience,* edited by Dwight Fee. Sage, 2000, pp. 1–17. *Ebscohost,* http://search.ebscohost. com/login.aspx? direct=true&scope= site&db=nlebk&db=nlabk&AN=45523. Accessed 13 Jan. 2019.

Flanzbaum, Hilene. "The Americanization of the Holocaust." *Journal of Genocide Research,* vol. 1, no. 1, 1999, pp. 91–104.

_____. "The Imaginary Jew and the American Poet." *The Americanization of the Holocaust,* edited by Hilene Flanzbaum. Johns Hopkins UP, pp. 18–32.

Fludernik, Monika. *Towards a 'Natural' Narratology.* 1996. Transferred to digital print. Routledge, 2006.

Foley, Matt. "Voices of Terror and Horror: Towards an Acoustics of Modern Gothic." *Sound Effects: The Object Voice in Fiction,* edited by Jorge Sacido-Romero and Sylvia Mieszkowski. Brill, 2015, pp. 215–242. *DQR Studies in Literature,* vol. 59.

Foucault, Michel. *Birth of the Clinic: An Archaeology of Medical Perception.* Translated by A. M. Sheridan. Routledge, 1973.

_____. "The Confession of the Flesh." Interview by Alain Grosrichard, et al. *Power/ Knowledge: Selected Interviews and Other*

Writings 1972–77, edited by Colin Gordon, translated by Colin Gordon, et al. Pantheon Books, 1980, pp. 194–228.

_____. *Discipline and Punish: The Birth of the Prison.* Translated by Alan Sheridan. Vintage, 1975.

_____. "The Discourse on Language." *The Archaeology of Knowledge & the Discourse on Language.* Translated by A. M. Sheridan Smith. Pantheon Books, 1972, pp. 215–37.

_____. *The History of Sexuality.* Translated by Robert Hurley, vol. 1. Vintage, 1978.

_____. *Madness and Civilization: A History of Insanity in the Age of Reason.* 1965. Translated by Richard Howard. Vintage, 1988.

_____. *Mental Illness and Psychology.* Translated by Alan Sheridan. Harper and Row, 1976.

_____. *Psychiatric Power: Lectures at the Collège de France, 1973–74.* Edited by Jacques Lagrange, translated by Graham Burchell. Picador, 2006.

Frank, Arthur. *The Wounded Storyteller: Body, Illness, and Ethics.* U of Chicago P, 1995.

Franke, Astrid, Stefanie Müller, and Katja Sarkowsky, eds. *Reading the Social.* Palgrave, 2021.

Franklin, Benjamin. *The Autobiography of Benjamin Franklin.* 1791. Edited by Charles W. Elliot. P.F. Collier & Son, 1909.

Freud, Sigmund. "Humour." *The Standard Edition of the Complete Psychological Works of Sigmund Freud.* Translated by James Strachey. et al., vol. 21. The Hogarth P, 1961, pp. 159–166.

_____. "The 'Uncanny.'" *The Standard Edition of the Complete Psychological Works of Sigmund Freud.* Translated by James Strachey. et al., vol. 17. The Hogarth P, 1955, pp. 217–56.

Fry, William F. *Sweet Madness: A Study of Humor.* 2nd ed. Transaction, 2010.

Garrison, William Lloyd. Preface. *Narrative of the Life of Frederick Douglass, an American Slave,* by Douglass. Anti-Slavery Office, 1845, pp. v–xiv

Gergen, Kenneth J. *The Saturated Self: Dilemmas of Identity in Contemporary Life.* Basic Books, 1991.

_____. "The Self: Transfiguration by Technology." *Pathology and the Postmodern: Mental Illness as Discourse and Experience,* edited by Dwight Fee. Sage, 2000, pp. 100–115. *Ebscohost,* http://search.ebscohost.com/login.aspx?direct=true&scope=site&db=nle bk&db=nlabk&AN =45523. Accessed 13 Jan. 2019.

Geyh, Paula, ed. *The Cambridge Companion to Postmodern American Fiction.* CUP, 2017.

Gibbs, Alan. *Contemporary American Trauma Narratives.* Edinburgh UP, 2014. *Ebscohost,* http://search.ebscohost.com/login.aspx?direct=true&scope=site&db=nle bk&AN=830678. Accessed 13 Jan. 2019.

Gilman, Sander L. *Seeing the Insane: A Visual and Cultural History of Our Attitudes Towards the Mentally Ill.* Echo Point Books & Media, 2014.

Gilmore, Leigh. "American Neoconfessional: Memoir, Self-Help, and Redemption on Oprah's Couch." *Biography,* vol. 33, no. 4, 2010, pp. 657–679.

_____. "The Mark of Autobiography: Postmodernism, Autobiography, and Genre." *Autobiography & Postmodernism,* edited by Kathleen Ashley, et al. U of Massachusetts P, 1994, pp. 3–18.

Goffman, Erving. *Asylums: Essays on the Social Situation of Mental Patients and Other Inmates.* Doubleday, 1961.

_____. *Stigma: Notes on the Management of Spoiled Identity.* Prentice-Hall, 1963.

Gordis, Lisa M. "The Conversion Narrative in Early America." *A Companion to the Literatures of Colonial America,* edited by Susan Castillo and Ivy Schweitzer. Blackwell, 2005, pp. 369–386. *Wiley Online Library,* doi: 10.1002/9780470996416. Accessed 13 Jan. 2019.

Gorman, David. "Russian Formalism." *A Companion to Literary Theory,* edited by David H. Richter. John Wiley & Sons Ltd., 2018, pp. 36–47. *Wiley Online Library,* doi: 10.1002/9781118958933. Accessed 10 Jan. 2019.

Gottschalk, Simon. "Escape from Insanity: 'Mental Disorder' in the Postmodern Moment." *Pathology and the Postmodern: Mental Illness as Discourse and Experience,* edited by Dwight Fee. Sage Publications, 2000, pp. 18–48. *Ebscohost,* http://search.ebscohost.com/login.aspx?direct=true&scope=site&db=nlebk&db=nlab k&AN=45523. Accessed 13 Jan. 2019.

Gramsci, Antonio. *Selections from the Prison Notebooks of Antonio Gramsci.*

Edited and translated by Quintin Hoare and Geoffrey Nowell Smith. International, 1971.

Gregory, Elizabeth. "Confessing the Body: Plath, Sexton, Berryman, Lowell, Ginsberg and the Gendered Poetics of the 'Real.'" *Modern Confessional Writing: New Critical Essays,* edited by Jo Gill. Routledge, 2006, pp. 33- 49.

Grob, Gerald N. *Mad among Us: A History of the Care of America's Mentally Ill.* The Free P, 1994.

Grobe, Christopher. *Performing Confession: Poetry, Performance and New Media since 1959.* 2011. Yale University, Dissertation. *ProQuest.*

Gross, Andrew S. *The Pound Reaction: Liberalism and Lyricism in Midcentury American Literature.* Winter. 2015.

Grosz, Elizabeth. *Volatile Bodies: Towards a Corporeal Feminism.* Bloomington, 1994.

Hacking, Ian. "Between Michel Foucault and Erving Goffman: Between Discourse in the Abstract and Face-to-Face Interaction." *Economy and Society,* vol. 33, no. 3, 2004, pp. 277–302.

Halberstam, J. Jack. *Skin Shows: Gothic Horror and the Technology of Monsters.* Duke UP, 1995.

Hall, Stuart. "Race: The Floating Signifier." *Media Education Foundation,* 1997. MEF Stuart Hall Collection.

Hawkins, Anne Hunsaker. *Archetypes of Conversion: The Spiritual Autobiographies of Augustine, Bunyan, and Merton.* Bucknell UP, 1985.

_____. *Reconstructing Illness: Studies in Pathography.* 2nd ed. Purdue UP, 1999.

Heller, Agnes. *The Power of Shame.* Routledge & Kegan Paul, 1985.

Helyer, Ruth. "Parodied to Death: The Postmodern Gothic of *American Psycho.*" *Modern Fiction Studies,* vol. 46, no. 3, 2000, pp. 725–746.

Hendler, Glenn. *Public Sentiments: Structures of Feeling in Nineteenth-Century American Literature.* U of North Carolina P, 2001.

Hermsen, Lisa M. "Knights of the Seal: Mad Doctors and Maniacs in A. J. H. Duganne's Romance of Reforms." *Demons of the Body and Mind: Essays on Disability in Gothic Literature,* edited by Ruth Bienstock Anolik. McFarland, 2007, pp. 157–169.

Herrera, Christopher D., and Alexandra

Perry. *Ethics and Neurodiversity.* Cambridge Scholars, 2013. *Ebscohost,* http://search.ebscohost.com/login. aspx?direct=true&scope=site& db=nlebk&db=nlabk&AN=860078. Accessed 13 Jan. 2019.

Heyes, Cressida. "Identity Politics." *The Stanford Encyclopedia of Philosophy,* 16 July 2002. www.plato.stanford. edu/archives/spr2018/entries/identity-politics/. Accessed 12 June 2018.

Hindmarsh, Bruce D. *The Evangelical Conversion Narrative: Spiritual Autobiography in Early Modern England.* OUP, 2005.

Hughes, Arthur. *Ophelia ("And He Will Not Come Back").* 1863, Ashmolean Museum, Oxford.

Hume, Kathryn. *Aggressive Fictions: Reading the Contemporary American Novel.* Cornell UP, 2012.

Hutcheon, Linda. *A Poetics of Postmodernism: History, Theory, Fiction.* Routledge, 2003.

Itten, Theodor, and Courtenay Young, eds. *R. D. Laing: Fifty Years since the Divided Self.* PCCS Books, 2012.

Iversen, Stefan. "'In Flaming Flames': Crises of Experientiality in Non-Fictional Narratives." *Unnatural Narratives—Unnatural Narratology,* edited by Jan Alber and Rüdiger Heinze. De Gruyter, 2011, pp. 89–103.

Jamison, Kay Redfield. *Touched with Fire: Manic-Depressive Illness and the Artistic Temperament.* Free P, 1994.

Johnson, Stephen, ed. *Burnt Cork: Traditions and Legacies of Blackface Minstrelsy.* U of Massachusetts P, 2012.

Jones, Adrian. "Oprah on the Couch: Franzen, Frey, Foucault and the Book Club Confessions." *Compelling Confessions: The Politics of Personal Disclosure,* edited by Suzanne Diamond. Fairleigh Dickinson UP, 2011, pp. 94–109.

Jones, Nev, and Timothy Kelly. "Inconvenient Complications: On the Heterogeneities of Madness and Their Relationship to Disability." *Madness, Distress and the Politics of Disablement,* edited by Helen Spandler, et al. Policy P, 2015, pp. 43–55.

Jurecic, Ann. *Illness as Narrative.* U of Pittsburg P, 2012.

Kelly, Lori Duin. "Out of Just Relation to the World: Weir Mitchell's Rest Cure and the Power of Stigmatization." *Bodily*

*Inscriptions: Interdisciplinary Explora-
tions into Embodiment,* edited by Lori
Duin Kelly. Cambridge Scholars, 2008,
pp. 40–55.

Kendell, R. E. "The Myth of Mental Illness."
*Szasz Under Fire: The Psychiatric Aboli-
tionist Faces His Critics,* edited by Jeffrey
Schaler. Open Court, 2005, pp. 29–48.

Kleinman, Arthur. *The Illness Narratives:
Suffering, Healing and the Human Condition.* Basic Books, 1988.

Kristeva, Julia. *Powers of Horror: An Essay
on Abjection.* Translated by Leon S.
Roudiez. Columbia UP, 1982. *European
Perspectives: A Series of the Columbia UP.*

Kungl, Carla T. "'The Secret of My Mother's
Madness': Mary Elizabeth Braddon and
Gothic Instability." *Demons of the Body
and Mind: Essays on Disability in Gothic
Literature,* edited by Ruth Bienstock
Anolik. McFarland, 2007, pp. 170–80.

Kupfer, David J., and Darrel A. Regier. Preface. *Diagnostic and Statistical Manual of
Mental Disorders.* 5th ed. American Psychiatric, 2013, pp. xli-xliv.

Laine, Tanja. "You Want to See? Well, Take
a Look at This!" *Shame and Desire: Emotion, Intersubjectivity, Cinema.* Peter
Lang, 2007, pp. 29–60. Rethinking Cinema No. 3.

Laing, R.D. *The Divided Self: An Existential Study in Sanity and Madness.* 2nd ed.
Penguin, 2010.

_____. *The Politics of Experience and The
Bird of Paradise.* Penguin, 1970.

Lang, Amy Schrager. "Class and the Strategies of Sympathy." *The Culture of Sentiment: Race, Gender, and Sentimentality
in 19th-Century America,* edited by Shirley Samuels. OUP, 1992, pp. 128–142.

Lee, Ji-Eun. "Mad as Hell: The Objectifying Experience of Symbolic Violence."
*Mad Matters: A Critical Reader of Cana-
dian Mad Studies,* edited by Brenda
LeFrançois, et al. Canadian Scholars P,
2013, pp. 105–121.

LeFrançois, Brenda A., et al. "Introducing
Mad Studies." *Mad Matters: A Critical
Reader in Canadian Mad Studies,* edited
by Brenda A. LeFrançois, et al. Canadian
Scholars' P, 2013, pp. 1–22.

Lehtinen, Ullaliina. *Underdog Shame: Philosophical Essays on Women's Internalization of Inferiority.* 1998. U of Göteborg,
Dissertation.

Lejeune, Philippe. *On Autobiography.*
Edited by Paul John Eakin, translated by
Catherine Leary. U of Minnesota P, 1989.

Levine, Robert S. "Identity in the Autobiog-
raphies." *The Cambridge Companion to
Frederick Douglass,* edited by Maurice S.
Lee. CUP, 2009, pp. 31–45

_____. *The Lives of Frederick Douglass.* Har-
vard UP, 2016.

Lewis, Bradley. "A Mad Fight: Psychiatry
and Disability Activism." *The Disability
Studies Reader,* edited by Lennard Davis.
Routledge, 2017, pp. 102–118.

_____. *Moving Beyond Prozac, DSM, and
the New Psychiatry: The Birth of Post-
psychiatry.* The U of Michigan P, 2006.
Corporalities: Discourses of Disability,
edited by David T. Mitchell and Sharon I.
Snyder. Stopped here

Lewis, Michael. *Shame. The Exposed Self.*
Macmillan, 1992.

Liegghio, Maria. "A Denial of Being: Psychiatrization as Epistemic Violence."
*Mad Matters: A Critical Reader in Cana-
dian Mad Studies,* edited by Brenda A.
LeFrançois et al., Canadian Scholars' P,
2013, pp. 122–129.

Lifton, Robert. *Death in Life: Survivors of
Hiroshima.* Random House, 1967.

Link, J. C., and B. G. Phelan. "Mental Illness Stigma and the Sociology of Mental Health." *Sociology of Mental Health:
Selected Topics from Forty Years
1970s-2010s,* edited by Robert J. Johnson,
et al. Springer, 2014, pp. 75–100.

Lofton, Kathryn. *Oprah: The Gospel of an
Icon.* U of California P, 2011.

Lott, Eric. *Love & Theft: Blackface Minstrelsy & the American Working Class.*
1993. OUP, 2013.

Lutz, Deborah. *The Dangerous Lover: Gothic
Villains, Byronism, and the Nineteenth-
Century Seduction Narrative.* Ohio State
UP, 2006.

MacAulay, Brian L. *Discourses of Sobriety:
Addiction, Consumption and Recovery
Television.* 2014. Pennsylvania State U,
Dissertation. *ProQuest.*

Magi, Jill, New Jones, and Timothy Kelly.
"How are/our Work: What, If Anything,
Is the Use of Any of This?" *The Edinburgh Companion to the Critical Medical
Humanities,* edited by Anne Whitehead
and Angela Woods. Edinburgh UP, 2016,
pp. 136–152.

Mahawatte, Royce. "Transitions: From
Victorian Gothic to Modern Horror,

1880–1932." *Horror: A Literary History*, edited by Xavier Aldana Reyes. British Library, 2016, pp. 103–130.

"Major Depression." *NIMH: National Institute of Mental Health*, Nov. 2017, www.nimh.nih.gov/health/statistics/major-depression.shtml. Accessed Oct 4, 2018.

Marshall, Kelli. "Slapstick." *Encyclopedia of Humor Studies*, edited by Salvatore Attardo. SAGE, 2014, pp. 700–702.

Martinez, Jermaine. *Rhetorical Dimensions of 20th Century Depression Memoirs: Sylvia Plath's The Bell Jar, William Styron's Darkness Visible, & Kay Redfield Jamison's An Unquiet Mind*. 2016. U of Illinois, Dissertation.

McAdams, Dan P.. *The Redemptive Self: Stories Americans Live By*. OUP, 2006.

McAfee, Noëlle. *Julia Kristeva*. Routledge, 2004.

McGee, Micki. *Self-Help, Inc.: Makeover Culture in American Life*. Oxford UP, 2005.

McGinty, Emma, et al. "Trends in News Media Coverage of Mental Illness in the United States: 1995–2014." *Health Affairs*, vol. 35, no. 6, 2016, pp. 1121–1129.

McHale, Brian, ed. *The Cambridge History of Postmodern Literature*. CUP, 2016.

_____. *Postmodernist Fiction*. 1987. Routledge, 1996. *Ebscohost*, http://search.ebscohost.com/login.aspx?direct=true&scope=site&db=nlebk&AN=96841. Accessed 10 Jan. 2019.

McWade, Brigit, et al. "Mad Studies and Neurodiversity: A Dialogue." *Disability and Society*, vol. 30, no. 2, 2015, pp. 305–309.

Meek, Heather. "Medical Men, Women of Letters, and Treatments for Eighteenth-Century Hysteria." *Journal of Medical Humanities*, vol. 34, no. 1, 2013, pp. 1–14.

_____. "Of Wandering Wombs and Wrongs of Women: Evolving Conceptions of Hysteria in the Age of Reason." *English Studies in Canada*, vol. 35, no. 2–3, 2009, pp. 105–128.

Menninghaus, Winfried. *Disgust: The Theory and History of a Strong Sensation*. Translated by Howard Eiland and Joel Golb. SUNY P, 2003.

"Mental Health: A State of Well-Being." *World Health Organization*, 14 Aug. 2014. www.who.int/features/factfiles/mental_health/en/. Accessed 13 Jan. 2019.

Menzies, Robert, et al. "Introducing Mad Studies." *Mad Matters: A Critical Reader in Canadian Mad Studies*, edited by Brenda A. LeFrançois, et al. Canadian Scholars' P, 2013, pp. 1–22.

Mercer, Joyce Ann. "Writing Transformation: Using Addiction Recovery Memoirs toward Personal and Social Change." *Reforming Practical Theology: The Politics of Body and Space*, edited by Vähäkangas, et al. Tübingen, 2019, pp. 69–75.

Mieder, Wolfgang. "'Paddle Your Own Canoe': Frederick Douglass's Proverbial Message in His Self-Made Man Speech." *Midwestern Folklore*, vol. 26, no. 2, 2001, pp. 21–40.

Mills, China. *Decolonizing Global Mental Health: The Psychiatrization of the Majority World*. Routledge, 2014.

Mills, Sara. *Discourse*. 2nd ed. Routledge, 2004. The New Critical Idiom.

Modleski, Tania. *Loving with a Vengeance: Mass-Produced Fantasies for Women*. 1982. Routledge, 1988.

Moers, Ellen. *Literary Women: The Great Writers*. Doubleday, 1977.

Monteith, Lindsey, and Jeremy Pettit. "Implicit and Explicit Stigmatizing Attitudes and Stereotypes About Depression." *Journal of Social and Clinical Psychology*, vol. 30, no. 5, 2011, pp. 484–505.

Montgomery, Kathryn. *Doctors' Stories: The Narrative Structure of Medical Knowledge*. Princeton UP, 1991.

Morrall, Peter. "Madness: Fear and Fascination." *Psychology of Fear, Crime and the Media: International Perspective*, edited by D. Chadee. Routledge, 2016, pp. 40–57.

_____. *Madness: Ideas About Insanity*. Routledge, 2017.

Morrison, Linda. *Talking Back to Psychiatry: The Consumer/Survivor/Ex-patient Movement*. Routledge, 2005.

Murphy, Bernice M. "Horror Fiction from the Decline of Universal Horror to the Rise of the Psycho Killer." *Horror: A Literary History*, edited by Xavier Aldana Reyes. British Library, 2016, pp. 130–57.

Nelson, Hilde Lindemann. *Damaged Identities, Narrative Repair*. Cornell UP, 2001.

Noll, Richard. *The Encyclopedia of Schizophrenia and Other Psychotic Disorders*. Foreword by Leonard Georg. 3rd ed. Facts on File, 2007.

Norton, Eric. "Temperance Friction."

Studies in the Novel, vol. 49, no. 2, 2017, pp. 170–188.

Novick, Peter. *The Holocaust in American Life.* Houghton Mifflin, 1999.

Nussbaum, Martha C. *Political Emotions: Why Love Matters for Justice.* Belknap P of Harvard UP, 2013.

Oliver, Michael. *Understanding Disability: From Theory to Practice.* Macmillan, 1996.

Olson, Greta. *Reading Eating Disorders.* Peter Lang, 2003. Neue Studien zur Anglistik und Amerikanistik, vol. 87.

O'Reilly, Michelle, and Jessica Nina Lester. *Examining Mental Health through Social Constructionism. The Language of Mental Health.* Palgrave Macmillan, 2017.

Ostendorf, Berndt. *Black Literature in White America.* Harvester P, 1982.

Paul, Heike. *The Myths That Made America.* Transcript, 2014.

Penson, William J. "Unsettling Impairment: Mental Health and the Social Model of Disability." *Madness, Distress and the Politics of Disablement,* edited by Helen Spandler, et al. Policy P, 2015, pp. 57–66.

Perring, Christian. "'Madness' and 'Brain Disorders': Stigma and Language." *Configuring Madness: Representation, Context & Meaning,* edited by Kimberley White. Inter-Disciplinary P, 2009, pp. 3–24.

"Personality Disorders." *NIMH: National Institute of Mental Health,* Nov. 2017, www.nimh.nih.gov/health/statistics/personality-disorders.shtml. Accessed Oct 4, 2018.

Peters, Gerald. *The Mutilating God: Authorship and Authority in the Narrative of Conversion.* U of Massachusetts P, 1993.

Peterson, Dale, ed. *A Mad People's History of Madness.* U of Pittsburgh P, 1982.

Philips, Robert A. Introduction. *When Rabbit Howls,* by Chase. Jove, 1987, pp. vii–xxiv.

Phillips, Wendell. "Letter: From Wendell Phillips, ESQ." *Narrative of the Life of Frederick Douglass, an American Slave. Written by Himself,* by Frederick Douglass. The Anti-Slavery Office, 1845, pp. xiii–xvi.

Plato. *Phaedrus and the Seventh and Eighth Letters.* Translated by Walter Hamilton. Penguin, 1974.

Plumb, Anne. "UN Convention of the Rights of Persons with Disabilities: Out of the Frying Pan into the Fire? Mental Health Service Users and Survivors Aligning with the Disability Movement." *Madness, Distress and the Politics of Disablement,* edited by Helen Spandler et al. Policy P, 2015, pp. 183–198.

Pols, Johannes Coenraad. *Managing the Mind: The Culture of American Mental Hygiene, 1910–1950.* 1997. U of Pennsylvania, Dissertation. *ProQuest.*

Poole, Jennifer M., and Jennifer Ward. "'Breaking Open the Bone': Storying, Sanism, and Mad Grief." *Mad Matters: A Critical Reader in Canadian Mad Studies,* edited by Brenda A. LeFrançois, et al. Canadian Scholars' P, 2013, pp. 94–104.

Porter, Roy. *The Faber Book of Madness.* Faber & Faber, 1991.

_____. *Madness: A Brief History.* Oxford UP, 2010.

_____. *A Social History of Madness: Stories of the Insane.* Phoenix Giants, 1987.

Porter, Roy, and David Wright, eds. *The Confinement of the Insane: International Perspectives, 1800–1965.* CUP, 2003.

Prendergast, Catherine. "On the Rhetorics of Mental Disability." *Embodied Rhetorics: Disability in Language and Culture,* edited by James C. Wilson and Cynthia Lewiecki-Wilson. Southern Illinois UP, 2001, pp. 45–60.

Pryal, Katie Rose. "The Genre of the Mood Memoir and the Ethos of Psychiatric Disability." *Rhetoric Society Quarterly,* vol. 40, no. 5, 2010, pp. 479–501.

"Public Policy Platform." *National Alliance on Mental Illness (NAMI),* 12th ed., 2016. www.nami.org/About-NAMI/Policy-Platform. Accessed 13 Jan. 2019.

Quesenberry, Krista, and Susan Merrill Squier. "Life Writing and Graphic Narratives." *Life Writing,* vol. 13, no. 1, 2016, pp. 63–85.

Radden, Jennifer. "My Symptoms, Myself: Reading Mental Illness Memoirs for Identity Assumptions." *Depression and Narrative: Telling the Dark,* edited by Hilary Clark, SUNY P, 2008, pp. 15–28.

Radstone, Susannah. "Cultures of Confession/Cultures of Testimony: Turning the Subject inside out." *Modern Confessional Writing: New Critical Essays,* edited by Jo Gill. Routledge, 2006, pp. 166–179.

Rak, Julie. "Are Memoirs Autobiography? A Consideration of Genre and Public Identity." *Genre,* vol. 36, no. 2, 2004, pp. 305–326.

_____. *Boom! Manufacturing Memoir for the Popular Market*. Wilfrid Laurier UP, 2013.

Reaume, Geoffrey. "A History of Psychiatric Survivor Pride Day during the 1990s." *Bulletin 374*, 14 July 2008, pp. 2–3, www.csinfo.ca/bulletin/Bulletin_374.pdf. Accessed 13 Jan. 2019.

Reyes, Xavier Aldana. "Introduction: What, Why, and When is Horror Fiction." *Horror: A Literary History*, edited by Reyes. British Library, 2016, pp. 7–18.

Reynolds, Simon, and Joy Press. "Open Your Heart: Confession and Catharsis from Janis Joplin to Courtney Love." *The Sex Revolts: Gender, Rebellion, and Rock'n'Roll*. Harvard UP, 1995, pp. 249–275.

Richardson, Brian. *Unnatural Narrative: Theory, History, and Practice*. Ohio State UP, 2015.

_____. *Unnatural Voices: Extreme Narration in Modern and Contemporary Fiction*. Ohio State UP, 2006. *Theory of Interpretation of Narrative*, series editors James Phelan and Peter J. Rabinowitz. Google Books. https://books.google.de/books?id=q dkENNIPNcIC&printsec=frontcover&dq=richardson+unnatural&hl=de&sa=X&ved=0ahUKEwiPqYLblOvfAhWLzqQKHUPfChEQ6A-EIKTAA#v=onepage&q=richardson%20unnatural&f=false. Accessed 13 Jan. 2019.

_____. "What Is Unnatural Narrative Theory?" *Unnatural Narratives—Unnatural Narratology*, edited by Jan Alber and Rüdiger Heinze. de Gruyter, 2011, pp. 23–40.

Roehring, James, and Carmen McLean. "A Comparison of Stigma between Eating Disorders and Depression." *International Journal of Eating Disorders*, vol. 43, 2010, pp. 671–674.

Rohr, Susanne. "Screening Madness in American Culture." *Journal of Medical Humanities*, vol. 36, no. 3, 1 Sept. 2015, pp. 231–240.

Rosenthal, Macha Louis. *Our Life in Poetry: Selected Essays and Reviews*. Persea Books, 1991.

Roth, William. "Politics and the Disabled Body: Diverse Thoughts About Human Diversity." *The Politics of Inclusion and Exclusion: Identity Politics in Twenty-First Century America*, edited by David F. Ericson. Routledge, 2011, pp. 151–176.

Rothe, Anne. *Popular Trauma Culture: Selling the Pain of Others in the Mass Media*. Rutgers UP, 2011. *Ebscohost*. http://search.ebscohost.com/login.aspx?direct=true&scope=site &db=nlebk&db=nlabk&AN=435118. Accessed 10 Jan. 2019.

Rubin, Lawrence C., ed. *Mental Illness in Popular Media: Essays on the Representation of Disorders*. McFarland, 2012.

Rush, Benjamin. *Medical Inquiries and Observations upon the Diseases of the Mind*. Kimber and Richardson, 1812.

Russo, Jasna, and Debra Shulkes. "What We Talk about when We Talk about Disability: Making Sense of Debates in the European User/Survivor Movement." *Madness, Distress and the Politics of Disablement*, edited by Helen Spandler, et al. Policy P, 2015, pp. 27–41.

Rutherford, Sarah. *The Victorian Asylum*. Shire, 2008.

Rylko-Bauer, Barbara, and Paul Farmer. "Structural Violence, Poverty, and Social Suffering." *The Oxford Handbook of the Social Science of Poverty*, edited by David Brady and Linda M. Burton. OUP, 2016, pp. 47–74.

Sadock, Benjamin James, and Virginia Alcott Sadock. *Kaplan and Sadock's Concise Textbook of Clinical Psychiatry: Derived from Kaplan and Sadock's Synopsis of Psychiatry, 10th Edition*. 3rd ed. Lippincott Williams & Williams, 2008.

Scheid, Teresa L., and Tony N. Brown. "Approaches to Mental Health and Illness: Conflicting Definitions and Emphases." *A Handbook for the Study of Mental Health*, edited by Scheid and Brown. 2nd ed. CUP, 2012, pp. 1–5.

Schiller, Marvin. "Scarsdale, New York, March 1982-June 1982." *The Quiet Room: A Journey out of the Torment of Madness*, by Schiller and Bennett, 1994. Grand Central, 2011, pp. 39–50.

"Schizophrenia." *NIMH: National Institute of Mental Health*, May 2018, www.nimh.nih.gov/health/statistics/schizophrenia.shtml#part_154880. Accessed Oct 4, 2018.

Schwalm, Helga. "Autobiography." *The Living Handbook of Narratology*, edited by Peter Hühn et al., 11 April 2014, www.lhn.uni-hamburg.de/article/autobiography. Accessed 11 Oct. 2018.

Scull, Andrew, editor. *Cultural Sociology of*

Mental Illness: An A-to-Z Guide. SAGE, 2014.

_____. *Hysteria: The Disturbing History.* OUP, 2009.

_____. *Madness in Civilization: A Cultural History of Insanity from the Bible to Freud, from the Madhouse to Modern Medicine.* Thames & Hudson, 2016.

_____, et al. *Masters of Bedlam: The Transformation of the Mad-Doctoring Trade.* Princeton UP, 2014.

Sedgwick, Eve Kosofsky. *The Coherence of Gothic Conventions.* Methuen, 1986.

Shakespeare, William. *The Works of Shakespeare: The Tragedy of Hamlet.* Edited by Edward Dowden. Methuen & Co, 1899.

Shea, Daniel B., Jr. *Spiritual Autobiography in Early America.* Princeton UP, 1968.

Shklovsky, Viktor. "Art as Technique." *Global Literary Theory: An Anthology,* edited by Richard J. Lane. Routledge, 2013, pp. 7–20.

Siebers, Tobin. "Disability Studies and the Future of Identity Politics." *Disability Theory.* U of Michigan P, 2011, pp. 70–95.

Sinclair, Jim. "Don't Mourn for Us." *Our Voice,* vol. 1, no. 3, 1993. www.autreat.com/dont _mourn.html. Accessed 13 Jan. 2019.

Singer, Judy. "Why Can't You Be Normal for Once in Your Life? From a 'Problem with No Name' to the Emergence of a New Category of Difference." *Disability Discourse,* edited by Mairian Corker and Sally French. Open UP, 1999, pp. 59–67.

Smith, Andrew. *Gothic Literature.* 2nd ed. Edinburgh UP, 2013.

_____, and William Hughes, eds. *The Victorian Gothic: An Edinburgh Companion.* Edinburgh UP, 2012.

Smith, Dorothy. *Institutional Ethnography: A Sociology of the People.* Altamira P, 2005.

Smith, Gordon T. *Transforming Conversion: Rethinking the Language and Contours of Christian Initiation.* Baker Acad., 2010.

Smith, Jeffrey. "Epilogue: Understanding DID Therapy: The Case of Robert B. Oxnam." *A Fractured Mind: My Life with Multiple Personality Disorder* by Robert B. Oxnam, Hyperion, 2005, pp. 261–285.

Smith, Sidonie, and Julia Watson. *Reading Autobiography: A Guide for Interpreting Life Narratives.* 2nd ed. U of Minnesota P, 2010.

Sonntag, Susan. *Illness as Metaphor.* Vintage, 1979.

Spandler, Helen, and Jill Anderson. "Unreasonable Adjustments? Applying Disability Policy to Madness and Distress." *Madness, Distress and the Politics of Disablement,* edited by Spandler, et al. Policy P, 2015, pp. 13–25.

Spandler, Helen, et al., eds. Introduction. *Madness, Distress and the Politics of Disablement,* edited by Helen Spandler, et al. Policy P, 2015, pp. 1–9.

_____. *Madness, Distress and the Politics of Disablement.* Policy P, 2015.

Spooner, Catherine. *Contemporary Gothic.* Reaktion Books, 2006.

Star, Shirley A. "The Public's Ideas About Mental Illness." Annual Meeting of the National Association for Mental Health, 5 Nov. 1955, Sheraton-Lincoln Hotel, Indianapolis, IN. www.norc.org/PDFs/publications/StarS_Publics_Ideas_1955.pdf. Accessed 10 Jan. 2019.

Starkman, Mel. "The Movement." 1981. *Mad Matters: A Critical Reader in Canadian Mad Studies,* edited by Brenda A. LeFrançois, et al. Canadian Scholars' P, 2013, pp. 27–37.

Stein, D. J., et al. "What Is a Mental/Psychiatric Disorder? From DSM-IV to DSM V." *Psychiatric Medicine,* vol. 40, no. 11, 2010, pp. 1759–1765.

Stevenson, Robert Louis. *Dr. Jekyll and Mr. Hyde.* 1886. Penguin Popular Classics, 1994.

Strahan, S. A. K. "The Propagation of Insanity and Allied Neuroses." *Journal of Mental Science,* vol. 36, 1890, pp. 325–338.

Strick, Simon. *American Dolorologies: Pain, Sentimentalism, Biopolitics.* U of New York P, 2014.

Sue, Derald Wing, et al. "Racial Microaggressions in Everyday Life: Implications for Clinical Practice." *American Psychologist,* vol. 62, no. 4, May-June 2007, pp. 271–286.

Surry, Tara. "Encounters with the Monster: Self-Haunting in Virginia Woolf's 'Street Haunting.'" *Demons of the Body and Mind: Essays on Disability in Gothic Literature,* edited by Ruth Bienstock Anolik. McFarland, 2010, pp. 97–107.

Szasz, Thomas Stephen. *The Myth of Mental Illness: Foundations on a Theory of Personal Conduct.* Revised ed. Harper Perennial 1974.

_____. *Psychiatry: The Science of Lies.* Syracuse UP, 2008.

Szmigiero, Katarzyna. "They Wouldn't Make Good Orphelias." *Configuring Madness: Representation, Context & Meaning*, edited by Kimberley White, Inter-Disciplinary P, 2009, pp. 49- 66.

Tal, Kalì. *Worlds of Hurt: Reading the Literature of Trauma*. CUP, 1996.

Tambling, Jeremy. *Confession: Sexuality, Sin, the Subject*. Manchester UP, 1990.

Taylor, Gabriele. *Pride, Shame, and Guilt: Emotions of Self-Assessment*. Claredon P, 1985.

Tell, Dave. "Jimmy Swaggart's Secular Confession." *Rhetoric Society Quarterly*, vol. 39, no. 2, 2009, pp. 124–146.

Todorov, Tzvetan. *Introduction to Poetics*. 1968. Translated by Richard Howard. U of Minnesota P, 1981.

Tomkins, Silvan. "Shame-Humiliation and Contempt-Disgust." *Shame and its Sisters: A Silvan Tomkins Reader*, edited by Eve Kosofsky Sedgwick and Adam Frank. Duke UP, 1995, pp. 133–178.

Tompkins, Jane. *Sensational Designs: The Cultural Work of American Fiction, 1790–1860*. OUP, 1986. *Ebscohost*, http://search.ebscohost.com/login. aspx?direct=true&scope =site&db=nlebk&db=nlabk&AN=143647. Accessed 10 Jan. 2019.

Trimble, Michael R., and Mark George. *Biological Psychology*. Wiley-Blackwell, 2010.

Trumm, Paulette. Afterword. *A Waltz through La La Land: A Depression Survivor's Memoir*, by Smola. Kirk House, 2010, pp. 213–14.

Turner, Victor. "Liminality and Communitas." *The Ritual Process: Structure and Antistructure*. 1969. Cornell UP, 1977, pp. 94–130. *Symbol, Myth, and Ritual Series*, edited by Victor Turner.

The United Nations. "Convention on the Rights of People with Disabilities." *Treaty Series*, vol. 2515, 2007, pp. 1–31. treaties.un.org/Pages/ViewDetails.aspx?src=IND&mtdsg_no=I V-15&chapter=4. Accessed 17 Jan. 2019.

Vath, Raymond E. "A Medical Perspective." *Starving for Attention*, by Boone-O'Neill. Continuum, 1982, pp. 184–187.

Vickroy, Laurie. *Trauma and Survival in Contemporary Fiction*. U of Virginia P, 2002.

Wahl, Otto. *Media Madness: Public Images of Mental Illness*. Rutgers UP, 1995.

_____. "Stop the Presses: Journalistic Treatment of Mental Illness." *Cultural Sutures: Medicine and Media*, edited by Lester D. Friedman. Duke UP, 2004.

Wallcraft, Jan, and Kim Hopper. "The Capabilities Approach and the Social Model of Mental Health." *Madness, Distress and the Politics of Disablement*, edited by Helen Spandler, et al. Policy P, 2015, pp. 83–97.

Walter, Madaline Reeder. *Insanity, Rhetoric and Women: Nineteenth-Century Women's Asylum Narratives*. 2011. U of Missouri, Dissertation. *ProQuest*.

Wasson, Kirsten. "A Geography of Conversion: Dialogical Boundaries of Self in Antin's *Promised Land*." *Autobiography & Postmodernism*, edited by Kathleen Ashley, et al. U of Massachusetts P, 1994, pp. 167–187.

Watkins, Owen. *The Puritan Experience: Studies in Spiritual Autobiography*. Routledge & Kegan Paul, 1972.

Weedon, Chris. "Discourse, Power, and Resistance." *Feminist Practice and Poststructuralist Theory*. Basil Blackwell, 1987, pp. 107–135.

White, Elizabeth. *The Experiences of God's Gracious Dealing with Mrs. Elizabeth White as They Were Written under Her Own Hand, and Found in Her Closet after Her Decease, December 5, 1669*. Kneeland and Green, 1741.

White, Kimberley, and Ryan Pike. "The Making and Marketing of Mental Health Literacy in Canada." *Mad Matters: A Critical Reader in Canadian Mad Studies*, edited by Brenda A. LeFrançois, et al. Canadian Scholars' P, 2013, pp. 239–252.

Williams, Bernard. *Shame and Necessity*. U of California P, 1993.

Williamson, Jennifer A. *Twentieth-Century Sentimentalism: Narrative Appropriation in American Literature*. Rutgers UP, 2014.

Wills, Garry. *Augustine's 'Confessions': A Biography*. Princeton UP, 2011.

Wise, Sarah. *Inconvenient People: Lunacy, Liberty and the Mad Doctors in Victorian England*. Vintage, 2013.

Wood, Mary Elene. *Life Writing and Schizophrenia: Encounters at the Edge of Meaning*. Rodopi, 2013.

Wurmser, Leon. *The Mask of Shame*. Johns Hopkins UP, 1981.

Wyatt, Richard. "Science and Psychiatry." *Comprehensive Textbook of Psychiatry*, ed. by Kaplan and Sadock. Wolters Kluwer, 1985, pp. 2016–28.

Wyllie, Irving G. *The Self-Made Man in America: The Myth of Rags to Riches.* The Free P, 1966.

Yagoda, Ben. *Memoir: A History.* Riverhead Books, 2009.

Yezzi, David. "Confessional Poetry and the Artifice of Honesty." *New Criterion,* vol. 16, no. 10, June 1998, pp. 14–21.

Young, Alexander William, III. *Speaking, Silently Speaking: Thomas Shepard's "Confessions" and the Cultural Impact of Puritan Conversion on Early and Later America.* 2012. U of Oregon, Dissertation.

Young, Elizabeth. "Memoirs: Rewriting the Social Construction of Mental Illness."
Narrative Inquiry, vol. 19, no. 1, 2009, pp. 52–68.

Zimmerman, Jacqueline Noll. *People like Ourselves: Portrayals of Mental Illness in the Movies.* Scarecrow Press, 2003. Studies in Film Genres, no. 3.

Zimmerman, Lee. "Against Depression: Final Knowledge in Styron, Mairs, and Solomon." *Biography,* vol. 30, no. 4, 2007, pp. 465–90.

Zimmermann, Anja. *Skandalöse Bilder—Skandalöse Körper. Abject Art vom Surrealismus bis zu den Culture Wars.* Reimer, 2001.

Zwerdling, Alex. *The Rise of the Memoir.* OUP, 2017.

Index

233

www.ingramcontent.com/pod-product-compliance
Lightning Source LLC
Chambersburg PA
CBHW031128270326
41929CB00011B/1546